The Book of INDIAN CRAFTS
and INDIAN LORE

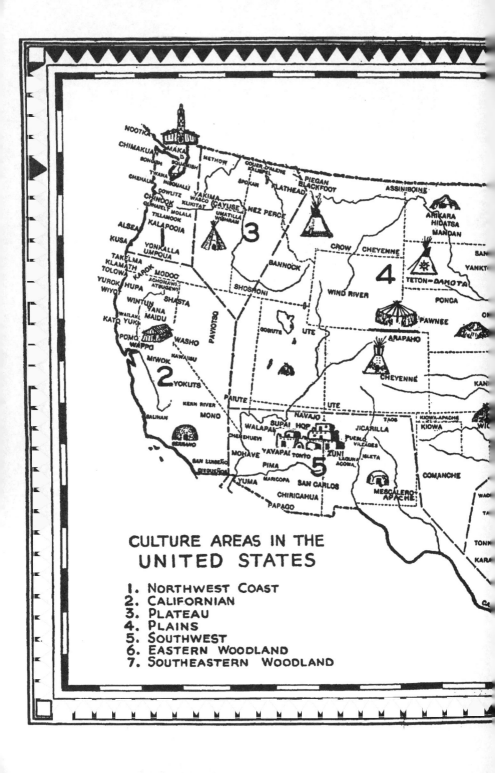

CULTURE AREAS IN THE
UNITED STATES

1. NORTHWEST COAST
2. CALIFORNIAN
3. PLATEAU
4. PLAINS
5. SOUTHWEST
6. EASTERN WOODLAND
7. SOUTHEASTERN WOODLAND

Curly Bear, Chief of the Blackfoot

The Book of Indian Crafts and Indian Lore

Julian Harris Salomon

DOVER PUBLICATIONS, INC.
Mineola, New York

Bibliographical Note

This Dover edition, first published in 2000, is an unabridged republication of the work originally published by Harper & Brothers Publishers, New York, 1928. It includes all illustrations from the original 1928 edition.

Library of Congress Cataloging-in-Publication Data

Salomon, Julian Harris, 1896–
    [Book of Indian crafts & Indian lore]
    The book of Indian crafts and Indian lore / Julian Harris Salomon.
       p. cm.
    Originally published: The book of Indian crafts & Indian lore. New York: Harper & Brothers, 1928.
    Includes bibliographical references and index.
    ISBN 0-486-41433-7 (pbk.)
    1. Indians of North America—Industries. 2. Indian craft—North America. 3. Indians of North America—Folklore. I. Title.

E77 .S2 2000
970'.00497—dc21

00-031397

Manufactured in the United States of America
Dover Publications, Inc., 31 East 2nd Street, Mineola, N.Y. 11501

TO
DOROTHY

WHOSE PRACTICAL HELP, INSPIRATION
AND ENCOURAGEMENT MADE IT POSSIBLE
FOR ME TO FINALLY BRING THIS BOOK
INTO BEING

For permission to use many of the illustrations that appear throughout the text the author is indebted to the following institutions:

American Museum of Natural History   (AMNH)
Smithsonian Institution   (SI)
Bureau of American Ethnology   (BAE)
United States National Museum   (USNM)
Junior Red Cross News   (JRCN)

The letters in parenthesis are used with these illustrations to indicate their source.

CONTENTS

ILLUSTRATIONS

Illustrations

PREFACE

THE idea of this book was really Curly Bear's, not mine. It came one night as I was seated in his lodge with Apikuni (James Willard Schultz), listening to Heavy Eyes, Many Tail Feathers, White Grass, and other old men tell stories of the days when the plains were black with buffalo. All these tales of wonderful adventure were told Apikuni so that he might preserve them in a book that he was writing. It was just as Heavy Breast finished telling us how he made the traps to catch the weasels, whose white skins decorated the costume he was wearing, that Curly Bear spoke.

"Our stories Apikuni keeps for our children by putting them in his thick writings [books] but our handwork will go with us to the Sand Hills."

"Yes, so it is," said White Grass; "our young men no longer know how to make traps of bark and sinew. They buy those of steel from the trader. So it is with all that they need."

"Yet the old ways were good ways," said Curly Bear, "and the things that Old Man taught us in the beginning should not be allowed to die. Would that they, too, might be put down in a thick writing."

And so to fulfill the desire of my old friend Curly Bear and also because I knew that boys and girls wanted

Preface

to learn how to do things the Indians did, this book was written.

Camp directors and leaders of the great outdoor movements such as the Boy Scouts, Girl Scouts, and Camp Fire Girls have found in Indian lore an opportunity to enrich their programs in handicraft, pageantry, and ceremonial and to give to their work more romance and color. The schools, too, have found in the almost universal appeal that the Indian makes to the child, a method of using Indian lore for teaching many subjects. A project in Science carried out by the Lincoln Elementary School, Teachers College, Columbia University, which began with a study of Indian methods of growing cotton, led the children to a general study of Indian life. When it was over it was found that in addition to Science the children had touched on the following subjects: Reading, through Indian stories; Spelling, through Indian words; Geography, from the study of the Indian's physical environment; History, through a study of the Indian's relations to the white race; Household Arts, by cooking Indian dishes; Fine Arts, by reproducing Indian designs; and Physical Education, through Indian dances. The report says, "It is a study that is rich in worth-while leads. It has a historical as well as a social significance for the child. It is a subject to which children continually return, even after it has been replaced by another central activity."

A summer camp, perhaps, offers the best opportunities for the development of a program of Indian lore, for it may be adapted to all parts of the camp's work. Tents, buildings, boats, and other equipment may be decorated with Indian designs. Indian meals may be occasionally served, made up of foods grown in an Indian garden. The handicrafts offer a variety of opportunities for indoor and outdoor activities, while field trips in search of materials will add new interest to nature study. Indian games, quiet and active, may well take their place with the better-known sports. Indian stories told round the camp fire and accompanied with ceremonials and dances provide an outlet for emotional expression and adventure through the imagination.

In the preparation of this book it was necessary for me to supplement my field work by drawing from the vast amount of ethnological data collected by scientific institutions. To the publications of these institutions I am especially indebted: Bureau of American Ethnology; Smithsonian Institution; American Museum of Natural History; Museum of the American Indian, Heye Foundation; Peabody Museum; Field Museum of Natural History; University of California; Canadian National Museum. I am also under obligation to the same institutions for the use of many of the illustrations.

To those ethnologists who have critically read over parts of my manuscript and have offered many helpful suggestions, I am profoundly indebted and here extend my grateful thanks: to Dr. Pliny E. Goddard of the American Museum of Natural History, who read Chapters I, III, IV, VI, and IX; to Mr. Francis La Flesche of the Bureau of American Ethnology, who read Chapter II; to Mr. William C. Orchard of the Museum of the American Indian, who read Chapter V; to Dr. Stewart Culin of the Brooklyn Museum, who read Chapter VII; and to Mr. Donald Cadzow, Mr. Arthur Woodward, Dr. Melvin R. Gilmore, and Mr. Louis Shellbach III, all of the Museum of the American Indian, who read Chapters VIII, X, XI, XII, XIII, and XIV.

I have also to express my obligation to many friends, Indian and white, for practical help and encouragement. Of these I want to specially mention Mr. Ernest Thompson Seton, who through his books and early camps encouraged me to continue and develop my interest in the Indians; Mr. Ralph Hubbard, with whom I was associated in the production of boy scout Indian pageants in this country and in Europe, who has been a source of constant inspiration; Mr. James Willard Schultz for many courtesies while I was on the Blackfoot Reservation; Mr. A. Verne Westlake and Mr. Fay Welch, who helped me with the music.

In recent years there has been a renewed and growing interest in the American Indian and with it a realization of the contribution to American art, music, and drama that he has already made. This has led to an effort to preserve some of his arts and crafts that still remain. It is my hope that this book may contribute to this movement by interesting boys and girls in reviving some of the arts of the first Americans.

JULIAN HARRIS SALOMON
"Apota"

Nyack, N. Y.

The Book of INDIAN CRAFTS
and INDIAN LORE

Chapter One

THE INDIANS OF THE UNITED STATES

In the dim mists long before the age of written history there began a series of migrations from northeastern Asia to Alaska that led to the gradual occupation of the American continents by the ancestors of the people known to us as the Indians. Living remnants of the old race that gave America its Indians and Eskimos have been found in parts of northern and eastern Asia, and the fact that it was possible for them to cross Bering Strait to North America and make even longer journeys along the Alaskan coast has been definitely proved. Pressure of foes and increasing numbers probably led the first pioneers to make the journey and in turn forced the gradual spread southward in the New World until both continents were entirely occupied.

Although this explanation of the origin of the Indian is generally accepted by scientists today, old fallacies still persist. According to one of these the Indians are descendants of the "lost ten tribes of Israel" while another traces them to a colony of Welshmen founded by Prince Madoc in 1170. Others have tried to identify the Indians of Central and South America with the Chinese and Pacific Islanders, but the evidence in all of these cases has either been proved false or insufficient to warrant its acceptance. The theory that the mound-builders and the cliff-dwellers were of separate races that had died out before America's discovery has also been disproved. Mounds have been built in historic times by tribes in the Mississippi Valley and in the

A Cliff Dwelling (JRCN)

South, while the cliff-dwellers and the basket-makers who preceded them were the immediate ancestors of the Pueblo tribes now living in the Southwest.

When Columbus landed, Indians were living in scattered villages in all parts of North and South America. Their ways of life had been influenced and developed according to the kinds of country in which they happened to live, so that although they were all of one race, they differed widely in customs, language, and the degree of civilization to which they had attained. Some were primitive hunters, others agriculturists, while in Mexico, Central America, and Peru were densely populated towns and cities with well-organized governments. In the empires of the Mayas, Incas, and Aztecs, Indian civilization reached its highest development. This civilization, which was destroyed by the Spaniards, produced some finely carved monuments, huge pyramids, and great cities with remarkable stone buildings. Many of these have recently been excavated, and an interesting result of the explorations is that architects are now considering ways in which Mayan designs may be adapted for use in the erection of skyscrapers in New York and Pittsburgh. Thus the oldest American architecture may contribute toward the development of the newest.

Here in the United States the tribes differed from one another as they did in other parts of the continent. They spoke so many different languages that, except in a very few cases, members of neighboring tribes could not understand one another. To overcome this difficulty the Indians of the plains invented a sign language that is said by some authorities to be the finest gesture language ever devised by man. By the use of sign talk, Indians could convey ideas to one another, no matter how unlike their spoken languages might be. In addition to this difference in language, the Indians also differed in their costumes, handicrafts, and general ways of life. However, ethnologists have found that tribes living in the same type of country were somewhat alike in their customs and habits, and so they have divided the Indians of the United States into seven culture

A Virginia Indian from an Early Drawing and the First Known Picture of an Indian Made in 1479

groups, as follows: Eastern Woodland, Southeastern Woodland, Northwest Coast, Californian, Southwestern, Plateau and Plains. In the descriptions of these groups that follow, the facts are based on the life of the tribes considered most typical of each area. The boundaries of these areas as given are merely for convenience, for if one were to travel from one group to another he would find that as the edges of the area

were approached the customs of the tribes living there
would resemble in some ways each of the two groups
near which they lived.

Eastern and Southeastern Woodland Groups

In the vast forests that once stretched from the Mississippi River to the Atlantic Ocean and from Hudson
Bay to the Gulf of Mexico lived the Woodland Tribes.
In the far north the Naskapi, Montagnais, Saulteaux,
Wood Cree, and Ojibwa hunted the caribou; south of
them the principal tribes were the Abnaki, Micmac,
Mohican, Pequot, Iroquois, Huron, Ottawa, Wyandot,
Erie, Susquehanna, and Delaware, while to the west
were the Menomini, Sauk and Fox, Pottawatomi, Illi-
nois, Peoria, Kickapoo, Miami, Shawnee, and Winne-
bago. In the far south lived the Cherokee, Creek,
Choctaw, Powhatan, Tuscarora, Yuchi, Quawpaw,
Atakapa, Alibamu, Tonkawa, Chickasaw, Biloxi,
Natchez, and Seminole.

Most of these tribes lived in villages fortified with
palisades of sharpened poles. Each village was made
up of a number of dwellings known as wigwams. These
differed from the tipi of the Plains Indian, to which
the name is often wrongly applied, mainly in that they
were intended to remain in one place for a length of
time and could not easily be moved about. They varied
in form from the tipi-shaped one of the Naskapi to

the gabled long house of the Iroquois and the dome-shaped shelter of the Ojibwa.

Wigwams were built on a framework of poles and saplings that was covered with the most suitable material the Indian could find in his own country. Thus in

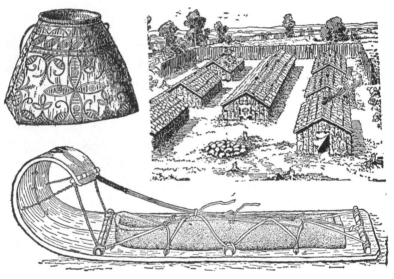

Penobscot Bark Kettle (AMNH). Replica of an Iroquois Village built by Boy Scouts. An Indian Toboggan (USNM)

the far north caribou skins were used, while in the south palmetto leaves and a plaster made by mixing clay and Spanish moss made excellent wall and roof coverings. Bark and mats made of cat-tail or other rushes were perhaps the most common materials for this purpose.

The rush mats woven by the women were made in

different sizes. When traveling these could be folded
up in long bundles that were easily stowed in a canoe.
When it came time to camp, a frame was made of saplings tied together with strings of fiber. The largest
mats were then tied to the sides and the smaller ones
thrown over the top so that they overlapped and formed
a waterproof roof. A small hole was left in the center
so that smoke from the fire could escape. The largest
of the eastern dwellings was the Iroquois long house,
which was built by setting up a framework of poles and
covering it with slabs of red elm or ash bark that had
been flattened and dried. These houses were about
twenty feet wide, nearly as high, and sometimes from
eighty to one hundred and fifty feet long.

One of the greatest achievements of these forest people was the formation of a highly developed political
organization known as the League of the Iroquois,
which was a "League of Nations" organized by five
powerful tribes that lived in New York State. Later
they admitted a sixth tribe, the Tuscaroras of North
Carolina. Each tribe in the League elected representa-
tives to a supreme council which made and enforced
laws and also sat as a court without a jury to try important cases. Its decisions were final and its power
over the individual tribes was absolute. The names of
its officers were the speaker, fire-keeper, wampum-
keeper, door-keeper and head war chief. This great

League succeeded in abolishing hatred between the nations that composed it and in putting a stop to wars of revenge within its membership. So powerful did it grow that at one time it was well on its way toward controlling the eastern half of North America. The coming of the white man marked the beginning of the decline of its power although even then it played a decisive part in the struggle between Britain and France for the control of the continent.

For their food supply the Woodland Indians depended mainly on agriculture. They were good

Penn Treaty Wampum Belt (BAE)

farmers and would raise each year large crops of corn, squash, beans, pumpkins, watermelon and sweet potatoes. Like most of the other tribes in the country they also raised some tobacco for ceremonial purposes. In the far north where farming was not possible, caribou were killed in great numbers by driving them into pens. The meat not needed right away was dried for future use so that there was always plenty to eat in the lodges. The other tribes did some hunting too. Deer were taken by still hunting or by a great tribal hunt in which an entire herd would be surrounded and slaughtered. The tribes living near the Great Lakes were expert at catching the great sturgeon and nearly all of the others knew how to catch fish with spears, hooks or nets. Maple sugar, made in New England,

Driving Deer into a Pen (after Champlain)

wild rice, gathered around the Great Lakes, berries, hickory-nut oil, persimmon bread, peanuts, hominy and small game were some of the other things that lent variety to their food supply.

Soft tanned deerskin was used for making clothing. The men wore leggins or kilts, breech-cloth and a sleeved shirt and the women a skirt and jacket. Their moccasins were soft soled with puckered fronts and were generally decorated with porcupine quillwork. Birch bark was used in making all kinds of utensils and many of the tribes made a little pottery. A plain

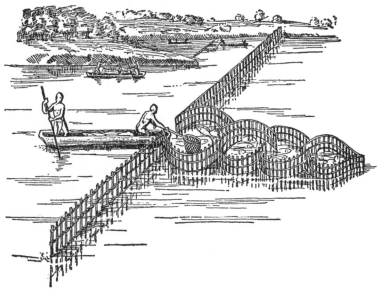

Fish Trap of the Virginia Indians (USNM)

wooden bow and wooden war clubs were their principal weapons.

It was rather natural that in their country of many lakes and rivers these Indians should develop the birch canoe, the pattern of which we follow in making the canvas covered craft that is so popular on our waters. We are indebted to them also for contributing to our outdoor life the game of lacrosse, snowshoes and the toboggan.

Northwest Coast Tribes

Along and near the Pacific coast from southern Oregon to Alaska lived the Northwest Coast Tribes, best known to us through their totem poles. Among these the most important were the Haida, Tlingit, Tsimshian, Kwakiutl, Bellacoola, Coast Salish, Nootka, Chinook, Kalapooian, Wailatpuan, and Chimakuan. These people lived in villages of wooden houses, near or on the seacoast, and depended for their food supply almost entirely on fishing. They were the best woodworkers of any of the Indians on the continent.

The excessive rainfall in the region led these tribes to develop permanent houses rectangular in shape with low gabled roofs and often of great size. On huge posts set in the ground a framework was built of heavy poles. To this were fastened the sides and roof which were made of planks split from the great white cedar trees that grow along the coast. The principal supporting posts of the house were sometimes decorated with paintings and carvings representing the characters in some tribal myth. Outside the house a skillfully carved and painted pole was erected bearing the crests or totems of the family and generally illustrating a legend or some important family happening. These were sometimes fifty or sixty feet tall. The peculiar decorative art of these Indians was highly developed and displayed on their houses, poles, ceremonial dress, and household implements,—in fact, on everything they possessed.

A Northwest Coast House. Decoration Shows a Thunderbird Carrying Off a Whale (BAE)

As nearly all of their traveling was done by water it is not surprising that the war canoe of these Indians was the largest boat built by any of the tribes. A canoe of this kind was often sixty feet long and was made by hollowing out a great cedar log. This was done by carefully burning the wood and chipping it out with stone adzes and bone chisels. When the sides were thinned down to the proper thickness the log was filled with water which was brought to a boil by dropping hot stones in it. After the wood had been softened by this process the sides were stretched and held apart by thwarts to give the canoe greater width. The high bow and stern were then made of sections of logs carefully hewn out and fitted together with twisted ropes of cedar bark and cedar pegs. So carefully was this done that the joints were made water-tight without the use of pitch. In these great canoes, paddled by slaves or under sails of thin wood or matting, the chiefs would make long journeys for war, or to pay a ceremonial visit to some friendly neighbor. Smaller canoes were used for hunting whales, for fishing and for sport by the children.

Porpoises and seals were harpooned from canoes in tribal hunts in which many men took part. Whales were taken in the same manner by two of the tribes, the Nootka and the Quileute. Fish were caught in traps and nets or taken by hook and line. In the north salmon were preserved by splitting and drying them, but in the south the dried salmon were pounded up fine and packed in basketry bags. Berries, roots, seaweed and crabapples, nearly all of which were cooked in fish oil, were the only vegetable foods. Very occasionally deer, bear or mountain goats were killed and eaten. The goats were killed mainly for their wool which was used in making blankets.

Baskets of all kinds were made but no pottery. Cooking was therefore done in peculiar wooden boxes, the sides of which had been bent in shape from a single piece of wood and sewn together with concealed stitches of spruce root. The bottom was attached in a similar manner, the joint being made water-tight. The workmanship displayed was truly remarkable when one considers the crudity of the tools with which it was done. Food and water were placed in the box and brought to a boil by dropping hot stones in it.

Despite the cold and often rainy climate in which they lived, little clothing was worn by these people. In the north, robes of tanned skins and fur were worn in winter, and in the south similar robes were made of cloth woven from twisted bark or mountain-sheep wool. These blankets, ornamented with black, blue, and yellow designs, were woven from cedar bark and mountain goat hair, by the Chilkat, a Tlingit tribe. Blankets of this kind were highly valued by all of the Coast tribes and were worn on ceremonial occasions. A broad-brimmed basketry hat and a poncho of tightly woven matting were worn in rainy weather. No moccasins or sandals such as were used by all of the other Indians were worn, the people going barefoot in both summer and winter. In war, armor made of thick folded hides, overlapping slats, or heavy rods of wood was worn, and also a wooden helmet. This offered good protection against the arrows, bone knives, and clubs which were their only weapons.

During the year, and especially in winter, great cere-

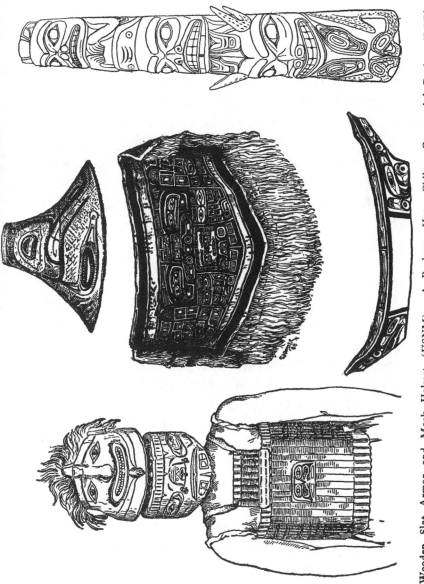

Wooden Slat Armor and Mask Helmet (USNM). A Basketry Hat. Chilcat Ceremonial Basket (BAE). Northwest Coast Canoe. Haida Totem Pole: From below upward, Sculpin, Dogfish, Sea Monster (AMNH)

monials known as potlatches were given on important occasions. After days of singing, dancing, and feasting the celebration would be brought to a close by the distributions of many gifts by the man who had given the potlatch. At such a time a wealthy man might give away all of his possessions except his house and in this queer way gain high social standing among his people. Although this left him poor for a time, at future potlatches he received gifts of greater value than those he had given and so eventually became richer than he had been before.

Californian Tribes

Perhaps the most primitive of all the tribes lived in the area that is now southern Oregon and the state of California. Here the principal tribes were the Pomo, Maidu, Wintun, Yana, Yuki, Kato, Mikwok, Wappo, Yokuts, Yurok, Hupa, Mono, Klamath, Shasta, Modoc, Mohave, and Yuma.

Strangely enough, acorns were the chief food used by the people. Small game and fish supplemented this vegetarian diet whenever they could be secured. From their northern neighbors the tribes on the coast and near the rivers in the interior learned how to gather sea food and to fish for salmon, so that they used less of the acorn mush than the tribes in the south. Flour for acorn mush was ground in a hopper-like basket placed on a flat stone. With a rounded pestle the acorns were pounded into a fairly fine flour. To remove the tannin the flour was spread in a basin of clear sand, and hot water was poured upon it. This process eventually removed the bitter taste. It was cooked by boiling it to a thin mush in a basket, the water being heated by hot stones dropped into it.

Basket Hopper and Mortar Slab for Grinding Acorns (AMNH)

Little or no clothing was worn by these people. A skin apron and a blanket of the same material were the commonest forms of dress. Woven rabbit-skin robes were worn in cold weather and were also used for bedding. Moccasins were of the forest type, with soft soles and puckered fronts. In the south sandals similar to those of the Southwestern Indians and to the Mexican *hueracho* were used.

Californian homes were simple shelters of brush, bark, grass, and tule, or rough lean-tos made of poles.

For crossing streams wooden canoes and a canoe-like raft of tule rushes, called a balsa, were used. Other boats were made of planks lashed together and of large baskets coated with pitch.

Though backward in many ways, the Californian tribes excelled all other Indians in making baskets. They developed a great variety of weaves and colors.

Basketry Water Bottle and Water-tight Cooking Basket (USNM)

Some were so tightly woven that they would hold water and so could be used for cooking by the hot-stone method. Into others decorations of beads and feathers were woven. Baskets of the latter kind are often very beautiful and show most delicate workmanship.

Southwestern Tribes

In the desert and semi-desert country of the Southwest, that is now the states of Arizona and New

Mexico, lived three groups of people, the Pueblos, the village tribes, and the nomadic Apache and Navajo. The pueblos, beginning with Taos on the north, are stretched along the Rio Grande almost to the city of Albuquerque. Three others, Laguna, Acoma, and Zuñi, are southwest of this main group, and in Arizona, not far from the Grand Canyon, are the pueblos of the Hopi. All are in, or near to the same places where they were when first visited and conquered by the Spaniards. The name Pueblo, meaning town, was given these Indians by the Spaniards because of the compact stone and adobe villages in which they live.

The Pueblos are a peaceful agricultural people, more civilized, according to our standards, than any of the other tribes that lived in this country. Long ago their villages were nearly always built on high mesas or other naturally protected spots, but as the need for protection against their more savage neighbors was done away with, under Spanish and American rule, they gradually moved down into the valleys so as to be nearer to their fields. Today only some of the Hopi villages and Acoma remain on their high rocky locations. In the old days the houses were built as high as five stories high, in terraces around a central court. Entrance to them could be made only through holes in the roof, which also served as smoke holes and windows. These could be reached only by ladders that were drawn up in times of danger. In this way the peaceful villages could hastily be turned into a strong fort under orders from its war chief. Coronado in 1540, and the other captains who, like him, expected to find the pueblos filled with gold and treasure, soon found out that, though they were only defended with stones and arrows, they could not, because of their location and construction, be easily captured.

Navajo Blanket, Zuñi Water Jar and Hopi Rabbit Stick (BAE)

The Pueblo men took care of the fields and did some of the weaving. Before the coming of the Spaniards they had learned how to irrigate the dry land in which they lived and to raise good crops of corn, pumpkins, melons, beans, and cotton. In the underground ceremonial rooms, called kivas, the men twisted the cotton into thread and wove it into clothing. Later on, when the Navajo secured sheep from the Spaniards, he learned how to weave from his Pueblo neighbors and so to produce the well-known Navajo rugs. Besides being the best weavers, the Pueblos were also the best potters of any of the tribes in the country. Beautiful jars, bowls, and other articles were molded and decorated by the women. These jars and rugs often were traded with the Apache and Navajo for meat and tanned hides.

To obtain meat in addition to that supplied by neighboring tribes the Pueblos often conducted hunts of their own. At Taos and other eastern villages long trips would be made out on the plains for buffalo. Rabbits would be surrounded in great numbers and killed with a curved stick something like the Australian boomerang. Deer, antelope, bear, and mountain lion were also hunted. Turkeys were domesticated and kept in large flocks for their feathers, which were used to make head-dresses and for ceremonial purposes. Eagles, too, were captured when young and raised for their feathers.

The ceremonial and religious life of the Pueblos was highly developed. Every tribe was divided into a number of clans and secret societies. Each society had its own series of ceremonies, some being held on the plazas. Perhaps the best known of these is the snake dance which is given each year at a different Hopi pueblo by the Antelope and Snake fraternities. Like most of the other pueblo ceremonies, it is a prayer for rain. During this dance the snake priests carry live snakes, of all varieties found in the Southwest, including rattlesnakes, in their mouths, and dance around the plaza with them. At the end of the dance the snakes are carried to the edge of the village and turned loose as messengers to the rain gods, with whom they are supposed to have especially strong powers. As far as we know, the fangs of the rattlers are not removed, but because of their skill in handling the snakes the priests are seldom bitten.

The Pima, Papago, and Maricopa live south and west of the Pueblo country in villages of dome-shaped houses built of saplings covered with thatch and mud. Unlike the pueblo houses, these dwellings are small and occupied by but a single family. The food of these people is almost the same as that of the Pueblos. In addition to what they raise they gather many of the wild desert plants such as the mesquite and the giant cactus. Cactus fruit is preserved or made into syrup and the seeds are ground fine and mixed with water to form a gruel known as pinole. Deer, antelope, and occasionally a mountain sheep formed their chief meat supply.

For clothing the men wore a cotton breech clout, a cotton or rabbit-skin robe, and in winter a deerskin shirt. Rawhide sandals were worn instead of the moccasins which were used in most of the other parts of the country. As in the pueblos, the weaving of the cotton blankets was done entirely by the men. The women made many beautiful baskets of different shapes and sizes.

Differing greatly in some ways from the other Southwestern tribes, were the Apache and the Navajo. Being

Pima House, Pueblo Kiva, Apache Brush House and a Navajo Hogan
(JRCN)

nomadic, they did not practice agriculture to a great extent, but secured their food mainly by hunting and by gathering wild berries. The Apache, with the exception of the eastern bands who used the tipi, lived in easily erected brush shelters of various shapes. The

Navajo winter lodges were made by setting up a framework of three forked poles and covering it with logs, small poles, brush, and earth to form a conical house. A doorway was left on the east side, and above it was a large opening which served as a combined window and smoke hole. Another type of hogan, as the Navajo house is called, was built by laying up logs horizontally to form a six-sided house. At the top the logs were brought in toward the center, where a small smoke hole was left. The roof was made by covering the top logs with brush and a thick coating of adobe. In the summer the Navajo camp consisted of a simple windbreak of brush or a stone wall.

Navajo and Apache pottery was crude, but the baskets made by the latter excelled those made in the pueblos. Silver-working and rug-making are other Navajo crafts. Silver work was not done in the old days, but in comparatively recent times many of the men have become clever silversmiths. From coins they fashion, with crude tools and homemade dies, rings, bracelets, beads, and large oval disks used in ornamenting belts. Often this jewelry is set with bits of turquoise matrix obtained from Indian mines. Rugs are woven by the women from native wool that they spin and dye themselves. The colors most commonly used are the natural white and brown of the wool, a gray made by mixing these, and a red made with native dyes. Before commercial dyes were introduced by the traders, red and one or two other colors were obtained by unraveling a heavy woolen European cloth called bayeta.

For many years the Navajo and Apache fought with the Mexicans and later with the Americans, mainly because of attempts to crowd them off reservations that had previously been guaranteed to them. Under their great war chiefs, Victorio, Cochise, and Manuelito, they made themselves feared on both sides of the border until they were finally captured and pacified by Generals Crook and Miles.

Plateau Tribes

In the mountain and desert country now comprising Idaho, Utah, eastern Oregon, Washington, Nevada, and western Colorado, lived the Plateau Tribes. Among them were the Shoshone, Nez Perce, Kutenai, Flathead, Yakima, Ute, and Paiute. These tribes led a more or less roving life. Their homes were mat-covered or skin tipis and rough shelters of bark, grass, brush, or poles called wikiups. So poorly were the tipis of the Ute constructed that they gained for the tribe the name "bad lodges" among the Indians of the plains.

The food used by these tribes varied according to the district in which they lived. In the east, buffalo, and in the west, deer, were hunted, while the far-

Western tribes depended on salmon that they caught with weirs, seines, and spears. In some of the more barren sections where little game larger than rabbits could be found, snakes, grasshoppers, and insects were eaten. Camas roots, berries, nuts, and the seeds of wild grasses were gathered for food wherever they could be found.

Rude dug-out canoes and rafts of rushes like the balsa of California were used for fishing and for ferrying across streams. Good baskets were made by most of the tribes, some of which were woven water-tight.

A Kutenai Canoe (USNM)

A conical pack basket was used for transporting food and firewood. Others were bottle-shaped, and after being made water-tight by pitching them inside and out were used as canteens. A basket of this type was also used in the Southwest.

Soft tanned skin clothing and robes of woven rabbit-skin were worn. To make a robe, the rabbit-skin was split in a long strip. These strips were then tied together and twisted into long ropes which were woven into a blanket on a framework of poles set in the ground.

Armor was made of the stiffest hides that could be obtained. The hides were first soaked until they were soft, and then doubled and shaped as they dried. Bows were ordinarily made of white cedar backed with a strip of sinew, but occasionally a finer one would be made of mountain-sheep horn. Horns to be used for such a bow were put in a hot spring or water until they were quite soft. They could then be cut into thin strips which were glued together with balsam gum and backed with sinew. Hunting and war arrows were sometimes poisoned by dipping the tips into a rotted deer liver or rattlesnake venom.

The most famous of the Plateau Indians was Chief Joseph, the Nez Perce, who, though he tried hard to maintain peace, was finally led to go to war against the whites to defend his lands and his people.

Plains Tribes

Ask the average person to name the most character-istic parts of an Indian costume, and the first thing mentioned will be a war bonnet of eagle feathers. Next will probably come beaded leggins, shirt, and mocca-sins. The description is that of the plains costume, for these Indians, because of their numbers and warlike exploits even in quite recent times, have impressed themselves on our minds as the most typical of all who lived in our country. Their homes were on the great grass-covered prairies and plains that stretched be-tween the Rocky Mountains and the Mississippi River.

They are undoubtedly the best known of all of our Indians, and the names of some of their great leaders, such as Sitting Bull and Red Cloud, are quite famous. The most typical tribes of this group are the Assiniboine, Blackfoot, Crow, Cheyenne, Gros Ventre or Atsena, Teton-Dakota, Kiowa, Kiowa-Apache, and Comanche. Other tribes that lived in this area in villages that were fairly permanent, were the Arikara,

Hidatsa Earth Lodge *

Hidatsa, Mandan, Omaha, Osage, Ponca, Pawnee, Oto, Iowa, Kansas, Missouri, Santee-Dakota, and Wichita. All depended on the buffalo for their chief food supply, but the village Indians also raised considerable crops of corn, beans, and pumpkins.

With the exception of the Wichita, the village tribes lived in earth lodges and tipis. The earth houses were thirty or forty feet in diameter, ten to fifteen feet high in the center, and five to seven feet high at the eaves.

* From "Goodbird the Indian." Courtesy of Fleming H. Revell and Co.

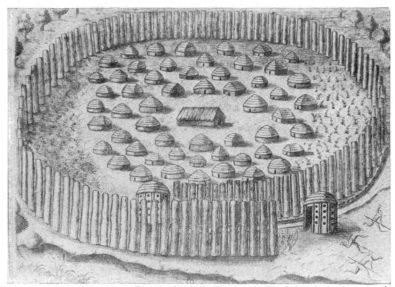

A Stockaded Village of the Florida Indians

A Piegan Blackfoot Camp

Taos—A Pueblo Village

Skidegate—A Haida Village of the Northwest Coast

To build them an excavation was first made and in this was set up a framework of heavy posts. This was roofed over with heavy beams, poles, hay, and earth. A hole was left in the center, which served as combined window and chimney. The Wichita house was a large beehive-shaped framework of poles carefully thatched

Wichita Grass House

with bundles of grass. The most typical tribes used only the tipi.

Before horses were introduced, when the tribe was on the march, everything had to be carried in packs on the backs of men and women or by means of travois drawn by dogs. This consisted of two poles attached at one end to a harness, while the others dragged on the ground. Between them was lashed an oval or square netted frame of rawhide to which bundles could be fastened.   Later on, this device was made larger for

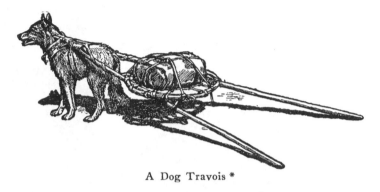

A Dog Travois *

use with horses.   For crossing streams a bowl-shaped bull boat, made of green buffalo hides stretched on a

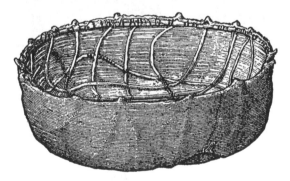

A Bull Boat

framework of willow saplings, was used.   In these the women would ferry equipment, while the men swam the horses over.   Once on the other side, the boat was

* From "Goodbird the Indian."   Courtesy of Fleming H. Revell and Co.

loaded on a travois or the hides would be folded for
future use and the march resumed. Horses were first
obtained by the Southern tribes after Coronado's expedition of 1540. In the two hundred years that followed they gradually spread north over the plains,
being stolen or traded from one tribe to the other.
After the introduction of horses the tribes made longer
journeys than they had been able to before, accumulated more property, and changed their hunting methods. Of the latter we will learn more later on.

The buffalo furnished them with practically all of
the necessities of life. From its hide they made clothing and shelters. Shields, packs, bags, ropes, snowshoes, boat covers, and many other articles were also
made from the skins. The horns were used for making
weapons, spoons, and ceremonial articles, and the hoofs
for rattles and glue. Bow strings, arrow points, and
sewing materials were fashioned from the sinew. The
hair was woven into pillows and saddle pads. Bones
were converted into various implements and the skull
had a prominent place in ceremonies. In fact, no part
of the animal was wasted. The meat was generally
cooked by roasting or broiling, but sometimes it was
boiled by putting it in a hole in the ground that had
been lined with a green skin and dropping hot stones
into it. It was from this custom that the Assiniboine
got their name, which means "stone-boilers." Pails
made of a buffalo paunch, wooden bowls, and spoons

made of buffalo and mountain-sheep horns were the only utensils used by the most typical tribes, as they made no pottery.

The Plains Tribes differed in their forms of government, but all had their unwritten tribal laws enforced by soldier societies or police. These men controlled the great tribal hunts and carried out the orders of the chiefs. They would punish a man who had acted against the general welfare by destroying his property or whipping him. In extreme cases they might drive the wrong-doer from the tribal camp.

Buffalo Horn Spoon (AMNH)

Men attained distinction by doing great and good deeds for the benefit of their fellow tribesmen. Wealth counted little if at all, and those in need of food or anything else obtained it from those who had in abundance. A man might often gain distinction by giving his property to those in need, and it was considered the chiefs' first duty to care for the widows and orphans and the needy members of the tribe.

At the end of the winter and after the great tribal hunt in the spring was held the sun dance, which was the greatest religious ceremony of the year. At that time all the bands of the tribe that had been scattered in winter camps came together. Under the direction of the police the bands erected their lodges in regular order, making camp in a great circle. Near the camp was erected a circular lodge of poles and brush in which the ceremonies, which lasted several days, took place. To the prairie people this was one of the most joyful times of the year. Food was plentiful, so that feasting and social activities had a prominent part in this annual religious revival.

Many of the things this book tells us how to make and do come from the Plains Tribes, so that we will learn a great deal more about them in the chapters that follow.

Northwest Coast Design. Mythic Raven

Chapter Two

WAR BONNETS AND HEAD-DRESSES

FOR rallies, pageants, and camp-fire ceremonials hardly anything is more effective than the appearance of a group in Indian costume. The most striking part of a Plains Indian costume is the large feather war bonnet. This can be made easily from materials which are inexpensive and can be purchased locally or from one of the large mail-order houses.

An Indian's war bonnet had a special significance to him and was worn only on special occasions. Of course, if you are going to make and wear one you will want to know what it was. Nowadays Indians of tribes that never saw or heard of bonnets wear them as a sort of tuxedo on dress occasions because they seem to realize that it is expected of them, but in the old days they were worn by comparatively few Indians. Many of the tribes wore feathered headbands and used feathers for decorating their costumes before the white man came, but the Plains tribes and they alone wore the large eagle-feather bonnets. The feather headband of the Woodland Indians differed from that of the Plains Indians in that its feathers stood erect instead of drooping back, it had no tail, and the feathers of other birds than the eagle, such as the turkey, crane, and heron, were used for it. To the Indian the bonnet's greatest value was not in its fine appearance, but rather in its great medicine, or sacred power, that protected the wearer in battle. In the old days a head-dress of this kind could only be worn by a man with the consent of his fellow warriors. This meant not only that he must

Counting Coup. From an Indian Drawing

have had the full respect of the leading men of the tribe, but that he had also received high war honors.

War honors, or *coups,* as they were called, were granted to men who had shown great bravery in battle. The highest honor that could be won was that given for touching a living enemy with the bare hand or with something held in it. Lesser honors were allowed for capturing a shield or gun and for killing and scalping an enemy. Greater credit was given for touching an enemy than for killing him, because it required more courage to touch an enemy and leave him unhurt than it did to attack him. High honors were also given to those who were the first to touch a fallen enemy, because in order to do this a man had to be at the very front of battle. To the Indian the eagle was the greatest of all birds and had great power in war, so that an eagle feather was worn in the hair for each *coup* won.

A very young man might sometimes gain the right to wear the bonnet among the Omaha through a peculiar custom which existed in that tribe which permitted the presentation of a bonnet as a challenge. The donor might be an enemy of the young man's family, so that the gift of the bonnet would really be an act of revenge. When rumors of the presentation reached the young man, he might retreat to the woods to avoid receiving it. If he did this the warriors would attempt to capture him and bring him back to the village. He would then be placed on a high seat and the bonnet formally presented to him. Immediately his relatives would begin to wail and mourn for him. The receipt of the bonnet was often equivalent to a sentence of death to a warrior so young and untried, for it meant that he was either compelled to start on the war trail at once and not return until he had killed an enemy, or that he must take a dangerous position in the next fight. If he survived he won the right to wear the bonnet.

Eagle-hunting

When a man had finally accumulated enough honors to entitle him to a war bonnet he set about to secure the eagle feathers from which it was to be made. In some of the tribes eagle-hunting was limited to certain men from whom the feathers could be purchased, but in others each man would secure them for himself. When the time came for the hunt the warrior would leave the tribal camp with his family and go to some rough hilly country where the eagles might be found. There he would make camp and conduct ceremonies to appease the spirits of the birds he was about to kill. On the top of a hill he would then dig a pit deep enough to stand up in. In doing this he was careful to carry away and scatter the earth as it was removed. The pit was then carefully covered over with sticks, brush, earth, and grass, so that when it was finished no trace of the excavation could be seen from above.

After sitting up all night, singing eagle songs and purifying himself in the smoke of sweet grass, the hunter would leave his lodge early in the morning and go to the pit on the hill. Before leaving he warned his wife not to use a sewing awl or any other pointed object while he was gone. He believed that if she did, he would be scratched by the birds he captured. Sometimes he would take a human skull with him because he believed it would make him as invisible to the eagles as was the spirit of the skull's owner.

Baiting the Trap

On top of the pit he would place a piece of buffalo meat or liver and near it, so that it appeared to be feeding on this bait, he would set up the stuffed skin of a coyote. He then climbed into the pit, carefully covering the entrance once he was inside. Small openings had been left in the pit cover so that he could see the sky above. Through these he watched as he waited for the eagles to come. If other birds or coyotes came near, he drove them away by poking a stick through the cover. When at last the eagle darted down, it would alight at one side of the trap and then walk over to the bait. Quickly the hunter would push his hands up through the branches and, seizing the bird first by one leg and then by the other, would pull it down into the hole, where he broke its back with his foot. By killing the bird in this way the wings would fall to either side and the feathers were uninjured. When the bird was dead the hunter placed a bit of pemmican in its mouth. This he thought would so please the spirit of the dead bird that it would hasten to tell other eagles how well it had been treated and so induce them to come and be caught.

When grizzly bears were about, eagle-hunting was

extremely dangerous. Once an Indian was in his eagle
trap when a big grizzly started to drag the bait away.
The man had a thong attached to the meat and with
this drew it into the pit. The bear turned back to
investigate. With a sweep of his heavy paw he tore
off the brush covering and, finding the man, dragged
him out and killed him.

The Making of the Bonnet

After the feathers and other materials for the bonnet
had been gathered, the man who was to receive it called
together the chief men of the tribe and invited them
to a feast at his lodge. As soon as the meal was over
those present counted *coup* on the feathers, which prepared them for use, and work on the bonnet began.
First a skullcap of soft buckskin, which formed the
foundation to which the feathers were attached, was
made. To this a long strip of buckskin was fastened,
if the bonnet was to have a trail. Before the day of
horses, the trail reached only to the waist, but after
they were introduced it was lengthened, so that when
a warrior dismounted it dragged behind him on the
ground. Sometimes a man would have so many honors
that two trails would be necessary to hold all the
feathers.
  Each feather as it was prepared was handed to the
bonnet-owner, who described the honor which en-

titled him to it. He then handed it to the man who was making the bonnet, and it was fastened in place. As a bonnet contained thirty or fifty or more feathers, and as each honor had to be recounted separately, it often took weeks to complete it. Finally, it was ornamented with a band of quill or beadwork and strips of white weasel skin. The weasel was skillful and

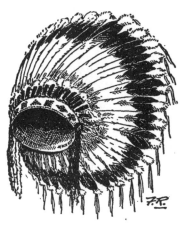

An Eagle Feather Bonnet

alert in evading pursuit, so that this power was supposed to come through the skins to the bonnet-wearer. When complete, the bonnet represented a council of warriors, each feather being a man, and the horsehair tip at its end his scalp lock. The peeled shaft of a long feather, to the end of which three or four fluffy feathers had been tied, was fastened to the hat so that it stood out in the center of the circle of feathers. This

was known as the "plume" and it represented the man
who owned the bonnet. Occasionally a warrior of very
great deeds was given the privilege of wearing horns
on his bonnet as a symbol of strength and power. Buffalo horns used on bonnets of this kind were hollowed
out or split, to make them light, and then highly
polished.

What to Get

When you make your bonnet you will probably find
it difficult to secure eagle feathers, so that white turkey,
swan, or goose feathers, which can be secured from
any millinery supply house, will have to be used as
a substitute. By dyeing the tips of these dark brown
or black they can be made to look very much like real
eagle plumes. Brown turkey-tail feathers and barred
turkey-wing feathers will also make up well. Your
butcher will be glad to save some for you at Thanksgiving or Christmas time. Be sure, though, that he
plucks the feathers while the bird is dry, as they will
be spoiled if he dips it in hot water. Such feathers
may sometimes be restored, and the appearance of all
feathers may be improved by passing them through
steam vapor and smoothing them with the fingers.
Turkey feathers were used by the Eastern Indians and
are now being used by Indians who can no longer capture eagles, while in the pueblos they are being raised

for their feathers just as young eagles were so reared
in days gone by.

You will need about thirty feathers for the crown of
the bonnet and an additional twenty or more if you
intend to add a tail to it. The other materials required
will be an old felt hat, an eighth of a yard of red
flannel, some pieces of thin soft leather, a small
chicken-feather duster or some turkey marabou, a red
horsehair harness tassel, three yards of different colored
ribbons, and three or four shoelaces. "Turkey marabou" is the trade name for small downy turkey feathers. Felt hats took the place of buckskin as soon as
they could be had from the traders, so that in using the
hat for the foundation we are following the Indian's
present method.

Making the Foundation

Begin by removing the brim, band, and sweatband
and fitting the crown to your head so that it forms a
close-fitting skullcap. The edges of it should be even
all around and should come well down on the forehead. When you are sure it fits, fold the hat double
from front to back and draw a pencil line from a point
an inch and a half above the front edge to a point a
half an inch above the back edge. Do this on both
sides, so that when you have finished there will be a
continuous line around the lower part of the hat. Start-

ing on this line at the front and center, cut with a small knife blade two slits about a quarter of an inch apart and a quarter of an inch long, at right angles to the pencil line. Continue to cut these slits in pairs all

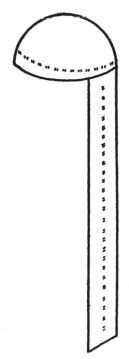

Fig. 1. Bonnet Foundation

around the hat, leaving a half-inch space between each pair. Now make a small hole in the center of each side of the hat, just above the edge, and tie a lace about a foot long to each hole. These are for tying under the chin to hold the bonnet in place.

If you are going to make a tailed bonnet you will need for the trail foundation a strip of colored cloth long enough to reach from your neck to your ankles and about eight inches wide. This should have pairs of slits cut in it the same as those on the hat, except that they should be spaced an inch apart instead of half an inch. They should be cut at right angles to the side of the strip along a line drawn along its center from top to bottom (Fig. 1). This strip can be made more attractive by binding its edges with cloth or ribbon of a contrasting color.

Preparing the Feathers

When the foundation is finished, begin to prepare the feathers. In doing this work the use of water-proof cement instead of sewing will save much time. First bind two or three of the turkey marabou or small chicken feathers, that you have removed from the duster, to the lower part of the shaft of each of the large feathers. These small feathers will form a ruff just above the red-flannel binding when the bonnet is finished, and so take the place of the down eagle feathers which were used by the Indians for the same purpose. For each feather then cut a piece of leather, a quarter of an inch wide and about three inches long, for a lacing loop. Fold and cement or sew this over the front and back of the lower part of the feather's

From Maximilian's Atlas

Sauk and Fox Indians Wearing Deer Tail Roach Headdresses

From Maximilian's Atlas

A Mandan Chief and His Exploit
Feathers

Dakota War Bonnet and Hair
Trimmed Shirt

A Horned Bonnet Worn by the Author

Courtesy of the Museum of the American Indian

An Oglala "Crow" or Bustle

shaft so that a loop is formed at the bottom about an eighth of an inch long (Fig. 2).

Next cut a piece of flannel two inches long and an inch wide. Wrap this around the leather above the loop so that it covers the ends of the small chicken or

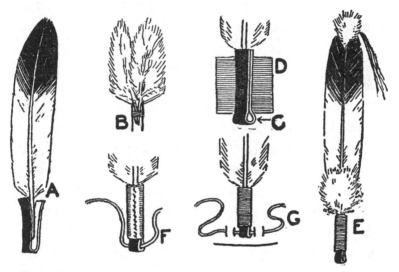

Fig. 2. (A) Feather and Leather for Loop. (B) Marabou Bound in Place. (C) Lacing Loop. (D) Flannel Binding. (E) Feather Complete. (F and G) Method of Lacing.

marabou feathers, and sew it on tightly, keeping your stitches to the under side of the feather. Now cut a small strand of horsehair, as long as your tassel will allow. Wind a thread around the end of the strand to hold it together and then carefully cement it to the outer side of the tip of the feather. A weight should be placed upon it to hold it in place while the cement is drying. Before it has hardened, a bright-colored chicken or fluffy turkey feather may be pressed on over the horsehair. The Indians sometimes used gypsum for putting the horsehair in place, so that a small white oval was made on the black tip of the feather. By using plaster of Paris you can get the same effect. Finish off each feather in this way.

Putting It Together

You are now ready to put the war bonnet together. Lay the feathers out on a table, putting the largest one in the center, the next in size to the right of it, the next to the left of the center, and so on until they are all laid out. Those that you intend using for the tail should be laid in a single line, with the largest feather at the left. If you have been fortunate enough to have secured feathers of a uniform size you will not have to do this.

Begin by assembling the crown at the front and center. Pass a shoelace through the slit at the front from the inside of the hat, then through the loop of the largest feather and then through the slit a quarter of an inch away, drawing the feather down tight. The feather next in size is laced on to the right of the first feather, and so on, until the feathers on the right side are all in place. The left side can then be finished in

the same way. After all of the feathers are in place
tie the lace together in the back. With a separate lace,
one end of which has been sewn to the under side of
the tail foundation at the top, the tail feathers are laced
on the same way, starting with the largest feather,
which goes on the top.

When the crown feathers are all laced on, you are
ready to put in the upper lacing which gives the bonnet
its shape and which holds the feathers upright. With
an awl make a small hole through the shaft on the

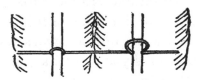

Fig. 3. Inner Lacing Thread

under side of each feather, four inches above the lacing loop. Then with heavy linen thread or string sew
through this hole, around the under side of the shaft,
and through the hole again. Allow about an inch of
thread between feathers and then sew the next feather
in the same way (Fig. 3). Start this sewing at the back
center of the war bonnet and continue all the way
around. Then shape the bonnet by adjusting the distance between the feathers, and tie the ends of the
thread together at the back. If you have made a tail,
sew the feathers in the same way, starting at the bottom
and sewing the end of the thread to the top of the hat.

Final Trimmings

Finish the bonnet by sewing some strips of bright-colored ribbon along the back edge of the hat. A good substitute for weasel-skins can be made from strips of white rabbit fur, an inch wide and about a foot long, which should be sewn on each side of the hat just over and in front of the chin tie strings. This fur is ordinarily used for trimming women's clothing and can be purchased by the yard from any of the big mail-order houses. Imitation ermine tails sewn to such strips make them look like the real thing. Indian bonnets generally had a strip of beadwork sewn across the front of the hat. This you can make, or if you do not care to spend the time on it you can sew a piece of ribbon in its place.

The "plume" which represents the bonnet's owner can be made by stripping the shaft of a long feather or from a piece of wire wrapped with ribbon. A small bunch of fluffy feathers is bound to one end of it, and at the other is a lacing loop for fastening it to the center of the hat. The hat itself is completely covered with fluffy turkey feathers which may be sewn or cemented to it (Fig. 4).

The Buffalo-horn Bonnet

When you have finished an ordinary bonnet you may wish to try to make the more elaborate and spectacular

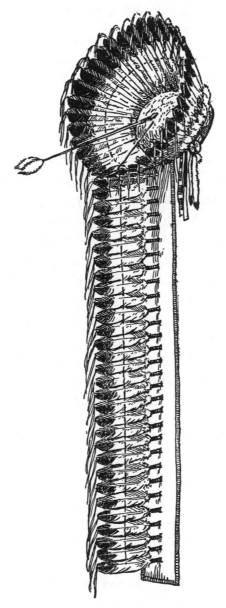

Fig. 4. Tailed Bonnet Complete

horned bonnet. The Indian used cow horns for his bonnet after the buffalo had disappeared from the plains. These you may be able to secure through a dealer in archery supplies. Painted with India ink and given a coat of shellac they look like the horns of a buffalo cow. If you can't get cow horns, good imitation buffalo horns can be whittled out of a block of white pine. They should be well curved and about seven inches from base to tip. Sandpaper them well and finish with black paint and shellac (Fig. 5).

Make the foundation exactly as described for an ordinary tailed bonnet except that the slits for the feathers are not cut all around the hat. Instead fold the hat double and draw a pencil line along the crease from front to back. Begin an inch above the front center of the hat and cut the pairs of slits a half inch apart and at right angles to the pencil line till you come to the back edge of the hat. Continue to cut them in the tail foundation, which is made the same as for an ordinary bonnet.

The horns should now be fastened to the hat. Drill small holes a half inch apart all around and close to the base of each horn. These holes are used in sewing the horns to the hat. Heavy waxed string should be used for this purpose. The horns should be sewn in the center of each side of the hat about one inch and a half above its lower edge.

The feathers are prepared in the same way as for

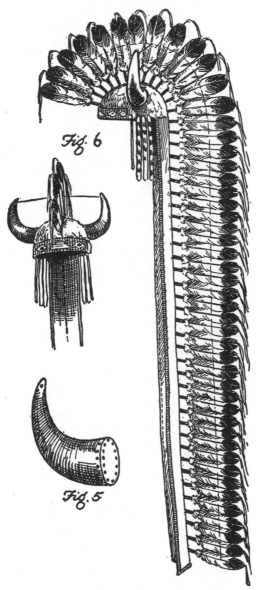

Fig. 5. Wooden Buffalo Horn. Fig. 6. Horned Bonnet Complete

an ordinary bonnet except that the marabou or small chicken feathers are fastened to both sides of the lower part of the feather. In lacing them to the hat, follow the directions given for an ordinary bonnet. The upper lacing is sewn fast to the foremost feather three inches above the lacing loop, and then through the next feather above. This lacing is passed from feather to feather until the lowest tail feather is reached, where its end is made fast. A thread fastened from tip to tip of the horns and tied in the center to the upper lacing helps to hold the top feathers upright. Many marabou or small chicken feathers should be sewn on the hat until it is almost completely covered. If you have been careful in your work, you will have succeeded in completing a bonnet such as many an old Indian scout would have been proud to wear (Fig. 6).

Exploit Feathers

Single feathers, or three or four of them, were worn in the hair by some of the Plains Tribes to designate war honors. By the way the feather was worn and decorated one could tell just what the wearer had done to earn the right to wear it. Thus among the Omaha an eagle feather was worn in the scalp lock to stand erect by the man who had struck an unwounded enemy with the hand or bow. This was an honor of the first grade because the feat required bravery and skill. The feather worn to project horizontally represented a second-grade honor, which was given for striking a wounded enemy. An honor of the third grade was awarded to the first two men to strike a dead enemy and was represented by a feather hanging down. The Hidatsa had a similar system in which the first man to touch and kill an enemy wore a feather with a horse-hair tuft. The second person to strike wore a feather with one red bar, the third two red bars, and the fourth three red bars. A man who had been wounded wore a feather dyed red, and one who had killed an enemy wore a feather decorated with a band of quillwork (Figs. 7A to 7F). Dakota feathers are shown in Figs. 7G to 7M. The first, with a red spot on it, is for killing an enemy, the notched feather for cutting an enemy's throat and taking his scalp, the cut top for cutting an enemy's throat, a notch at the top for being third to strike, notched sides for being fourth to strike, cut sides for being fifth to strike, and split for being wounded many times.

Feathers worn in the hair were first bound to a small wooden pin and fitted in a split stick as shown in Fig. 8, or fitted in a rawhide holder. A completed decoration made of partially stripped feathers is shown in the same drawing.

Feather hair decorations often had a religious significance and sometimes whole skins of birds, shells, claws, and bone were worn in the hair. A decoration

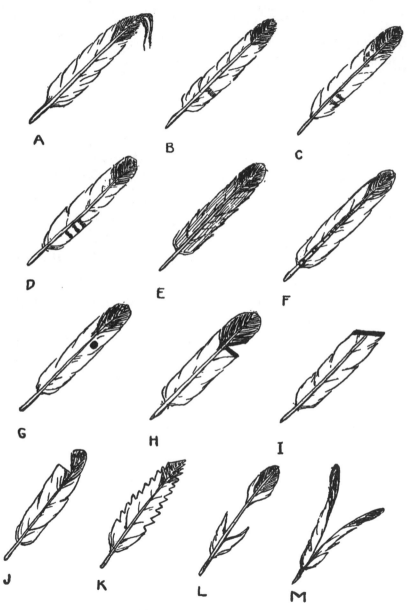

Fig. 7.   Exploit Feathers

of this kind is shown in Fig. 9. It consists of a morn-
ing-star cross cut from rawhide to which have been
fastened downy eagle feathers. When worn, decorations of this kind should be sewn to a wig.

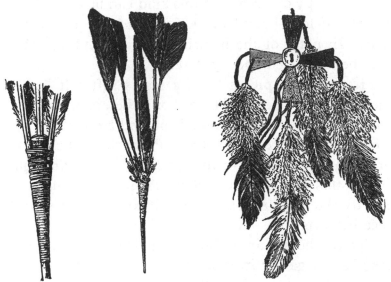

Fig. 8.   Method of Mounting Head Feathers
Fig. 9.   Feather Head Decoration (AMNH)

Deer-tail Head-dress

A roach made of a deer's tail dyed red and turkey
neck-hair could be worn by the Omaha warrior who
had won any of the first three honors. This type of
head decoration was also used by many other tribes
in the East and on the plains. The hair was woven
and fastened to a bone spreader, so that when worn it

stood erect. A feather or feathers were attached to its center. It was held in place by drawing a lock of hair through a hole in its forward end and then tying it in a knot.

A fair copy of a roach of this kind can be made from a piece of long-haired black fur and some red horsehair. In place of the horsehair, hemp binding twine may be unraveled and dyed red.

First cut two pieces from a man's soft felt hat in the shape of Fig. 10. These should be about two and a half inches wide at the broad end and ten inches long. The thicker the felt the better. Place these one on top of the other and sew them together. Now trim your fur so that it is bristly and brush-like, and cut it in exactly the same shape as the felt to which it should then be sewn.

Cut the horsehair or binding twine in twelve-inch lengths and gather it in bundles about an eighth of an inch in diameter. Bend them double and bind them with thread to form bundles as in Fig. 10. These bundles are sewn to the edges of the roach so that they stand nearly upright. They are placed close together at the front and back and about an inch apart in between.

To the top of the roach a feather is fastened so that it may twirl about in the wind. This is done by cutting off its end and forcing it on a small wooden pin held inside a bone socket which is sewn to the roach. The

socket is made from a piece of bone about two inches
long and a half inch in diameter, with a tapering hole
through it. The larger opening is reamed out to make
the opening still wider. A wooden pin is now whittled
out with a ball at one end just large enough to fit in the

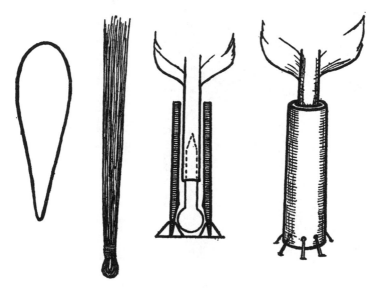

Fig. 10. Roach Foundation and Hair Bundle
Fig. 11. Bone Feather Socket

large opening, and a point at the other. The pin is
placed inside the bone, which is sewn to the center of
the roach about three inches from the wide end. When
in place the feather is pushed over the pin. The construction of the socket is shown in the sectional drawing in Fig. 11, and the completed roach in Fig. 12.
The roach may be held in place with tie strings or

sewn to a wig. It can also be worn on a beaded headband with cross straps similar in construction to the
frame of an Iroquois cap.

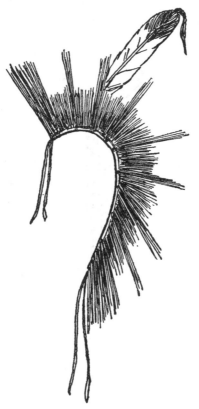

Fig. 12. Completed Roach

Winter Cap

The Blackfoot and other northern Plains Tribes
wore a fur cap without a top in winter, made from a

band of fur from some smaller animal such as the coyote, badger, or otter.   Caps of this kind were also worn by the Omaha, Osage, and Ponca.   Among the latter tribes they were ornamented with quillwork and painted designs on rawhide.   Feathers were often fastened to them to stand upright in the back.

Such a cap may be made from a discarded lady's fur neckpiece.   Simply sew it into a circle to fit your

Fig. 13.   Winter Cap

head and attach a large feather to the back of it as shown in Fig. 13.

Iroquois Head-dress

The Eastern Indians wore head-dresses of animal skins, caps, turbans of soft buckskin, and feathered headbands.   One of these that you can make is the feathered cap of the Iroquois called by them the *gus-to-weh,* or real hat.   The feathers required for it are one large eagle feather, real or imitation, and a number of small feathers, including some turkey marabou. White chicken feathers with their tips dyed and small turkey feathers will do nicely.

The cap, which is round and fits the head closely, is made of any kind of cloth or soft leather, such as sheepskin. The first thing to make is the frame. Cut a strip of felt from a hat an inch and a half wide and

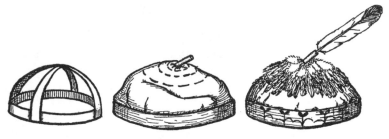

Fig. 14. Frame for Iroquois Head-dress
Fig. 15. Covered Frame Showing Basting Stitches
Fig. 17. Head-dress Complete

long enough to fit closely around your head. Then sew to it two felt cross-pieces as shown in Fig. 14. The covering of cloth or leather is now sewn to the frame. The cloth should be cut to cover the frame rather loosely and not so that it will be tight and smooth. To the top of the hat a bone socket is now sewn in place. This is exactly like the one used on the roach and is, of course, used for the large feather. In the old days this feather was removed while traveling through the woods. Two inches from the socket a circle of basting stitches an inch long are now made around the hat. A similar circle is then made a half inch closer to the center (Fig. 15). These stitches are made with doubled waxed linen thread, as the small feathers are to be fastened to them. A third circle, which is the smallest, is made about a half inch from the socket. This should be sewn through the hat in

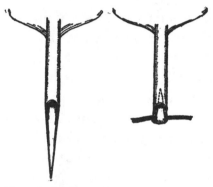

Fig. 16. Method of Fastening Feathers

not more than three places, so that the feathers attached to it may fly rather freely.

The feathers are placed in three overlapping rows, the ones farthest from the center being put in place first. To prepare the feathers, their ends are whittled off to a point as shown in Fig. 16. They are fastened to the threads simply by passing the pointed end of the quill over the top and around the thread and then tucking it into its own quill as shown in the drawing. The smallest circle is made entirely of turkey, marabou or other fluffy feathers. Don't make the mistake of putting the feathers too close together. When all of the small feathers are in place, put the large feather in its socket. The hat may be finished by sewing a beaded band around its rim (Fig. 17).

"The Crow," or Bustle

Among the Omaha and other plains tribes men who had won high war honors were permitted to wear a feather decoration known as "the Crow." By white men it is often called a dance bustle. From those who had the right to wear it the "dog soldiers," or tribal police, were chosen. They wore it as a badge of office during the great tribal hunts and in certain ceremonial dances. "The Crow" was worn at the back, being held in place by a belt of buckskin. It consisted of a rawhide frame covered with the entire skin of an eagle and from which two buckskin pendants hung down the wearer's legs, like the trail of a war bonnet. Projecting from it were two upright feather shafts tipped with red horsehair. Fur, loose feathers, and entire birdskins were often used on it as further decorations. "The Crow" symbolized a battlefield and only the feathers of birds that appeared after a battle were used in its construction. It took its name from an entire crowskin, which in the old days was one of its important parts, because the keen scent of this bird brought it to the battlefield before any of the others. Feathers of buzzards, magpies, and eagles were used because they were the second, third, and fourth birds to arrive. The eagle was also associated with war and the power of the thunder. The two upright shafts symbolized slain warriors and the arrows that had killed them. The one on the left represented an enemy and the one on the right a friend. In modern times this old symbolism has been forgotten, so that feathers of all sorts, together with decorations furnished by the traders, go into the making of a "Crow."

For the foundation of the "Crow" you are going to make you may use a section of an ordinary cardboard mailing tube. Get the heaviest one you can find, about two inches in diameter, and cut it down to eight inches in length. Reinforce it by covering it with adhesive tape or muslin which may be glued on. If you can get it, make the tube of rawhide as the Indians did.

The uprights are whittled from two slender sticks, which when finished will be fifteen inches long and tapering from a quarter of an inch at the bottom to an eighth of an inch in diameter at the top. These take the place of the eagle wing-feather shafts used by the Indians. Before being put in place they should be decorated. Leave the lower end bare for about three inches and wrap the rest of the stick with colored ribbon which should be held in place with glue. To the tip of the stick bind a tuft of red horsehair, a downy feather, or a bit of fur and some short streamers of narrow ribbon. Two or three large feathers may be tightly bound to the lower end of the shaft where the ribbon wrapping begins. A string of small brass costume bells may be tied the length of the shaft. The complete shaft is shown in Fig. 19. When both are finished put them in place on the foundation by inserting them in holes made an inch from its ends, as shown in Fig. 20. The lower end of the shaft projects for about a quarter of an inch through the foundation. In this end, and also through the shaft where it enters the tube, a brad is driven to hold it in place. A wrapping of string is also made at these points to hold the shaft firmly in place and to prevent its slipping around. The upper wrappings are covered by circles of smaller feathers prepared in the same manner as those for the Iroquois head-dress. Six or more are strung on a cord which is tied around the shaft at the point where it enters the foundation. A thread is then run through the inside of the shaft of each small feather halfway to its top, like the inner lacing in a war bonnet. This holds the feathers upright so that they form a cone as shown in Fig. 21a. Two or three of these decorations may be placed about each shaft. Others should be made and tied to the ends of the cardboard foundation which they will serve to cover.

The tail foundation is made from a piece of card-

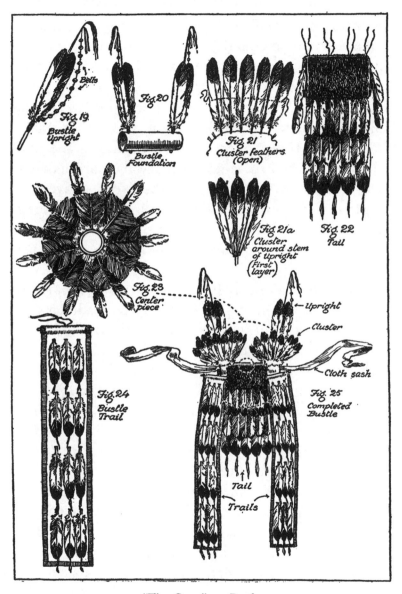

"The Crow" or Bustle

board or rawhide five by ten inches, folded double to make a five-inch square. In the fold, about an inch apart, five large feathers are inserted and sewn in place so that they lie flat and their edges just overlap. These are tipped with horsehair and decorated with small colored feathers cemented to them. A row of smaller feathers is lapped over them and sewn to the cardboard, and when these are in place they are half covered by a row of still smaller feathers sewn above them. A piece of fur or a small mirror is used to cover the ends of the quills. The tail is finished by sewing a few feathers loosely to the sides of the foundation (Fig. 22).

Nowadays a circular feather decoration is sometimes used in place of the tail. This may be made on a circular foundation of two pieces of cardboard, five inches in diameter. Between these, feathers are sewn in a circle as shown in Fig. 23. A row of other feathers with their ends cut off square is sewn over them, and a third row cut the same way is sewn on top of the cardboard to overlap the second row. A small round mirror is then sewn to the center to hide the ends of the top row of feathers. Some downy feathers may then be cemented under the edge of the mirror.

The two trails are made of bright-colored cloth, four inches wide and about two feet long. At their upper ends they are hemmed over and a small stick is inserted to make them hang flat. The feathers on the trail lie flat instead of projecting as they do in the trail of a bonnet. They are decorated like bonnet feathers, but their ends are prepared like those for the Iroquois hat. The feathers are fastened to the cloth in rows of three or four, so that each row just touches the one below. A complete trail is shown in Fig. 24.

To assemble "the Crow" tie the trails to the ends of the foundation. Do this by tying a thong around the center of the small stick on the upper end of the trail and then to the edge of the tube. Then fasten the tail or the circular ornament to the center of the foundation between the two uprights. This is best done by first punching holes in the cardboard and making the fastenings with heavy string or leather thongs. The sash or belt which holds "the Crow" in place may be made from a piece of cloth six inches wide and long enough to go around the waist and be tied in a bow. The center of it is tied to the back of the tube foundation in such a way that the two upright shafts will be at an angle of about thirty degrees to the back of the wearer when the bustle is worn. The bustle complete is shown in Fig. 25.

Chapter Three

WAR SHIRTS, LEGGINS, AND WOMEN'S COSTUME

IN THE old days the plains Indian's clothing was made entirely of skins. Buffalo, elk, antelope, mountain-sheep, and mountain-goat hides were used for this purpose. These were secured by the men and tanned by the women. Buffalo cowskins were commonly used for robes, breech clouts, leggins, moccasins, and shirts. Ordinarily the man wore only the breech clout, but he always had his soft tanned robe handy, so that it could be put on at once if visitors arrived or if he were summoned to a gathering of importance.

How Buffalo Were Trapped

Before horses were introduced, buffalo were often taken in great numbers in traps built on the edge of a cliff or cut bank. Such places were not common on the prairies, so that, once constructed, the traps were used for many years. Traces of some of them can be clearly seen today, so that we can tell exactly how they were made. Along the edge of the cliff an open space a hundred to two hundred feet wide would be left, and from its ends two diverging lines of stone piles would

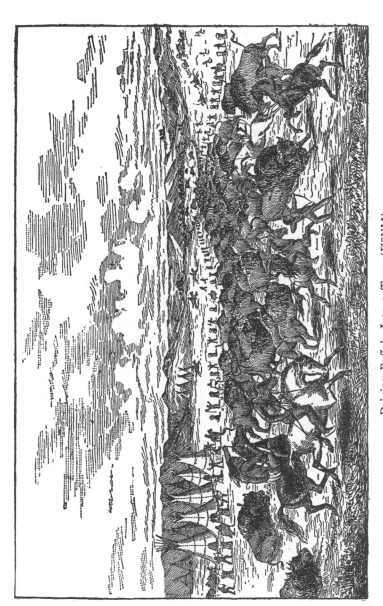

Driving Buffalo Into a Trap (USNM)

be built out on the prairies for a mile and a half or more, so that when finished they resembled a large V with the narrow end at the cliff. The stone piles were built about five paces from one another and the two lines of them were about two miles apart at the wide end of the trap. Directly below the opening a round log corral would be made, but if the cliff was very high, or the ground below miry, this was not needed.

When a hunt was to take place the tribal camp was moved near the trap and scouts sent out to watch the movements of the buffalo. When they reported that the herd had come close to the trap the buffalo caller, who was a man having great medicine power over the buffalo, began to prepare himself for the hunt. All night long he would sing his buffalo songs and pray to the Above People for help. Before dawn the buffalo caller would put on his horned head-dress and leave the camp, followed by the men and women who were to take part in the hunt. These people would hide behind the stone piles while the buffalo caller went off alone toward the herd. He would get as close as he could to the leaders of the herd and then try to attract their attention. To do this he would hide, jump about, and softly call to the buffalo. After a while the old bulls might walk toward him. As soon as they moved, he would edge off toward the trap. If they kept following and others joined them, the caller

would move faster and faster, until finally the entire
herd was following him at a trot. Once they were well
between the rows of stone piles, the people behind
would rise up shouting and waving robes, until the
whole herd was in a stampede. The buffalo caller by
this time had turned aside to safety between the walls
but the herd kept crowding and thundering on until a
veritable waterfall of buffalo went tumbling over the
cliff to the corral below. Many were killed by the
fall, but often some fell into the corral alive. Here
they would mill around until they were killed by men
armed with stone mauls or by arrows shot from the
walls. Soon there was plenty of meat, hides, and sinew
in the camp, and the making of new clothing and
lodges would begin.

The Meaning of the War Shirt

Like the war bonnet, the war shirt trimmed with
hair or weasel skins was considered to have great medicine power and could be worn on special occasions
only by men in authority or those who had distinguished themselves in battle. Among the Dakota and
Cheyenne these shirts were trimmed with hair, but the
Blackfoot and Crow often used white weasel skins in
the place of the hair fringe. Though called scalp
shirts by the whites, the hair used in trimming the shirts
did not always come from enemy scalps. A man

might cut off some of his own or his wife might give some of hers for these decorations.   Each lock on the shirt represented a *coup* won by capturing a horse, taking prisoners, getting wounds, or saving the life of

Blackfoot Shirt Trimmed with Weasel Skins (AMNH)

a friend.   The hair or weasel-trimmed shirt and the leggins which were similarly decorated were made at a feast with a great deal of ceremony.   They were worn only on very important occasions or when going into battle.

Indian tan buckskin is very difficult to obtain nowadays, but genuine buckskin from which gloves are made can still be had from leather dealers, although it is rather expensive. For the most part it comes from Mexico and Brazil. The skins are usually smaller than those of sheep and are seldom perfect because of wounds or thorn scratches. The best substitutes for our purposes are ooze split calfskins, suède, or buff tanned sheepskins.

Making a War Shirt

To make a war shirt you will need four skins, if it is to be of leather, or five yards of white or khaki cloth. Hair for scalps may be obtained by buying black "switches" at a five-and-ten-cent store or by purchasing black Chinese hair fringe from a hair-goods dealer or wig-maker. The latter is the least expensive and the easiest to make up. Black horsehair may also be used, but because of its coarseness it is not entirely satisfactory. Instead of weasel skins you may use the white rabbit fur trimming mentioned in the previous chapter. Enough will be needed to make eighty-four strips a foot long, or about twenty-eight yards of the half-inch-wide fur. You will also need three yards of inch-wide red ribbon.

The old Indian pattern is quite a simple one, and this we shall largely follow. As you can see from the diagram (Fig. 25a), it was the easiest way to cut two skins to make a shirt. The small foreleg section was used for a sleeve and the larger piece for the front or back of the shirt. Begin to make your shirt by cutting a paper pattern for it. Enlarge the pattern (Fig. 26) given here, using a shirt of your own as a guide to the

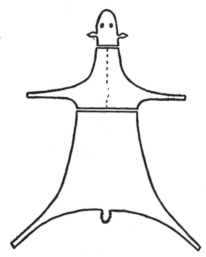

Fig. 25a. Indian Method of Cutting Shirt from Deer Skin

size. In cutting the pattern remember that a war shirt should be loose-fitting and that it should be long enough to reach halfway to the knees. Cut the front and back of the shirt first. In doing this make the neck opening just large enough to slip your head through. Next cut the two triangular neck flaps and the sleeves. You are now ready to begin sewing.

First sew the neck flaps to the front and back along

the edge of the neck opening, BC. Then bind the neck opening by sewing over its edges red flannel or ribbon. This binding should be about a half inch wide. Now sew the back and front sections together at the shoulder seams, AB and CD. The sections should be turned

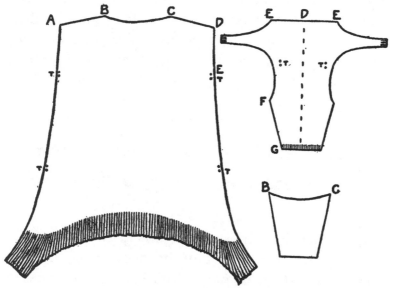

Fig. 26. Shirt Pattern

inside out while this sewing is done. The sleeves should then be sewn in at the shoulders, EDE. Next sew the lower part of each sleeve together, FG. Your sewing is now finished except for the beaded strips or substitute decorations, which should now be attached. Directions for making these are to be found in the chapter on beadwork. The strips that go over the shoulders should be three inches wide and twenty-four inches long. The sleeve strips are two inches wide and eighteen inches long. If you are a rather small chap the sizes just given will have to be cut down in length.

After the strips are in place put in the tie strings, TT. These should be strips of skin or tape nine inches long and about one-quarter inch wide. They hold the loose edges of the shirt together. Besides those indicated in the diagram, tie strings may also be placed on each side of the neck opening.

Fig. 27. Hair Locks

Now that the shirt is put together, we are ready for the most important part of its decoration—the hair locks or the strips of fur. Each hair lock or piece of fur is attached to the shirt with a thong or piece of tape six inches long. Eighty-four of these thongs and locks should be prepared. If you are using hair, first cut off a lock about an eighth of an inch in diameter. Double the cut end over for about a half inch and bind it tightly with heavy cotton thread (Fig. 27). Then bind to it the end of your thong or piece of tape. Next cut off an inch of the inch-wide red ribbon and after

Kilted Antelope Priests in the Hopi Snake Dance

An Indian of Manhattan Island   Plains Woman's Costume

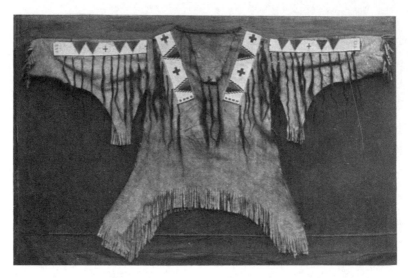

Hair Trimmed Shirt

A Northwest Coast Chief

Washakie—Chief of the Shoshone

coating one side of it with water-proof cement wrap it around the binding so that it completely conceals the thread. If you use fur, cut it in strips a half inch wide and a foot long and attach the thongs or tape in the same way. The hair locks or fur strips are attached to the shirt under the bead strips as shown in the illustration. To fasten them in place make small holes an

Crow Beaded Vest (AMNH)

inch apart. Through these push the thong, and after the lock is drawn up fairly tight tie a large knot in the thong on the inside of the shirt.

Finish the shirt by fringing the bottom. Do this carefully, cutting each strip of fringe about a quarter of an inch wide and four to six inches deep. The fringe around the cuff is of the same width, but it should be cut to a depth of only two inches. Sometimes the Indians colored the upper half of the shirts blue to represent the sky, and the lower half yellow to represent the earth. Leather may be colored in this way with ordinary aniline dyes or paint. Prepare the dyes according to the directions on the package and apply them with an ordinary one-inch paint brush. Paint must be thinned out with turpentine and brushed well into the leather. When it is dry go over it with the varnish used as a finish for parchment lamp-shades. This keeps the paint from peeling off.

How to Make Leggins

Leggins are easily made of split calfskin, sheepskin, or outing flannel. The average boy's size takes two yards of material twenty-four inches wide. Cut this length in half and fold the two pieces lengthwise (Fig. 28). From A, at the bottom center of the leggin, sew a single seam diagonally to B, which should be at about the same height as the lower end of the hip pocket opening on an ordinary pair of trousers. Pin the goods together and try it on before sewing. Next cut out the curved sections, BC and DE, which permit the leggin to fit under the crotch. The upper edge, CD, should be folded over and sewn down to form a belt loop. The back of under side of the leggin is cut out as indicated by the dotted line, BE, and is left open like a cowboy's chaps. Turn over and over and bind all edges so that they will not fray or rip.

The old Indian pattern (Fig. 29) was open in both front and back, and when worn was fastened to the belt with a thong. Instead of being sewn, the front and

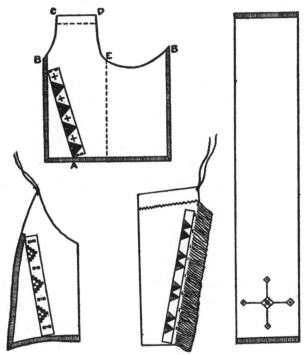

Fig. 28. Leggin Pattern
Fig. 29. Old Indian Leggin Pattern
Fig. 30. Crow Leggin
Fig. 31. Breech Clout Pattern

back were held together by thongs tied about three inches apart along the diagonal seam line. Sometimes the flaps were cut into fringes. This was particularly true of the leggins made by the Crow (Fig. 30).

Often scalp locks or weasel-skins were sewn or tied along the seam as an additional decoration. To decorate your leggins you will need two stenciled or beaded strips about three inches wide and twenty inches long, which should be sewn on the front along the seam. Directions for making these are to be found in the chapter on beadwork. The edges of flaps and the bottom of the leggins may be bound with bright-colored satin ribbon. This will add to their attractiveness. If you make them of leather, three hides will be required. Fold and sew the largest two skins in the same way as you would the cloth. The third skin will be needed to piece the tops in order to get the proper length.

The Breech Clout

With the leggins a breech clout (Fig. 31) must be worn. This is simply a piece of cloth a foot wide and six feet long. Its ends are drawn between the legs and over the belt in front and behind. It may be decorated with beadwork and with strips of colored ribbon sewn to its edges and ends.

Both men and women wore robes that were originally of buffalo-skin but later on were made from a blanket or heavy red or blue flannel. To make such a robe simply sew the cloth in a six-foot square. The edges may be bound with silk ribbon three inches wide of a contrasting color. The seam in the robe's center is covered with a strip of beadwork or a stenciled substitute four inches wide. Cotton duveteen is an excellent and inexpensive material to use for a robe of this kind.

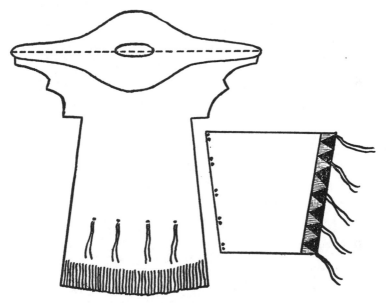

Fig. 32. Woman's Gown Pattern
Fig. 33. Pattern for Woman's Leggin

Woman's Costume

The plains woman's costume consisted of a plain knee-length gown, a belt, moccasins, and pair of leggins. The gown (Fig. 32) is cut in much the same way as the war shirt and the front and back are sewn together along the sides. There are no regular sleeves, but the upper part of the gown, which is cut separately, hangs cape-like over the shoulders and arms. This extra curved yoke may be omitted if desired and elbow-length sleeves may be cut to take its place. This curved yoke on old costumes is always heavily beaded and many pendants are hung from its edges. These pendants nowadays are sometimes made of thimbles which rattle and jingle as the wearer moves about. The bottom of the gown is deeply fringed. Extra fringed ornaments are made by drawing a long lace through two holes spaced a half inch apart so that its ends hang out evenly on the front or back of the gown.

Women's leggins cover the ankles and calf of the leg. They can be made from cloth or leather. They are decorated with a painted or beaded strip on one side, as shown in Fig. 33, or with a broad band of solid beaded work that covers the part of the leggin that goes around the ankle.

Round nickel-plated disks were introduced by the traders and became a common ornament for women's belts. As a substitute for them disks may be cut from tin cans, made concave by hammering and fastened to a cloth or leather belt by perforations made in their edges.

Like the men, the women wore many necklaces and often long earrings made of shells or bits of bright-colored stone. Occasionally they wore feathers in their

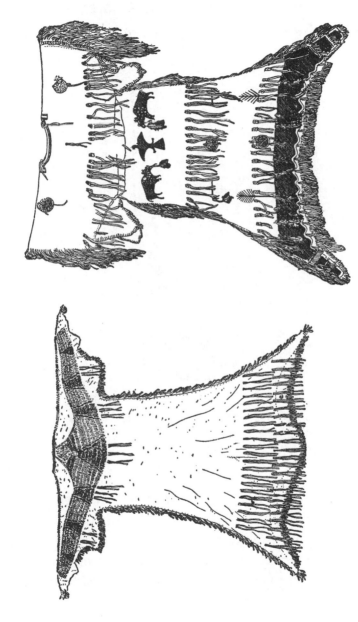

Yakima Woman's Dress and Arapaho Girl's Ceremonial Dress (AMNH)

hair, and in some ceremonies wore a regular war bonnet.

Crow Woman's Leggin (AMNH)

Pueblo Costumes

In reproducing Pueblo dances boys may wish to use the kilts and sashes worn by the men in these ceremonies. These were made from a coarse soft cotton cloth and were decorated with woven and embroidered designs in colors. Copies of them may be made from a

good grade of unbleached muslin, white drill, or other
heavy cotton cloth. Decorative designs can be embroidered in colored yarn in the way of the Indians or
simply painted on.

The kilt (Fig. 34) is thirty inches long and eighteen inches wide. It is fastened about the waist with

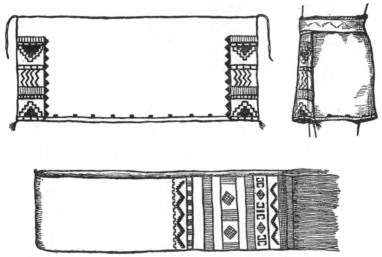

Fig. 34. Pueblo Kilt and Method of Wearing It
Fig. 35. Pueblo Sash

the tie cords at its upper ends. Tassels of colored
yarn are on its lower corners. The opening of the kilt
is on the side and is covered by the long fringed sash.
This sash (Fig. 35) is six feet long and ten inches wide.
It is worn by passing it around the waist over the kilt
and looping one end over the other. A wolf or fox
skin was generally suspended from it in the back.

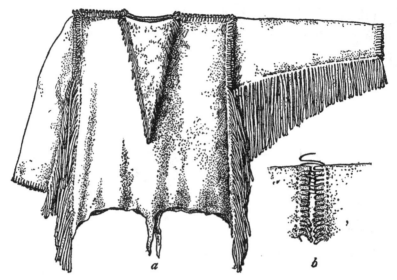

Fig. 36. (a)   Hopi Man's Buckskin Shirt.   (b)   Detail of Seams (USNM)

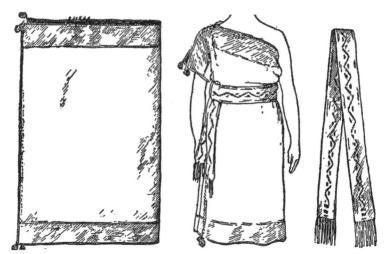

Fig. 37. Southwestern Woman's Dress.   Fig. 38. Method of Wearing Blanket
Dress.   Fig. 39.   Woman's Woven Belt

In ancient times the kilt and a cotton or skin robe was the man's ordinary costume. It is not known whether or not shirts and leggins similar to those worn by the Plains Indians were used by the Pueblos before the coming of the Spaniards. Such shirts and leggins have, however, been used by these Indians in recent times, one from the Hopi being shown in Fig. 36.

The costume of women in the Southwest consisted of a cotton dress without sleeves that was fastened over the right shoulder. Nowadays these are nearly always of a dark blue color. A sash, generally red with designs in black, green, and white in it, is worn about the waist (Figs. 37, 38, 39).

Eastern Costumes

Eastern Indians wore breech clouts, leggins, and shirts somewhat similar to the Plains costume. The men of the Iroquois sometimes wore a kilt similar to the Pueblo one in style, but made of soft buckskin instead of cotton. Their leggins differed from those of the Plains in that they had the seam to the front and were without the triangular flaps or fringe. They were curved at the bottom from front to back, so that there was an opening over the instep. In common with other Woodland Indians, the men often carried a square bag which hung at the side from a broad band over the shoulder (Fig. 40). Although used in early

Colonial times, it may be that the Indians copied these bags from the bandoleers carried by the soldiers. Robes of fur, feathers, and buckskin were worn by the men and women.

Fig. 40.   Iroquois Chiefs

Northwest Coast Costumes

Ceremonial clothing on the Northwest Coast was decorated with the "totem pole" type of design common to this area. A shirt worn in ceremonies is shown in Fig. 41. This is woven in the same way as a Chilkat blanket. A copy of it can be made of cotton cloth and the designs painted on it. In modern times these

Northwest Coast Chief's Costume (USNM)

Fig. 41. Chilkat Ceremonial Shirt (BAE)

Fig. 42. Northwest Coast Shirt with Appliqué Design (BAE)

Indians have been making clothing of cloth and carrying out their designs in appliqué. A shirt made in this
way is shown in Fig. 42. Trousers or leggins fringed

Fig. 43.   Leggin with Appliqué Design (AMNH)

at the bottom and with rows of fringe around the leg
are worn with shirts of this kind (Fig. 43).

Chapter Four

MOCCASINS AND TANNING METHODS

THE comfortable and easily made moccasin was the first part of the Indian costume to be adopted by the white man and is generally the last part of his native costume that the Indian discards as he takes the trail toward civilization. Perhaps the first white men to wear them were the early French explorers, who found their stiff-soled and heavy boots unsuited for woodland travel by canoe and snowshoe. Frontiersmen, trappers, and scouts wore them because of the advantages they possessed over the shoe in hunting, for life in the woods and on the plains. Today they are recognized as the best type of footwear for campers and outdoorsmen.

Nearly every tribe had its own pattern and method of decorating moccasins, so that it was possible for an Indian scout to tell a man's tribe by a glance at his moccasins. In some cases an expert tracker might do this merely by seeing the moccasin tracks. To deceive their enemies the Omahas often wore the moccasin of another tribe while on the war trail. Other Indians made moccasins with a heavy fringe at the heel which obliterated the tracks as the wearer walked along. Some years ago Chief Noisy Owl of the Oglala Dakotas made the drawings reproduced here (Fig. 44) for an

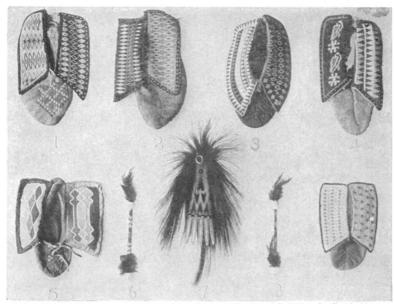

Woodland Moccasins and Deer Tail Head-Dress

Plains Moccasins

Making Moccasins in Camp

Tanning Hides in a Crow Camp
From a painting by George Catlin

artist, to show him the difference between the tracks of some of the plains tribes.

Moccasins were made wholly of soft tanned skins or with soft uppers and rawhide soles. In winter the hair was left on the hide and turned on the inside. The Indians never wore stockings, but sometimes moccasins were made with very high tops that covered the calf

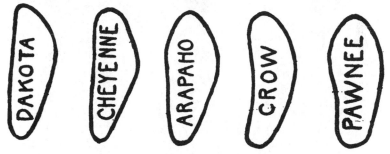

Fig. 44. Moccasin Tracks

of the leg. These kept out the cold and snow and with the leggins gave excellent protection.

Although moccasins were of many different patterns, there were but two principal types, the soft sole of the Woodland Tribes and the hard sole of the Plains and the Southwest. You can easily make a pair of either type by following the directions given here.

Making Hard-sole Moccasins

A pair of beaded moccasins that will give good service in camp and at home can be made from materials

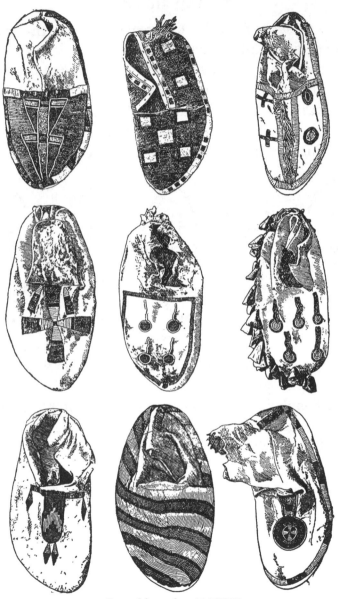

Crow Moccasins (AMNH)

that will cost no more than seventy-five cents. These are of the type used by the Plains Tribes, which in the old days were made with uppers of soft buckskin and soles of stiff rawhide. In place of buckskin we will use ooze calf or sheepskin, and as a substitute for rawhide thin sole leather, which may be purchased at the five-and-ten-cent stores. Some heavy linen thread, shoemakers' needles, and a thin curved awl will be the other materials required.

Begin by making a paper pattern and be sure your pattern fits before cutting the leather. Make the sole pattern first by placing your right foot, with the shoe removed, on a piece of wrapping-paper, and drawing an outline of the foot on it. Lengthen the outline that you have made by one-quarter of an inch and at the same time make it conform as nearly as possible to the shape of the dotted outline in Fig. 45. From this pattern the moccasin sole may be cut. With the sole pattern as a base the pattern for the upper is made according to Fig. 45. It should be about half an inch longer than the sole. Its width will depend on the size of your foot and can be determined by a little experimentation.

When your outline is drawn, cut it out and make the T-shaped cut, BYZ. Now try the pattern on over your foot, and if it fits cut the uppers from it. At the same time cut the flaps according to Fig. 46. The length of the edge, CD, must be the same as that of the cut, YZ, in the diagram.

You are now ready to sew the upper to the sole. The upper may be beaded with Indian patterns, but this work must be done before it is attached to the sole.

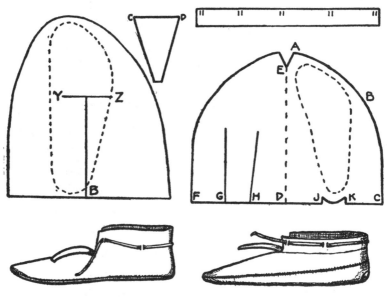

Fig. 45. Plains Pattern. Fig. 46. Tongue
Fig. 47. One-piece Plains Pattern. Fig. 48. Top Piece

The upper and sole are sewn together, turned inside out. First soak the sole in water until it is soft and pliable. Then, beginning at the toe, start your sewing. Make holes in the leather with your curved awl as you go along and do your stitching with well-waxed thread. Sew halfway back on each side and then turn the toe of the moccasin right side up. Complete your sewing down each side and around the heel. Sew up the vertical heel seam and turn the entire moccasin right side up. The small triangular toe flap is now sewn to the edge of the slit, YZ. Complete the moccasin by cutting small slits along the edge of the upper and inserting the lace. To make the left moccasin reverse the pattern.

The One-piece Plains Moccasin

Another type of moccasin used by the Northern plains tribes was the one-piece soft-sole type. The pattern given here (Fig. 47) is based on a Dakota moccasin now in the National Museum. This moccasin is made entirely of ooze calf, sheep, or any other soft skin. In making the pattern begin with an outline of the foot. Locate the point A about a half inch from the tip of the toe. Draw a line AE, which is about an inch and a half long. Then draw the line ABC. At B, it should be a quarter of an inch from the sole outline, and at C it is about three inches from the center of the heel and a quarter of an inch below it. Now draw the line CD, which will be approximately six inches long. Next cut out the drawing you have made so far and fold it over on the dotted line, DE. Then draw the pattern of the upper exactly the same size as that of the sole. The flap cuts, G and H, are now made at an angle and about six inches long. The curved heelpiece, JK, is about a half inch deep and an inch and a quarter wide. Notice that KC and FG are exactly the width of HJ. When you have made your paper pattern fit, cut the leather from it.

Fold the leather along the line ED, so that points F and C touch. Then sew the long seam, EABC. The vertical heel seam is now made by sewing KC and FG, which are now joined, to JDH. The curved heel flap, JK, is then turned up and sewn in place. The sides of this moccasin are not quite high enough so that a top piece (Fig. 48) two inches wide and long enough to go around the opening must be cut and sewn in place. Through slits made in this extra top piece the tie lace is passed. When this is done your moccasin is complete.

Woodland Moccasins

A third type of moccasin which you may wish to make is the soft-sole one of the Woodland Indians. It differs from the soft-sole plains moccasin in that it was generally made on a two-piece pattern with a puckered front. The Chippewas, one of the great woodland tribes, get their name from these moccasins; as translated it means, "people of the puckered moccasin."

As in the others, an outline of your foot serves as a basis for the pattern. However, as in this type there are no rights or lefts, you will not have to reverse the

pattern to cut the pair. After making the sole outline, lay off points about two inches from the toe and

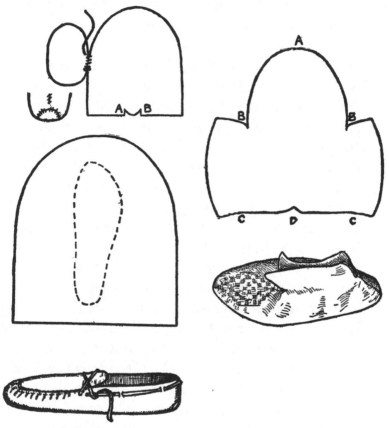

Fig. 49. Woodland Pattern. Fig. 50. Method of Stitching Sole to Tongue
Fig. 51. Heel Seam. Fig. 52. One-piece Pattern

sides and cut your pattern to the shape of Fig. 49.
Now cut the tongue pattern, which, except for the
slightly curved end, is exactly the same shape. This

should be half as long as the sole piece, and its width is a bit less than a third the distance around the ball of your foot. The best way to get this measurement is by taking a piece of string and passing it around the foot while you are putting your full weight on it. The full measurement thus obtained should equal the width of both pieces placed edge to edge.

When you are sure the pattern fits, cut your leather from it. Place the large and small pieces edge to edge and begin to sew them together as shown in Fig. 50. As the distance around the edge of the sole piece is about twice as long as that of the tongue, it is necessary to pucker it about every quarter of an inch. To do this take a stitch through the sole twice the length of the corresponding stitch in the tongue. If the puckers are correctly made the two sides will have the same number of stitches in them when you have finished.

After sewing the tongue in, put a board inside the moccasin and with another piece of wood pound the stitching down flat. Then try it on and mark the point where your heel will come. If the sole piece is too long remove the surplus leather with a straight cut. Next cut the notches and curved heelpiece, AB. The point A should be sewn to B, and the back stitched up. When this is done turn up the curved heelpiece and sew it down as shown in Fig. 51. Finish the moccasin by putting in a tie lace which is run through pairs of slits cut in the sides of the upper.

Assiniboine Moccasin Decorations (AMNH)

Another type of one-piece moccasin, such as many tribes used, is shown in Fig. 52. This is made entirely of soft leather and is cut to fit in about the same way as the moccasin we have just described. When you have cut the leather fold it down the middle from heel to toe and sew the edges AB together. This seam is puckered, and near the toes it is gathered so that the stitches do not go beyond, but end about a half inch from the toe. The heel is sewn up from D to C, the upper section forming the ankle flaps.

Indian Tanning Methods

After you have moccasins from commercial leather you may wish to try making them from hides prepared by yourself. The Indian method is a rather laborious but not difficult process. It can best be done in the summer when you are in camp.

For rawhide which is used for plains moccasin soles use a raw calfskin which you can get through your butcher. Such a hide will cost about one dollar and will provide soles for several pairs of moccasins. Soak the hide in warm water overnight, then stake it out on smooth ground, hair side down. The stakes should be driven about six inches apart and the hide stretched as tight as possible. The hide will have clinging to it pieces of flesh, fat, and tissue. This is removed by a first treatment which is called fleshing. The work can be done with a sheath knife or a light ax blade, but better results can be obtained with a simple hoe-shaped tool (Fig. 53) which you can make or which a blacksmith can make for you in a few moments. This tool is fashioned from a piece of one-eighth-inch by one-and-a half-inch band iron fifteen inches long. Three inches from one end the piece is bent over at a right angle. The outer edge of the short piece is then sharpened with a file and three or four teeth are nicked in it. The tool is used as a hoe. With it your work can be done more quickly and you are less likely to cut

Fig. 53. Hide Scraper

holes in the hide than you would be with the knife or ax.

If the hide dries or hardens while you are working, dampen it with warm water. When the upper surface is clean and smooth allow it to dry and bleach in the sun for two days. The next step is to again soak the hide, turn it over, and once more stake it out, this time with the hair side up. The hair is scraped off in the same manner as the flesh. If the hair does not come off easily it will be necessary to resoak the hide in wood ashes and water. Mix the ashes and water in a bucket to a consistency of pancake batter. Put the hide in this mixture and leave it soak overnight. In the morning wash out every trace of the wood ashes in cold water and stake it out again. The hair can now be removed with little effort. Allow this side of the skin to dry and bleach in the sun for two days, which completes the process and leaves the rawhide ready for use.

Making Buckskin

To make soft tan buckskin the hide is first put through the rawhide process. The rest of the treatment is more difficult and expensive. In addition to the hide you will need to purchase from the butcher the calf's brains and liver. These are used for the tanning mixture. To prepare them for use mash the brains and liver together with a quarter of a pound of lard. Add a small amount of water and cook the mixture slowly for about an hour, when it will be ready for use. A less expensive but also less satisfactory substitute for the brains and liver can be made from lard, baking flour, and warm water.

While the hide is staked on the ground the mixture is thoroughly worked into it first on one side and then on the other. This can best be done with the hands and with a smooth round stone. After it has been spread evenly over the hide the stakes should be withdrawn and the hide rolled or folded. It should then be left overnight, to allow the tanning mixture to soak in. The next day it should be washed in cold water and dried. This will cause it to shrink and thicken, so that before graining it will have to be pulled and stretched to its original shape. Two people working together can do this part of the work best.

To grain the hide its entire surface should be rubbed with a rough stone. A piece of pumice, coarse sandpaper on a block of wood, or the rough edge of a tin can can also be used for this part of the work. Finally, the hide should be worked back and forth with a seesaw movement through a loop of manila rope. The rope should be fastened to a branch of a tree or to an inclined pole well overhead. The friction generates considerable heat, which dries the skin and gives it its smooth texture.

Smoking the Hide

The buckskin process is now finished, but the hide may be smoked if you care to do it. Some Indians claim that smoking makes the skin dry out soft and smooth after it has been wet. Smoking, of course, colors the skin a light yellow, tan, or dark brown, according to the length of time it is smoked and the kind of skin.

To smoke the hide, sew the skin up to form a conical bag and suspend it over a smudge fire as shown in Fig. 54. The fire is built in a pit, and after it has burned down to a good bed of coals, punk, rotten wood, and chips of green wood are piled on it. A small hole is tunneled under from one side to keep the fire supplied with air.

The hide must be watched constantly to see that it is smoked evenly and that the fire does not blaze up.

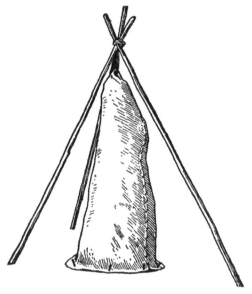

Fig. 54. Arrangement for Smoking a Tanned Hide (AMNH)

If you have a good smudge the skin will turn yellow in ten or fifteen minutes and dark brown in about three-quarters of an hour. It is only necessary to smoke one side, but both may be done if desired. Fold the hide with the smoked side on the inside and leave it set for a few days before using it.

Chapter Five

BEADWORK, BREASTPLATES, AND NECKLACES

THE beadwork which is so prominent in the decoration of an Indian costume owes its origin to the introduction of small Italian glass beads by the white traders. But beads of many kinds were made by the Indians before the advent of white men, and the designs later used in beadwork largely originated in the beautiful porcupine-quill embroidery developed by many of the tribes. Shell, bone, horn, teeth, claws, stone, and seeds were the most commonly used of natural materials for bead manufacture.

The Story of Wampum

Of the beads made by the Indians, wampum, the cylindrical shell bead of the Eastern tribes, is the best known and most interesting. It was used by the Indians for personal adornment, ceremonial purposes, conveying messages, ratifying treaties, making records, and in the same way that money is used by civilized people. The first white traders adopted this currency which all of the tribes were accustomed to: receiving it as pay for their merchandise and with it buying furs from the Indians. This and the fact that the Colonists brought little money with them led to the adoption of wampum as legal money in the Dutch and English settlements. The Dutch established factories where, with the aid of steel drills and grindstones, wampum could be turned out in such quantities that it soon gave them a monopoly of the supply for the Indian trade.

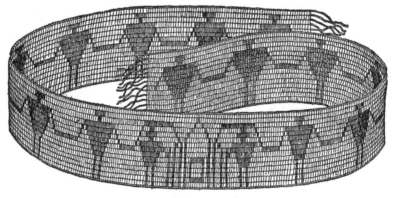

A Wampum Belt

Some of these wampum factories were still doing business fifty years ago with the Indian traders of the West.

Wampum was of two colors, white and dark purple. White wampum was the most plentiful and its value was about one half that of the purple. The white was made from the central part of the coiled shell of the whelk or periwinkle, and the purple from the shell of the quahog or hard clam. The beads were from an eighth to a half an inch in length and about an eighth

of an inch in diameter. Because of their small size and
the brittleness of the shell, the labor of making them

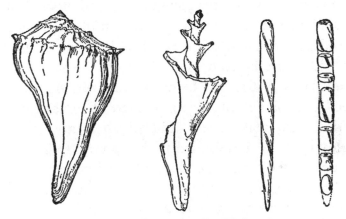

How Wampum Was Made

A Pump-drill

with the Indian's tools was difficult and tedious. Just
how they managed to drill these small beads with stone

drills is unknown, but there is plenty of evidence that they did it before the introduction of steel tools.

Beads made of the tusk-shaped dentalium and abalone shells were also used as a medium of exchange by the Indians on the Pacific coast and were there, too, adopted for use by traders and settlers. Another type of shell bead that is still being made is the small disk-shaped one that is highly prized by the Navajo and Pueblos. To make them, bits of shell are chipped roughly in shape and drilled with a pump-drill. Then they are rubbed between slabs of sandstone and on a grooved stone until they are of uniform thickness and diameter. They are generally strung with bits of turquoise and coral or with pendants of shell that have been inlaid with turquoise and jet.

Porcupine-quill Work

The large areas of beadwork on costumes, in most cases, takes the place of similar decorations formerly worked in the quills of the porcupine or occasionally with bird quills. In this work the quills were first dyed, then flattened, either with a bone tool or by the finger nails, and finally sewed down on the buckskin. As the quills were short, only a few stitches could be made with a single quill, so that in working with them their ends had to be frequently spliced together. You may be lucky enough to come into possession of some

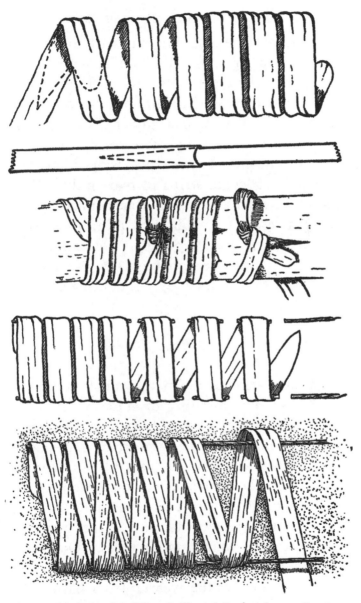

Fig. 55. Methods of Splicing Quills and Sewing them to Leather
Courtesy of the Museum of the American Indian

porcupine quills at some time, and may wish to try your hand at this ancient art. For this reason, some of the simpler ways of using them are shown in Fig. 55.

Beadwork is not at all difficult, but it requires a certain amount of patience and steady application. The speediest way of doing it is by the cross-stitch canvas method which is described later on. Using it, any boy can make a pair of leggin strips in two or three days spare time, or a headband for a war bonnet can be turned out in a few hours. The first thing to do is to decide on the designs you are going to use and then to make a pattern. For pattern-making the paper ruled in small squares that is used by draughtsmen is the handiest and best.

The Meaning of Bead Designs

Indian patterns were made up of symbols combined in various ways. The meaning of these designs was not fixed, so the same symbol would often have different meanings to people within the same tribe and among the different tribes which might use it. The Indian artists pictured in their work the common objects of everyday life, the great powers of nature, the sun, moon, stars, the winds, trees, animals, birds, or whatever might suit their whims and fancies. On clothing, designs were sometimes used that were supposed to have power to protect the wearer from harm. In

Designs from the Iroquois, Ojibwa and other Woodland Indians
Courtesy of the American Museum of Natural History

modern beadwork, one often sees a series of numbers or letters apparently copies from flour sacks, packing-cases, or other articles not of Indian origin. These are explained as "white man's medicine." That is, the Indian reasoned that, like himself, the white man covered his belongings with protective patterns. Knowing the many wonderful things the white man could do, it was certain that his "medicine" must be very strong and so his "designs" were often borrowed with the hope that some of their great medicine power might come with them. An example of this type of decoration, the gauntlets with "5-20 lbs." on them, is shown in the illustration.

The designs used by the Plains Tribes were geometric —that is, they were made up of squares, triangles, and other straight-sided figures, while those of the Woodland Tribes were mainly representations of flowers and plants. One of the commonest designs in Plains beadwork is the pointed triangle, either divided into halves of different color or including a small rectangle. This generally represents a tipi. A triangle built up of a number of small squares often is interpreted as a hill. Another common design is made up of a number of parallel lines sometimes broken up by short patterns of a different color. These lines represent trails, and the breaks in the lines camping-places or other stops made on the journey. A number of Dakota (Sioux) designs and their meanings are given in Fig. 56. Similar de-

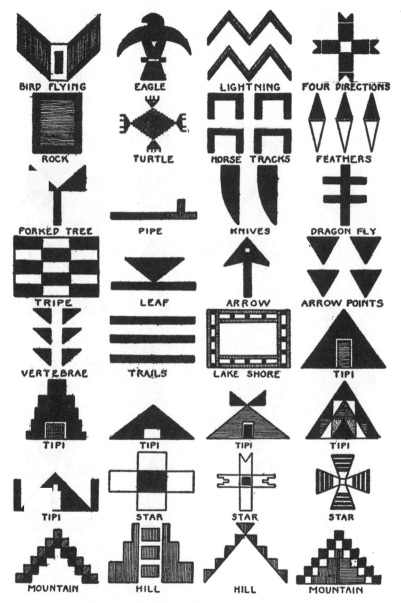

Fig. 56. Elements of Dakota Beaded Designs

Fig. 57. Elements of Arapaho Beaded Designs (See explanation on page opposite.) *Courtesy of the American Museum of Natural History*

signs from the Arapaho are illustrated in Fig. 57.
Colors are indicated in the drawings as follows: vertical shading, red; horizontal, blue; diagonal, green;
dotted, yellow; black and white as indicated. Nearly
all of the Dakota designs are done on a white background, which represents the snow-time or winter
which was the great time of the year for men to go on
the war trail and achieve honors and glory. Other
colors, which had a symbolic value in designs representing military achievement: were red, which indicated wounds inflicted or received; blue or black,
victory or enemies killed; yellow, horses, for tawny or
dun-colored war horses were especially prized; and
green, which represented the grass-time or summer.

EXPLANATION OF FIG. 57.

1. Deer Hoof	25. Swallow	48. Cricket
2. Ant Hill	26. Lizard Markings	49. Spider
3. Person	27. Snake	50. Crayfish
4. Tree on Mountain	28. Lizard	51. Centipede
5. Mushrooms	29. Buffalo Horns	52. Turtle Claw
6. Mountain	30. Coyote Tracks	53. Brush Hut
7. Dwarf	31. Turtle	54. Person
8. Rocks	32. Eye	55. Person
9. Crossing Paths	33. Bear Den	56. Morningstar
10. River	34. Mountains	57. Caterpillar
11. Head	35. Frog	58. Caterpillar
12. Eye	36. Fish	59. Willow Leaf
13. Lake	37. Bee	60. Meat Rack
14. Star	38. Elk Leg	61. Star
15. Morningstar	39. Elk Hoof	62. Star
16. Buffalo	40. Butterfly	63. Morningstar
17. Cloud	41. Buffalo Eye	64. Snake Rattles
18. Cloud	42. Buffalo Skull	65. Paths
19. Eagle	43. Tree	66. Bear Foot
20. Tipi	44. Beetle	67. Bear Foot
21. Camp Circle	45. Tipi	68. Bear Foot
22. Saddle Blanket	46. Tipi	69. Buffalo Path
23. Thunderbird	47. Dragon Fly	70. Life, Prosperity
24. Magpie		

In religious and ceremonial designs, red represents the sunset or thunder; blue, the sky, the west, water, or day; yellow, the dawn or sunlight; and black, the night.

You will secure the best results if you work out a pattern on cross-ruled paper before you try to start beading. Draw it full size and color it with crayon. Keep the design as simple as possible and do not try to use too many colors. On your first attempt it will be well to limit yourself to red, blue, and yellow in addition to the chalk-white beads for the background. If you are going to do a large piece of work it will pay to buy beads in hanks, but for small articles they may be bought in bottles from five-and-ten-cent stores. The best sizes to use are 2-0 and 3-0, the former being slightly larger and more easily handled. Whenever possible, use letter D silk buttonhole twist, but when this cannot be easily had No. 60 white linen thread makes a good substitute. The threads should always be kept well waxed while you are working. A special bead needle, or one size No. 11 or 12, must be used, as others are too large to pass through the beads.

The Cross-stitch Method

There are three ways to do beadwork—on cross-stitch canvas, on a loom and directly on the leather or cloth that forms a part of the article to be decorated. For leggin strips, belts and bags or other articles on which one side only of the work will show and large surfaces are to be covered, the cross-stitch method is to be preferred because of the speed and ease with which the work can be done. A further advantage of this method is that it gives the banded effect that is so noticeable in the fine old work that is done with sinew or buckskin. Loom weaving is useful in producing hat bands, watch fobs, and belts, and in copying old woodland designs which were woven on looms. The third method is the Plains Indian way, but because it is rather slow you will probably want to try it only on moccasins, breech clouts, knife sheaths, small pouches, and other articles which cannot be decorated in the other ways.

Cross-stitch canvas can be had from almost any dry-goods store or mail-order house. It resembles a stiff mosquito netting and has blue parallel lines running horizontally through it, spaced a half inch apart, just about the width of the bands in Plains beadwork. You will need a piece a few inches longer and a bit wider than the piece of work you are going to do. For example, a headband for a war bonnet eight inches long and an inch and a half wide will require a piece of canvas ten inches long by two and one-half inches wide. To begin, sew one end of the thread to the uppermost blue line and about one inch in from the edge of the canvas. Take a stitch from the under side of the canvas so that the end of your thread will be resting on the upper

side of the blue thread which will mark the upper edge
of your design. Now string ten beads or enough to
reach exactly to the blue line just below. Using the
vertical lines in the canvas as a guide, take a loop
stitch around the next blue thread below the one on
which you started (Fig. 58). Thread ten more beads

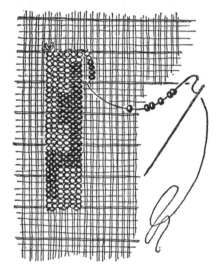

Fig. 58. Cross-stitch Canvas Method

and repeat the process until your beading has reached
the desired width. When you reach the bottom blue
thread, turn back and work up, sewing a string of beads
alongside the first line laid down. Sew back and forth
across the canvas until the design is completed. To
finish the work, turn the unused edges of the canvas
under and sew them down. It may then be sewn to

a strip of soft leather or directly on the article which
it is to decorate.

Making a Bead Loom

Looms for bead weaving can be bought ready made,
but it is easy and more Indian-like to make one yourself. The only materials needed are a cigar box, a
piece of broom handle, some screws, three small hooks,
and a round-head brass tack. Cut off an inch of the
upper sides of the box, then fasten in the bottom of one
end of the box a block of wood at least an inch thick

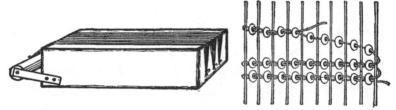

Fig. 59.   Cigar Box Bead Loom.   Fig. 60.   Double Weft Bead Weaving

and about three inches wide. This is merely a reinforcement and can best be held in place by small brads
driven in through the bottom and sides of the box.
At this end of the box screw to each side the two diagonal arms, Fig. 59. These should be six inches long
and should extend three inches beyond the end of the
box. Cut a piece of broomstick just long enough to
fit tightly between the two arms and drive the brass-

headed tack partly into its center. Fasten the broom-stick between the arms by a screw driven through the arms into each end of it. Holes slightly longer than the screws should have been drilled in the broomstick so that when it is in place it can be twisted around with-out coming loose. In the opposite end of the box place the small hooks about a half inch from the bottom and an inch apart. Then with a fret saw cut a number of notches, a sixteenth of an inch apart and about the same depth, along the top of the ends of the box. The loom is now ready for use.

Bead Weaving

In weaving, first cut your warp threads. Of these there should be one more than the number of beads in the width of your pattern and they should be a foot longer than its length. Knot one end of the threads and hook it over the tack on the roller. Then bring them across the ends of the box, fitting each thread in a notch and fastening the surplus thread around the hooks. Turn the roller until the warp threads are drawn up taut. Hold the loom with the roller away from you. Thread your bead needle and tie the end of the thread to the left-hand warp string close to the roller end of the box. Bring the thread out to the right under the warp, and thread enough beads to go once across the pattern. Push these beads up between the warp threads. Going above the warp, the needle is run through the beads again from right to left, Fig. 60. The needle is again brought out below the work, where another row of beads is strung and the process repeated. When you have finished the length of the loom, let out the threads, wind up the work on the roller, and continue as before.

Beading on Leather

To bead on leather, you will need a fine awl in addition to your needle and thread. The design is traced on the leather with a soft pencil and the beads sewn over it. The rows in Plains designs, which are about a half inch wide, are formed by stringing about ten beads at a time and sewing them down by going back and forth along the width of the band as shown in Fig. 61.

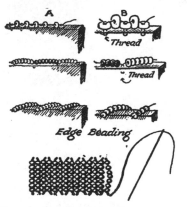

Fig. 61. Beading Directly on Leather

A hole must be made in the leather with the awl before the needle is inserted.   Failure to use an awl will result in many broken needles unless the leather you are working on is very soft.   It is also necessary to keep your thread well waxed at all times.   Pull your stitches up firmly, but do not draw them too tight or your work will be pulled out of shape.   Patterns for beading moccasins by this method are illustrated in Fig. 62 and in Chapter Four.   The edges of pouches, knife cases, and other articles of leather may be beaded by the methods shown in the diagram.

An effective substitute for beaded strips on shirts and leggins can be made by stenciling patterns on strips of white muslin.   If your stencils are carefully cut and

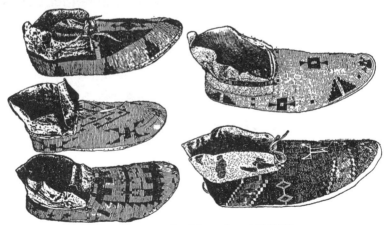

Fig. 62.   Arapaho Moccasins (AMNH)

the patterns and color combinations kept simple, it will be hard to tell them from real beadwork at a short

Pomo Men Making Shell Beads—Grinding and Drilling

Plains Beadwork

Woodland Beadwork

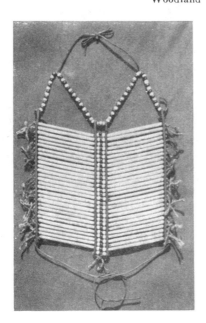

A "Pipestem" Breastplate

Low Dog, a Sioux, Wearing Bone
Breastplate and Bead Collar

distance or in the campfire light. Moccasins and other articles may also be decorated with painted designs.

Necklaces

Both Indian men and women wore necklaces of many different kinds. One of the easiest types to make is illustrated in Fig. 63. The beads are large glass ones that can be bought in five-and-ten-cent stores. The other materials needed are some pieces of sole leather and some light cord to string the beads on. The leather is cut in six strips an inch and a quarter long and a quarter inch wide, and two strips of the same width three inches long. With a red-hot wire or leather punch make three holes in each of the small pieces, and seven in the large ones.

Cut six pieces of string twenty inches for the main strings. Make a big knot in the end of each string and draw them through the holes in the piece of leather that will form the bottom of the necklace. Then string four blue beads on each string. Next draw the strings through the second long piece of leather. Knot the end of the center string on top of it. Twelve more beads—four yellow, four red, and four yellow—are now strung and a short piece of leather is strung over them on each group of three strings. This process is repeated in the next two sections with black, red and black and blue, yellow and blue, beads and the top pieces of leather are put in place. The central string in each of the groups is knotted over the leather. On the ends of the others three red beads are strung, after

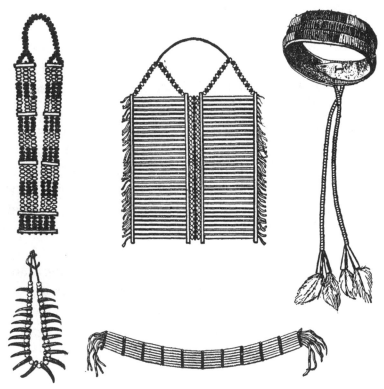

Fig. 63. Apache Necklace. Fig. 64. Bear Claw Necklace. Fig. 65. Bead
Collar. Fig. 66. Breastplate. Fig. 66. Arm Band

which the pair on each side is tied together to form a small loop. Twenty more red beads are strung on a separate piece of string the ends of which are tied to the center of the small loops, which finishes the necklace. Of course, the color scheme suggested here can be varied to suit your fancy.

Necklaces of grizzly-bear claws were worn as a mark of honor by a man who had killed one of these animals (Fig. 64). Such a necklace can be imitated by carving imitation claws out of soft wood, staining dark brown, and stringing them with glass beads. Rooster spurs also make good imitation bear claws.

Collars of the type shown in Fig. 65 were made of quills, bone, and glass beads. You can make one by cutting small hollow chicken bones in one-inch lengths or by using the long tubular glass beads which are known as bugles. Twelve strips of leather similar to those mentioned before and an inch and a half long will be required, as well as strong cord to string the beads on. The number of holes to be punched in each strip will depend on the diameter of the bones or the size of the beads that you are going to use. Knot the ends of the strings after putting them through the first piece of leather and alternate beads and leather until all are strung. Knot the ends of the strings again on the outside of the last leather piece and tie a cord to the center of each end. This is used to tie the necklace on.

The Breastplate

Another ornament worn by most of the Indians of the plains was a breastplate made of bone beads that were known to the traders as hair pipes. You can easily make one of these spectacular decorations of chicken leg bones cut to a uniform length or of corn-cob pipe stems as shown in Fig. 66. These reed pipe stems can be bought very cheaply in quantities through your local cigar store. If you will string them on a wire and give them a coat of cream-colored enamel before you use them, they will be hard to tell from the real thing. They can be strung on soft leather thongs in imitation of buckskin, or on ordinary heavy brown string which may be left with long ends and fringed out. Other materials needed for the breastplate will be some large glass beads and four strips of heavy strap leather about fifteen inches long and three-eighths of an inch wide. Small holes a half inch apart should be burned or pricked along the full length of each piece of leather.

Knot the string or lacing thong an inch and a half from its end and, starting at the top, string one of the leather pieces, then a bone or pipestem, another leather, three glass beads, a leather, a pipe bead, and the fourth leather. Knot the string on the outside and cut off the thong an inch and a half from the knot. Repeat this process until the breastplate is finished. The neck string is made of three separate strings of beads in a way similar to that described for the necklace. At each lower corner a thong is fastened. These are passed around the waist and tied at the back when the breast-plate is worn.

Arm Bands

Beaded armlets, tied above the elbow, were worn in dances, when making medicine or in war. One of these with a beaded and feathered pendant appears in Fig. 67. These are best made of rawhide or other stiff leather that is not too thick. They should be about two or two and half inches wide and just long enough to barely go round the arm. The ends are laced together with a light thong. Cut the arm band to the proper size and make a piece of beadwork to fit by the cross-stitch method. When the beading is finished sew it to the arm band with the aid of an awl and using waxed thread. To one end of each band sew two or three pieces of narrow ribbon about eight inches long which will hang down as pendants.

Chapter Six

TIPIS AND WIGWAMS

PERHAPS the most serviceable, comfortable, and beautiful tent ever devised is the lodge of our Plain Indians, better known by its Dakota name, tipi. It is so well adapted to the country in which it was invented that General Sibley used it as a model for the tent that with some modifications is still the standard for our army and which, since the war, has been so popular in summer camps. But the modern pyramidal tent lacks the picturesqueness of the lodge, so that if for no other reason than its beauty, every camp should include at least one decorated tipi. Then again, the tipi is an all-year-round tent and is so especially suited to the scout who is an all-season camper. In summer with its sides partly rolled up it is cool and breezy, while in winter a small fire suffices to keep it warm and comfortable.

The origin of the tipi is lost in the Long Ago but most authorities consider that it is a comparatively recent invention. Some of the tribes believe it was the accidental discovery of a man who, while playing with a cottonwood leaf, twisted it in the shape of a cone and then used it as a pattern for a dwelling, different from the earth lodges in which the people then lived. This story may be wholly imaginary, but we know that the

Blackfoot Water Monster Tipi. From an Indian Drawing (AMNH)
The bands at the top are red, green, yellow, blue and black; the sections of
the serpent are blue, red, yellow and green; the door is striped with the
same colors; the border at the bottom is in red and the top is black

children of the Plains Indians make model tipis from cottonwood leaves even to this day.

In the old days tipis were made of tanned buffalo-cow skins sewn together with sinew thread. From ten to forty hides were required, depending on how large the lodge was to be. The average size was about sixteen feet in diameter. Except for the play tipis of the children and the great council, or medicine, lodges, they were seldom made smaller than ten feet or larger than twenty-five feet. The largest tipi of which we have any record is one observed by Maximilian in 1832 in a camp of the Piegan Blackfoot. This great lodge was between forty and fifty feet in diameter. For scout use the best size will be between twelve and eighteen feet. Very small tipis are hardly worth making, while poles for very large ones are difficult to secure unless you live in the West.

How Tipis Were Made

Because of the hard use to which they were put, Indian tipis were renewed once a year. The new lodges were made in the spring when the buffalo had shed their hair and their skins were thin. They were finished in time for the great tribal encampment which was held in connection with the medicine lodge, or sun dance, in June. At that time all of the divisions of the

tribe that had been scattered during the winter came together. The lodges of the different bands were grouped
three and four deep to form a great camp circle.

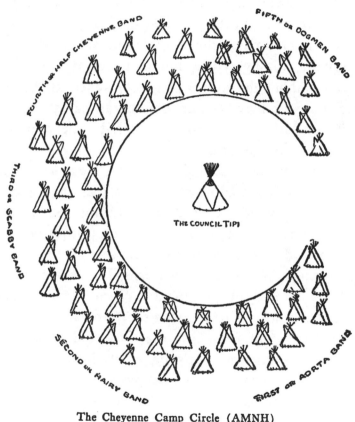

The Cheyenne Camp Circle (AMNH)

Each band had its own portion of the circle which
always remained the same, so that a person coming into
camp at night had no difficulty in locating his home,

even though the entire camp had been moved in his absence. In the central space but one or two lodges were pitched, the council lodge or the lodges containing the tribe's sacred medicines. These tipis were always the first to be taken down when the camp was moved, and their falling was the signal to break camp. New tipis were shining white, but in time they gradually browned about the middle and blackened at the top. After long use they became almost transparent, and accounts of early travelers often describe the beauty of the glowing lodges at night.

When a woman decided to make a lodge she called all of her friends and neighbors to a feast, and after it was over they helped with the cutting and sewing, much in the fashion of the old-time quilting bee. A woman who was especially skilled was intrusted with the cutting. She had no patterns, but depended entirely on her eye and judgment. When it came to sewing on the smoke flaps the women were very careful to see that this important task was intrusted to one who was known to have a happy, cheerful disposition, for it was their belief that if this work were done by a person who was cross and ugly, the flaps would fail to work properly and the lodge would always be smoky. In recent times the use of canvas and the sewing-machine has lessened the labor required to make a lodge, but the old methods are still largely followed.

Making a Tipi

Making a tipi is not too difficult a task for any live group of boys to undertake. The pattern given here is for a sixteen-foot tipi, which will require fifty yards of yard-wide eight-ounce duck, not including what will be needed for the dew-cloth, or lining, which will be described later. You will also need twenty yards of quarter-inch rope, some stout string or heavy thread, beeswax, seventy one-half-inch galvanized iron grommets which can be purchased from an awning-maker, and a sailor's palm and needle. If you can secure an old pyramidal or other tent for the purpose, you will save expense and perhaps some labor. Colored canvas, when it can be secured in some woodsy color, will make a very beautiful lodge.

Begin by cutting your canvas into five lengths, thirty-three feet, thirty-two feet, twenty-nine feet, twenty-four feet, and sixteen feet long. The smoke flaps, or ears, are to be cut later from the material remaining. With a pencil make a straight line across the center of each strip which is to serve as a guide in sewing the strips together. Sew the two longest pieces together first with a seam an inch wide, which should be made with a double row of stitching. When all the strips have been sewn together your canvas should resemble the dotted outline, ZZZZZ, in the diagram

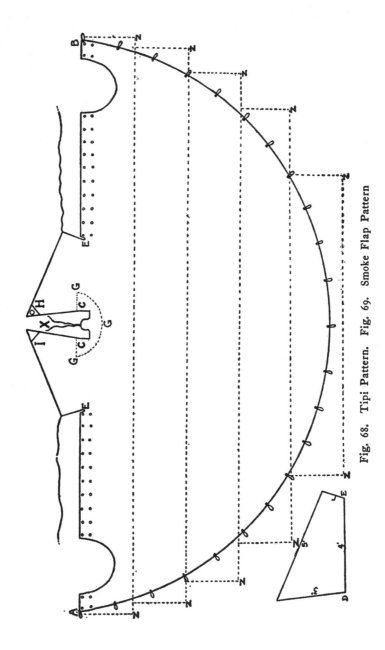

Fig. 68. Tipi Pattern. Fig. 69. Smoke Flap Pattern

(Fig. 68). Now spread the canvas out on a smooth flat surface and locate the point X. This should be eighteen inches from the center of the long straight edge of the canvas. With a crayon or pencil tied to a stout string exactly sixteen feet long, draw the curved line AB. With scissors trim the canvas down to within six inches of this curved line. This six inches of extra canvas should be turned under and sewn down to serve as a reinforcement for the lower edge of the tipi.

The top opening, CDC, and the tie flap, D, may now be cut. The two notches on either side of the flap are six inches deep and six inches wide, and the flap is of the same dimensions. Considerable strain is put on this part of the cover so that an extra reinforcement of canvas, GGG, should be sewn to it after the smoke flaps have been attached. The two small notches below the smoke flaps, EE, are one inch wide and three inches deep. They, too, should be reinforced with an extra piece of canvas and a half-inch hem. The door openings are three feet high and two feet across. Their lower edge should be one foot above the bottom of the tipi cover. Edges of these openings should be hemmed or bound with tape. Next cut out the smoke flaps according to the pattern (Fig. 69) and sew them on along the line DE. There are two ways of finishing off the upper corners of the flaps. One way is to make a hole, H, about three inches in diameter, through which the smoke pole is thrust, and the other is to make a pocket, I, by sewing a triangular piece of canvas to the upper corner in which the end of the pole is put.

Grommet holes may now be made and ropes attached. The holes for the lacing pins, AE, EB, are made in pairs, five inches apart and one inch from the edge of the canvas. The pairs are spaced nine inches apart. To make these grommet holes, cut a small cross in the canvas and bind the ring around it, buttonhole fashion, with waxed thread. Two ropes two feet long should now be strongly stitched to the tie flap, D, and a sixteen-foot rope sewn to the lower corner of each smoke flap. Small loops of rope spaced two feet apart should be tied through grommet holes around the curved edge of the canvas. The tipi cover is now finished.

Setting It Up

To set up the tipi, sixteen to twenty poles will be needed which may be anywhere from eighteen to twenty feet long. These should be smooth and straight, and, if possible, peeled of bark and seasoned. The Indians used lodge-pole pine or cedar and traveled long distances to get good ones. Once a good set was secured it was moved from camp to camp, the poles being fastened over the horses' shoulders with the ends dragging on the ground. The work of erecting a tipi was reduced to a regular system so that the lodge could be rapidly erected. I have seen two Blackfoot women erect a fifteen-foot tipi in three minutes, while it is recorded that two women of the same tribe put up a similar lodge in a competition in one minute and forty seconds.

In erecting the tipi, first pick out the best three poles for the tripod. Then lay aside two slender poles for the smoke flaps and a good stout one for the lifting pole. Spread the canvas on the ground and lay two of the poles across its center so that their butts project about six inches beyond the curved edge of the cover. The third pole, which is known as the door pole, is then laid along one of the straight edges of the canvas. Its butt should project equally with the others. The poles should cross at the tie flap. There they should be tied together by the Teton method or by simply passing a rope around them three or four times and tying a square knot (Fig. 70). Thus the tripod is made.

The door of an Indian tipi always faces the east, so that the back of the lodge is in the direction from which come the prevailing winds. The door pole is to the left of the door as you enter, so that it is carried to the east of the proposed site of the tipi and the two back poles to the west as the tripod is erected. In separating the back poles care should be taken to place the butt of the under or inner one to that side on which the door pole is tied; otherwise the tripod will not lock securely above. The back poles should now be spread equidistant from the door pole and a less distance apart. The other poles are then laid in, in the order indicated by the numbers in the diagram, leaving a space for the lifting pole, L (Fig. 71). The circle formed by their

Fig. 70. Teton Tie and Simple Method of Lashing Tripod

butts should be slightly less than the diameter of the tipi. If the tipi is to stand for some time the end of the tripod rope should be sufficiently long so that it may be wrapped around the outside of all the poles at the point where they come together. Its end is then spiraled down one of the poles. In windy weather it is fastened to stakes driven near the center of the lodge (Fig. 72). When the lodge was to remain in one place for a long period the poles were sunk in the ground to a

A Tipi made in a Boys' Camp

A Blackfoot Tipi

Tipis made by Boy Scouts at the Eastern States Exposition

Ojibwa Rush Mat and Bark Wigwam

Courtesy of the Bureau of American Ethnology

Framework and Completed Southern California Gani House

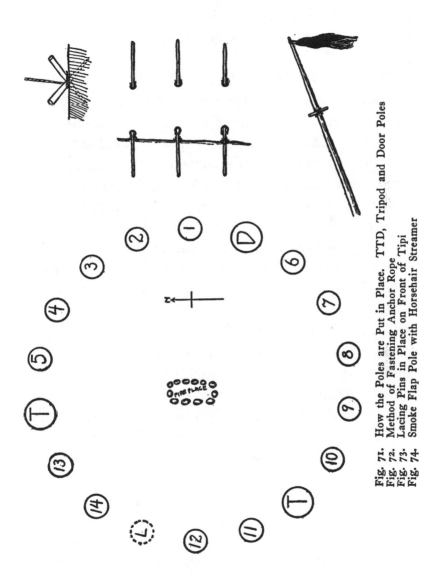

Fig. 71. How the Poles are Put in Place. TTD, Tripod and Door Poles
Fig. 72. Method of Fastening Anchor Rope
Fig. 73. Lacing Pins in Place on Front of Tipi
Fig. 74 Smoke Flap Pole with Horsehair Streamer

depth of twelve to eighteen inches, extra allowance for this having been made when the tripod poles were measured off.

The cover should now be folded and tied to the lifting pole with the tie-flap ropes. This pole with the canvas is raised and lowered to its place in the back of the lodge. The canvas is now spread round the poles and the opening between the door and smoke hole laced from the top down, with straight wooden pins, which should be of about the same diameter as a pencil and fifteen inches long (Fig. 73). The poles may now be gently shifted outward, from the inside, until the canvas is stretched taut. Pegs should now be driven through the loops all around the bottom of the lodge. The smoke poles are now poked into the pockets in the flaps or through the holes, whichever have been made. To keep the end of the smoke pole from going too far through the hole, a small cross-piece should be lashed to it about two feet from the end (Fig. 74). To the ends of the poles the Indians often fastened streamers of cloth, buffalo or horse tails. The latter were supposed to bring fortune and many horses to the tipi's owner.

The cords on the bottom of the smoke flaps are tied to a peg placed well in front of the door. By swinging the smoke poles around according to the direction of the wind, a good draft for the fire may always be had.

The Inner Lining

A most important part of the tipi is the dew-cloth or lining (Fig. 75). This is made of strips of cloth four to six feet wide, which are fastened to the poles on the inside of the lodge. The upper edge of each

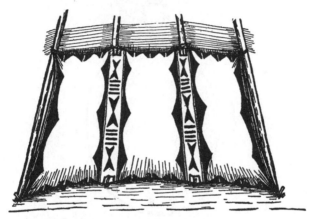

Fig. 75. Decorated Section of Dew-cloth in Place

strip has tie strings on it for this purpose, and the lower is provided with rope loops one foot apart, so that it may be staked close to the ground. It is best made of drill or light canvas in six-foot sections and should be long enough to extend entirely around the lodge. Its purpose is to keep the lower part of the lodge free of smoke and the rain which runs down the poles from the beds. The cold air which enters under the lower edges of the lodge cover is turned up along the roof by this

lining and out the smoke hole.   In the winter the lodge
may be made warmer by filling the space between the
lining and cover with straw.   Another method used by
the Indians in winter was to dig the earth out in the
center of the lodge and pile in on the edges.   The fire-
place was an excavation surrounded by stones a little

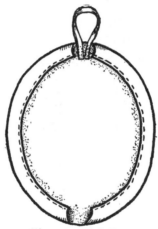

Fig. 76.   Tipi Door

to the back of the center, about twelve by eight by six
inches deep.   Wood for the fire is kept piled just outside of the door.   For the door an oval-shaped piece
of canvas is cut larger than the door opening.   Its edges
are hemmed over to form tubular pockets.   In these
flexible sticks are inserted.   Their ends are bound together where they protrude at the top and bottom, so
that a hoop is formed which holds the door taut and in
shape.   A loop sewn to the door's upper edge is hung

over a lacing pin to hold the door in place. An additional loop may be made at the bottom for use in inclement weather (Fig. 76).

The Indians observed certain forms of etiquette in the lodge that all users of the tipi may well adopt. The place of honor was at the back of the tipi, opposite the door. Here were the bed and seat of the owner, which he relinquished only to honored guests. Between this place and the fire no one need pass, nor was it good form for one to pass in front of others who might be seated. When a person moved about the tipi he did so by going around the edge, the people bending forward to let him get by.

Decorations

Tipis were often decorated with colored designs which had either a religious or a historical significance and among some tribes indicated the family to which the lodge's owner belonged. In decorating your tipi you may copy the designs given here or invent some of your own. The pattern given in Fig. 77 is typical of the Blackfoot. The lower border represents the mountains and lakes of the Blackfoot country, and the circles in the black top represent the Pleiades and the Big Dipper in the night sky. Some of the older Indians, though, say that the lower circles do not represent lakes, but "dusty stars" which are puffballs that grow on the

prairie that disappear in a cloud of dust when they are
broken.   The green Maltese Cross at the back top of
the tipi represents the morning star.   In this place the

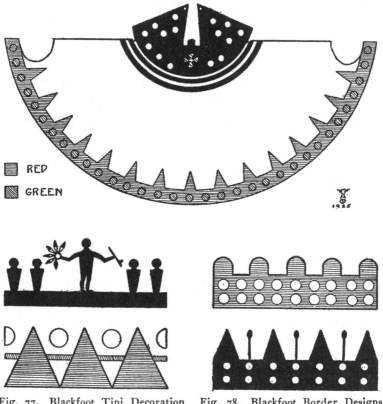

RED

GREEN

Fig. 77. Blackfoot Tipi Decoration   Fig. 78. Blackfoot Border Designs

totem of the lodge's owner was often painted.   Other
Blackfoot borders are given in Fig. 78.   One, as you
can readily see, represents a council being addressed by
a chief who holds a peace pipe in one hand and his

war bonnet in the other. This standing figure is always painted at the back center of the lodge.

In decorating the tipi, first sketch in the design with crayon. Use a sponge and a bucket of water or a garden hose to wet the canvas thoroughly before applying the paint. This will save paint and will also keep the lodge cover lighter and more pliable than it would be if the paint were applied to the dry canvas and allowed to soak through.

When your lodge is decorated and erected properly you will not only have the satisfaction of having completed an excellent outdoor dwelling, but of also knowing that you have helped to preserve for those who are to follow in our trail, the staunchest, handsomest, and most comfortable of tents.

Back Rests and Beds

Tipi furnishings consisted of beds and back rests and rawhide cases for the storage of food and clothing. Back rests were made of smooth, straight willow rods woven together with sinew. They were of various sizes and styles. Dimensions of one of fair size would be five feet long and tapering from thirty inches at the bottom to eighteen inches at the top (Fig. 79).

The rest is made on warp cords of fish line fastened to stakes driven in the ground as shown in Fig. 80. The rods are fastened down with other cords passed through the rod and about the warp as shown in Fig. 81. The rest may be finished off by binding its edges with cloth and sewing a heavy cloth loop to the top. It is set up for use against a tripod of sticks, two of which are against the rest, with the other as a support. The cloth loop at the top is hooked over the tripod to keep the rest from slipping down.

Fig. 79. Willow Bed or Back Rest Fig. 80. Frame for Weaving Willow
Bed (AMNH) Fig. 81. Method of Fastening Rods

Beds were made by placing two small logs parallel about a yard apart and fastening them in place with stakes. The space between was filled with fresh-cut prairie grass and covered with buffalo robes, as shown in Fig. 82. Grass, leaves, or pine boughs may be used to make a bed of this kind. The logs keep the bedding material from spreading out and catching on fire.

A Model Tipi

Before you make your full-size tipi it may be well to make a few models on which to try out various schemes of decoration. These models also make interesting decorations and with a bit of Chinese incense burning inside them are quite realistic (Fig. 83).

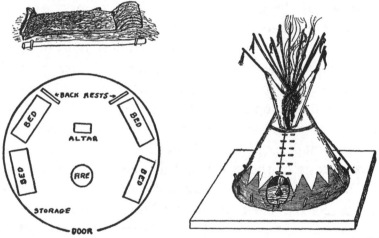

Fig. 82. Grass Bed and Tipi Interior Arrangement   Fig. 83. Model Tipi

The first thing to do is to determine the size of your model and to cut a pattern from stiff wrapping-paper the exact size it is to be. In order to make our decorations clearer we will presume you are going to make a twelve-inch tipi. For this the materials needed will be a baseboard of white pine or whitewood seven-eighths of an inch thick and fourteen inches square; twenty pieces of No. 4 basketry reed or other light, smooth sticks, fifteen inches long; some small twigs for ground pegs and lacing pins; and a piece of material for the cover, fourteen by twenty-four inches. The cover may be made of thin leather, parchment lampshade paper, or cloth. It should be decorated with water- or oil-colors before being put in place.

Pin the paper pattern together and measure its diameter at the base. Then, with a compass draw a circle of the same size on the baseboard. Divide this circle in eighteen equal parts and mark the points of division. On them, with a drill, bore holes at an angle about halfway through the board. These are for the poles, which should next be inserted and tied where they come together at the top. The cover is now put in place and laced up. Holes are then made in the bottom edge of the cover and drilled in the baseboard for the ground pegs. Two holes are then drilled in the baseboard back of the tipi for the smoke poles, which are next put in place. Carry out the detail as closely like a full-size tipi as possible and you will succeed in making a model of which you can well be proud.

Wigwams

Wigwams are as worth while making as tipis. They have been rather neglected by us for the better known tipi in our pictures and books, so that we should do our best to preserve this type of Indian dwelling, which has the advantage of being very easy to make. One or more of them might be built as part of the Indian village in your summer camp. In the East, all of the materials the Indians used in wigwam construction can still be found, and where the cutting of the necessary trees may be done exact reproductions of this type of Indian home may be built. However, so many trees would have to be destroyed if bark covering was used that it will be better for us to use canvas for our lodge covering instead, just as the Indian has done in modern times. Cornhusks, sedge grass, and mats made of cat-tail leaves were also used by the Indians for coverings, but they cannot be made as water-proof as canvas and in some localities they will be difficult to secure.

Wigwams, as we have said, were of different shapes and sizes. The type used by most of the Eastern tribes was the dome-shaped round or oval winter lodge. This was much warmer than the square summer house of bark or the long-house of the Iroquois. It is also the easiest kind of wigwam to build and requires less material than either of the other types. It is suitable for use in all seasons.

For an oval wigwam about twelve feet in diameter sixteen saplings are required for the uprights, about fifteen feet long and an inch and a half in diameter. Four of the stoutest of these are set in the ground so as to form a rectangle three feet by twelve feet. Two of these will be the doorposts when the wigwam is completed. By means of ropes tied to their ends the poles are bent toward the center of the long sides of the rectangle, where the ends of each pair are lashed together about seven feet above the ground to form two arches. Heavy cord may take the place of the bass-wood bark the Indians used for this purpose.

The floor plan of the wigwam will be slightly oval and not a perfect circle as it is flattened at the sides. Because of this the next two uprights are placed ten feet apart, and when lashed together will form an arch at right angles to the two already erected. The other uprights are now set in place in the same way about two feet apart, bent over, lashed together, and also tied to the first two arches. Lighter saplings are now lashed at right angles to the uprights, so that except for the door space a horizontal ring is formed of them, thirty inches above and parallel to the ground. A second ring of this kind is made thirty inches above the first. This one extends completely around the frame and forms the top of the door opening. The frame of the wigwam is now complete (Fig. 84).

The canvas used in covering the frame is in several strips a yard wide, with hemmed edges in which grommets have been stamped two feet apart on the sides, and one foot apart on the ends. Three strips, twelve feet long, and eleven, six feet long, are required for the roof covering. These strips are put in place by tying one edge of the canvas to the horizontal saplings. The lower strips, which are twelve feet long, are put in place first, and their lower edges are drawn out tight and staked to the ground by means of rope loops attached to the grommets. The ends are overlapped for at least six inches wherever they come together. The next set of strips are tied to the upper horizontal ring

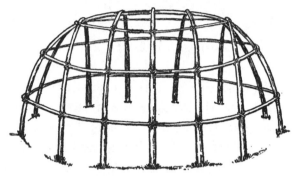

Fig. 84. Wigwam Frame

in the same manner, their lower edges overlapping the first strips by about six inches. The other short strips are used to cover the roof and one is used for the door. Each strip is so placed that it overlaps the one below it. When all are in place, cords are passed through the exposed grommets and fastened to stakes in the ground. These keep the strips from getting loose in windy weather. A rectangular hole about two and half feet square is left in the center of the room as a smoke hole. A piece of canvas is used to close this in rainy weather.

The fire was built in a shallow pit dug in the center of the floor. The floor itself was covered with balsam fir or spruce boughs or hay. In winter snow was heaped up about the sides for a depth of about eighteen inches so as to prevent cold from coming in from the bottom and to keep out drafts. As in the tipi, the place of honor was in the rear and behind the fire. Here also were kept the family medicine-bundles or other sacred objects.

Californian Grass House

Some of the southern Californian Indians built a circular grass house that closely resembled a wigwam such as we have just described. It was dome-shaped, with a circular floor plan. The frame was made by placing slender willow poles in the earth and then bending them over and lashing their ends together to form arches. As in the Eastern wigwam, horizontal poles were then lashed at right angles to the uprights at intervals of about one foot. Mescal fiber was used for the lashing. Tule, carrizo brakes, or grass was tied in bunches and used for the thatching. These were laid on in tiers, the lowest tier standing upright with the butt end to the ground, so as to form a firm base. The other tiers were placed upside down, as the inverted leaves shed the water better. The thatch when finished was about four inches thick and practically impervious to wind and rain. Other horizontal poles were lashed over the thatch to help hold it in place. An opening was left at the top center for a smoke hole and another in the front for a door. The latter was about a yard high and two feet wide and was closed, when necessary, with a mat of tule (see illustrations).

Chapter Seven

BOWS, ARROWS, AND QUIVERS

Bows and arrows are perhaps the best-known parts of the Indian's equipment, and of everything he owned, nothing was more important to him than these. On them depended his ability to furnish himself and his family with food and to protect them from his enemies. The bow remained the Indian's favorite weapon long after firearms were introduced, because, until repeating rifles were invented, it was, in many ways, superior to the smooth-bore muzzle-loading gun. Many arrows could be fired in a fight at close quarters in the time it took to load and fire a gun once.

Indian Warfare

Warfare among the Indians of the plains was almost constant, and it is probable that this was also true of the tribal groups in other parts of the country. Tribes migrating in the plains area were bound, in their travels, to cross and settle on the hunting-grounds of others, so that disputes and war would follow. In times when game was scarce, men would wander far from their own territory and so encroach on the land of their neighbors. Such invasions often resulted in

An Assiniboine Bowman (AMNH)

fights that were followed by long wars of revenge. In later years the introduction of the horse became a chief cause of intertribal warfare.

Horses were the most valuable property a Plains Indian could possess. They enabled him to accumulate

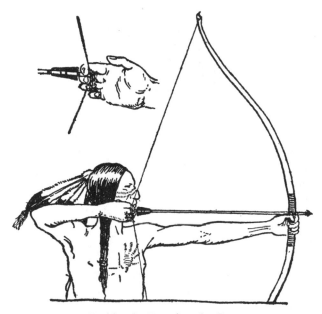

Position in Drawing the Bow

and move about more property than he had been able to when all of his belongings had to be transported on his own back and on the small dog travois. They also made hunting, his hardest work, easier than it had ever been before. The horses were first obtained by the Southern tribes, so that the Northern Indians were obliged to raid their Southern neighbors in order to get them. Horse-stealing soon developed into a regular business between tribes, and, though they tried to avoid open warfare, fights were bound to take place whenever the raiders were discovered.

Men were trained in the use of the bow from early boyhood and were taught that war honors were the highest to which they might attain. Without *coups* won on the war trail a man could not advance in rank. In the Plains Tribes the warriors were organized into societies graded according to their ages and attainments. Nearly all of these warrior societies had dances of their own in which weapons were carried and used as part of the dance paraphernalia. It is mainly because of this that directions of making weapons are given here.

English and Indian Bows

For target work the English bow is far superior to the Indian bow, so that you will do better to make your tackle according to the directions in one of the standard books on archery if you are interested in doing expert target work. The Indian bow, however, does not require the expensive materials used in making a good English bow, nor is it so difficult to construct. Materials for making good Indian bows can be found in almost every part of our country, and the Indian's method of bow-and-arrow making is simple enough to be followed by any good camper.

The best bow-makers on the plains were the Sioux and the Crows. Like nearly all of the other Indians in the West, they used a bow about four feet long. In the East a longer bow was used by some tribes, but the short bow is the common Indian type. This short length is one of the chief ways in which Indian bows

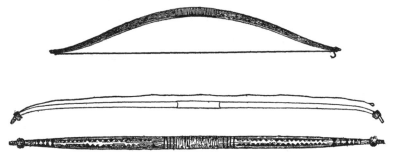

Sinew Backed and Decorated Plain Wood Bows (SI)

differ from the English. The proper length of an Indian bow was sometimes determined by holding the bow-stave diagonally across the body, with one end of it held in the right hand at the hip and the other just touching the finger tips of the left hand when held straight out to the side, shoulder high.

Bows were made of wood, wood backed with sinew, and of mountain-sheep, buffalo, or elk horn. Almost every wood found on and around the almost treeless prairies was utilized for bow-staves, Osage-orange, or *bois d'arc,* as it was called by the French voyageurs, was considered to be the best wood, but, because it grew in a small area and so was difficult to obtain, hickory, juniper, oak, ash, white elm, cedar, ironwood, and willow were more commonly used. The Eastern Indians made their bows from shagbark hickory, ash, red cedar, white oak, willow, birch, and hemlock, while in California hickory, ash, mountain cedar, juniper, willow, elder, and yew were used. The latter is considered to be the best wood of all.

Omaha Bow-making

The Omaha considered the "month of the return of the geese," or February, to be the only safe time to cut green wood for bow-staves. Then the sap was down, so that the stave would season with little danger of splitting by shrinkage. A young ash killed by a prairie fire was especially good bow material, for it was generally well seasoned, and so unlikely to be affected by rain or dampness. When cut and trimmed, the green stave was rubbed with bear's grease and hung from the upper part of the tipi poles in the smoke of the fire, but well out of reach of the flames, until it was well seasoned. When the wood was ready for use it was carefully shaped out with a knife and rubbed smooth with a piece of sandstone. The work might take a week, or on a fine horn bow the warrior might spend a month or more.

Ordinarily, the bows were perfectly flat when unstrung, but they were sometimes gracefully curved. The curves were put in the wood by greasing the part and holding it over the fire until it was quite hot, and then bending it with the foot. It was held in place until cool, when the curve would be permanent. Sinew backing was applied with hot glue to the flat back of the bow, which had been roughened with a stone. The sinew was lapped at the middle and ends and on the middle of the bow. Horn bows were made of thin slices of horn that had been rubbed down until they fitted nicely together. Four pieces were glued together, and a fifth piece fitted and glued over the center. All were then rubbed down until they were of correct proportions, after which they were tightly bound with strips of the small intestines of deer or strips of sinew which were applied when wet. As it dried, the sinew shrunk, so uniting all of the parts and making a bow that was said to be tougher, stronger, and more elastic than a bow of other materials. The chief disadvantage of horn and sinew-backed bows was that they were likely to become useless in wet or damp weather.

For bow-strings twisted sinew or vegetable fibers were used. The string was tied to notches in one end of the bow, while its noosed end could be slipped over a notch in the other.

How the Indian Made Arrows

Arrows were more difficult to make than bows. Generally, each man made his own, so that it was only by chance that the arrows of two men in the same tribe would be of the same length. Because of this and also because each man could recognize his own handiwork, the arrows in a carcass served as a means of settling disputes of ownership, which often arose after a great tribal buffalo hunt. Ash, birch, cane, dogwood, willow, and wild cherry-tree saplings were used for arrows. Like the bow-staves, the arrow wood was cut in winter. Sticks were selected that were free of branches, straight, smooth, and about the thickness of one's little finger. They were cut to proper length, put up in bundles of twenty or twenty-five, wrapped tightly with raw-hide or elk-skin, and hung in the smoke of the tipi fire for several weeks. When seasoned, the bundles were taken down and the bark was removed from the sticks. They were then scraped, smoothed, and straightened. This was a difficult and tedious process. Wherever a crooked place was found, it was greased and heated until the wood could be easily bent, after which it was held securely until it cooled. Sometimes the sticks were drawn through a stone or deer's horn, in which holes had been drilled, as a part of the straightening process. Grooved sandstone polishers, between which the sticks were twirled, were used in

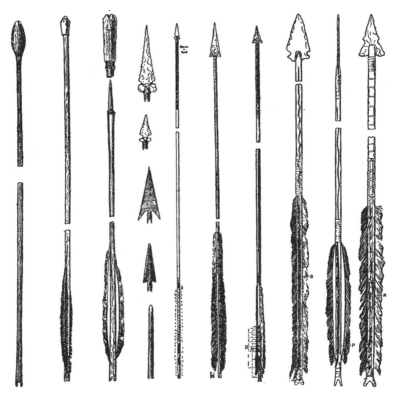

Bird Bolts and War Arrows from Various Tribes (SI)

the final shaping process. A U- or V-shaped notch, or nock, as it is called, for the bow-string was made in one end of the shaft.

The arrowhead was now fastened in a notch in the

shaft with glue and a binding of sinew. In the old days it was made of flint, obsidian, and other varieties of stone, as well as of sinew, horn, bone, shell, wood, and copper. Later traders introduced the sheet-iron arrowpoint, which soon displaced the native materials. Arrowheads made of turtle, bear and panther claws were supposed to strike the enemy with magic power as well as with the force of the bow. Sinew arrow-points were made from the hard sinew that lies along the top of the buffalo's neck and holds his head up. They were considered to be of special value in hunting buffalo because the sinew point striking a rib would go round it, whereas a flint point hitting the bone would often break off. The heads of war arrows were loosely fastened, and so shaped that they would split the shaft and remain in the wound when the shaft was withdrawn.

After the point was in place, the shaft was grooved with three zigzag lines. Just why this was done is not exactly known. Some claim that the grooves represented lightning, others that they caused the wounded animal to bleed more freely, while the Omaha state that they help to keep the straightened shaft from warping.

Finally, the arrow was feathered with two or three trimmed feathers of the eagle, owl, hawk, or other bird. These were glued and bound in place with sinew. The glue used was made from shell of a soft-shell turtle, deer hoofs, or chippings from a rawhide. Between the points where the feathers were fastened were painted bands of color, generally black and red. These colors represented night and day and were a symbol of precision.

Making an Indian Bow

For our bow we will take as a pattern a common type used by the Sioux or Dakota. When finished, it will be forty-four inches long, an inch and a quarter wide at the center, and five-eighths of an inch at the ends

Fig. 85.   Dakota Bow

(Fig. 85). You may cut and season your own stave, or, if this is not possible, a bow-stave may be purchased from a dealer in archery supplies. A piece of wood bought at a lumber-yard is not likely to prove satisfactory, as lumber is often kiln dried, which makes it too brittle for use. If you cut your own wood, you can do no better than to select one of the woods used by the Indians.

The first thing to do is to dress the sides and ends of the stave smooth with a jack plane. Two of the sides will, of course, be parallel to the grain. Select the smoothest of these sides, or, if you have cut your own stave, the one that was nearest the bark, for the back of the bow. On this side lay off the middle line AB (Fig. 86). Now carefully dress the stave down so that it will be forty-four inches long, an inch and a quarter wide, and three-quarters of an inch thick. Next determine the exact center of the stave, CD, and square lines around it two inches above and two inches below the center mark. This space is for the hand grip. At each end of the stave, now mark off points three-eighths of an inch on each side of the middle line and draw to them the tapering lines YZ. Lay off the same lines on the

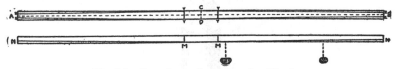

Fig. 86. Bow Stave Laid Out for Planing

under or belly side of the bow and plane the stave down to them.

Turn the stave on its side and mark the point N at each end, which is one-half inch from the edge of the back. Draw the diagonal lines MN on each side of the stave and plane down to them on the belly side. Now, with a spoke-shave and plane carefully round the belly so that it conforms to the sectional diagrams. Here again the Indian bow differs radically from the English. In the latter the belly is rounded to a perfect arch, while the Indian bow has almost flat sides. Only the edges of the back are rounded. Notches in the ends of the bow, for the bow-strings, are made as indicated in Fig. 87. They are best made with saw and small round file. The bow-string itself can be made by twisting three triple and well-waxed strands of heavy linen thread together, or it may be purchased ready made from a sporting-goods store.

Don't try to complete the work, especially the planing, too quickly. Many a good bow has been spoiled because the maker was too anxious to try it out. Set your plane fine and go slowly when using it. Test the

Fig. 87.   Bow End with Notches for String

bow carefully, when it is finished, to see that it bends evenly. If it does not, plane a bit off the stronger end. When finished, it may be rubbed with linseed oil or painted with Indian decorations. Keep it unstrung when not in use.

Arrow-making

Making a good arrow has always been considered a harder task than making a bow, but this need not dis-

courage you. With the materials and tools of civilization you will have a much easier job than did the
Indian boy who attempted his first arrow. Cut and
season your own wood and follow the Indian method
of making arrow shafts or, if you want to make the task
as easy as possible, purchase ordinary commercial
dowels from a lumber-yard or sash-and-door mill.
These are generally made of birch, which is an excellent arrow wood. The size you will want is five-six-
teenths of an inch in diameter.

Pick out the straightest and clearest shafts, and with
sandpaper remove any slight inequalities they may
have. Pick the best end for that in which the head is
to be fitted, and in the opposite one saw the nock, which
should be one-quarter of an inch deep. Finish it with
a small file and carefully round its edges with sandpaper so that it snugly fits the bow-string.

Feathering comes next. Turkey-wing feathers, secured from the butcher at Thanksgiving and Christmas, or purchased from a millinery supply house, are
the best. Use those from the same side of the wing
for the same arrow. With a sharp knife split the
feather. Then clean out the pith and with scissors trim
off the excess quill. With the scissors cut feathers to
shape as indicated in Fig. 88. The full length of the
finished quill should be six and a quarter inches; that
of the vane, five and a half inches. The latter is one-
quarter of an inch wide at the front, and three-quarters

of an inch at the rear. Finish them in sets of three and
put them aside until you are ready to feather the
arrows.

With a pencil, now mark off on the shaft the places
where the feathers are to go. One inch and a quarter
from the end of the arrow draw a circular line. This
is for the rear binding. Four and three quarters inches
from this draw a similar line which marks the begin-

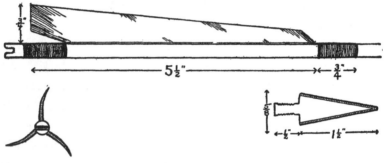

Fig. 88. Method of Feathering Arrow   Fig. 89. End View of Arrow
Fig. 90. Iron Arrow Point

ning of the front binding. At right angles to the nock
draw a perpendicular line which indicates the position
of the cock feather. Two similar lines are drawn equidistant from this, for the other feathers. When all are
set they will appear as in Fig 89.

We are now ready to glue and bind the feathers. Put
a thin coating of glue on the feather and on the pencil
line indicating its position, and allow it to partially
set before pressing both together. Pins may be used
in each end of the quill to hold the feathers in place

until all three are glued to the shaft. When they are in
place baste them down by a spiral binding of cotton
thread wrapped between the bristles of the feather. If
necessary, adjust the position of the feathers as this
basting is put in place. When the glue dries, remove
this basting and wrap and glue the permanent bindings
of colored silk thread to each end of the feather. The
hardest part of the work is now over.

Now for arrowheads. The easiest to make are those
of iron, like the ones the Indians first got from white
traders and which they later made from scraps of iron
that happened to fall into their hands. These varied in
style in the different tribes and according to the use to
which they were to be put. For them you will need
some one-sixteenth by five-eighths inch spring steel or
band iron, which you can get from a hardware store or
blacksmith shop. With a hack saw roughly shape the
point according to Fig. 90. Use a file to trim up and
sharpen the edges and to make the notches for the
binding cord in the shank.

Round off the end of the arrow and saw a notch in it
three-quarters of an inch deep, to receive the head.
Glue the point in place and bind it, while the glue is
soft, with button-hole silk thread. You now have an
Indian bow and Indian arrows such as were carried on
buffalo hunts and the war trail by the warriors of the
plains a hundred years ago.

Chipping an Arrowpoint

Some day you may wish to try your hand at chipping out flint arrowheads. The drawings in Fig. 91 show how to do it. Flint, quartz, or obsidian, suitable for this purpose, can be found in almost every part of our country, and if you have trouble in finding suitable natural material, remember that with care and practice good heads can be chipped from pieces of glass bottles. The equipment needed is simply a pad of heavy leather for the palm of the hand and a chipping tool of deer horn, bone, or steel. The piece of flint or glass to be chipped is held in the left hand on the pad and the chipper is pressed firmly against the edge of the flint until a chip breaks off. Take off but a small chip at a time. Patience and care are needed if you are going to master this ancient art.

The Quiver and Bow-case

A quiver and bow-case of the plains style can be made from two sheepskins or other leather. The quiver, or arrow-case, is made from a piece of leather two feet long, ten inches wide at the top, and six inches wide at the bottom, cut to the shape shown in Fig. 92. Through the holes indicated, a half inch above the lower edge of this piece, are drawn laces one foot long,

Mandan Chief with Lance

Crow Warrior with Coup Stick and Shield

A Dakota Shield

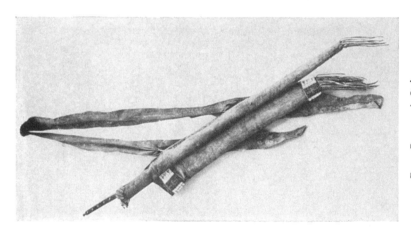

Bow Case and Quiver

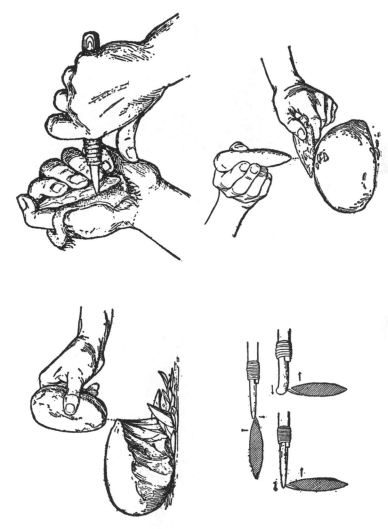

Fig. 91. Chipping Flint Arrow Points (BAE) (A) Making Flakes (B) Chipping a Flake with a Bone-pointed Tool (C) Position of Tool and Flake in Chipping (D) Chipping with a Hammer Stone

Dakota Quiver and Bow Case (SI)

which form a fringe on the finished quiver. The fringe
at the lower end of the bow-case is made in the same

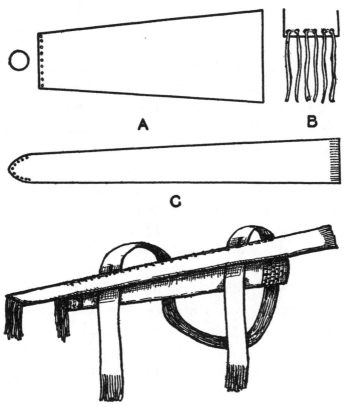

Fig. 92.   (A) Quiver Pattern   (B) Method of Making Fringe   (C) Bow.
Case Pattern   (D) Case and Quiver Complete

way.   The bottom of the quiver is made from a circular
piece two inches in diameter, cut from the thickest part
of the hide.

The bow-case is three feet long, five inches wide at

the top, and three inches at the bottom. The upper edge is fringed to a depth of one inch. The only other part of the case is the shoulder strap, five and a half feet long and three inches wide. It is best made from two pieces joined at the center.

Assemble the quiver first by sewing to it, with strong linen thread, its circular bottom. Then insert the fringe lacings and sew up the side to the top. Insert the fringe in the bottom of the bow-case, fold it in half and sew its edges together. Now place the bow-case on top of the quiver so that the sewed edges of both come together with the ends of the latter, equidistant from the ends of the bow-case. Beginning two inches below the upper end of the quiver, lash the edges of both case and quiver together for a distance of about one foot. This lacing should be done with a thong wrapped in a spiral through holes made close to the edges with an awl. The shoulder strap is fastened on with separate thongs drawn through its center and the edges of the case at each end of this binding. It is attached one foot from its ends, which are fringed to form pendants.

When complete, the ends of the quiver may be decorated with bands of beadwork, as shown in the drawing.

Chapter Eight

WEAPONS AND WAR PAINT

THE shield of buffalo-bull hide, carried by most Plains warriors, was valued more for its medicine power and the spiritual protection it gave the owner than for its practical use in warding off arrows and spear thrusts. To the man who carried one it was considered his most sacred possession and on its manufacture and care he bestowed infinite patience and thought. To carry one in battle was considered something of a distinction, as the shield-bearer was more conspicuous and so more likely to be shot at, and also because shields were always desired for capture. On the other hand, the shield gave the bearer some physical protection because it was strong enough to stop arrows or even the bullets of a smooth-bore gun.

The medicine power of the shield was contained in the design painted on it and in its other decorations. These designs were drawn on the front of the shield and on the soft buckskin cover which was laced over it. Some of the patterns contained pictures of animals, symbols of the elements, or other natural objects, that were considered by the warrior to be his special helpers. These designs were received in dreams along with the ceremonies and taboos connected with the shield.

A drawing of a bear might mean that the owner believed it would give him the strength of that animal. If the tortoise appeared in the pattern, it was probably

Blackfoot Shield of Buffalo Hide (AMNH)

because the shield-bearer believed that he would live even though he were severely wounded in battle, for the tortoise is long-lived and it will move about even though its head be cut off. Special medicines made of

parts of animals or birds were often tied to the shield
or placed under the outer cover, and pendants of soft
buckskin or cloth decorated with eagle feathers were
fastened to it. These were supposed to endow the warrior with the courage and swiftness of that bird. Miniature shields, in exact representation of the larger ones,
were sometimes made because they could be more
easily carried. These small shields possessed the same
spiritual protective properties of the full-sized ones
from which they were copied. In camp the shield
hung in an honored place.

In some of the tribes, shields of the same pattern
were carried by members of a society who used the
same war cries, body paint, horse decorations, and
songs. Among the Cheyenne, all of the shields were
made by one of the societies whose members carried a
plain red shield with a buffalo tail hanging from it.
These red shields were particularly powerful, for the
pattern was supposed to have been made originally by
the great Prophet who brought the tribe its medicine
arrows. When swung in a circle before the enemy,
they were thought to prevent enemy arrows from hitting either the shields or the men who bore them.

How the Shield Was Made

The making of a shield was a mysterious process,
often conducted in secret. A piece of hide was cut

from the neck or breast of a fresh hide about twice as large as the shield was to be when finished. The average size was about seventeen inches in diameter, although they varied from one foot to twenty-six inches. The hide was shrunk by heating or steaming it until it was almost twice its original thickness. This was done in one of two ways. The simplest method was to cover

Mounted Warrior with Shield. From an Indian Drawing

the hide with a thin layer of clay on which burning coals were placed until the skin hardened. The more common way was to peg the hide down over a hole in the ground about eighteen inches deep. One edge of the hide was left loose. This was lifted and red-hot stones were dropped in the hole. On these, water was poured until the steam had caused the hide to shrink to the desired size. The hair was then removed with a stone and the still soft hide was pegged down over a small mound of earth. This gave it a dish shape that increased its power to ward off lance thrusts. With a stick its circular shape was marked on it and the edges were trimmed smooth to this pattern. Finally it was laid on a rawhide and the wrinkles and dents were pounded with a smooth stone until the shield was smooth. Before it was decorated it was tested by having the warriors shoot arrows at it. If they bounded back from the hide, leaving it uninjured, the shield was considered fit for use. If not, it was rejected.

The decoration of the shield was done with special ceremonies conducted by medicine men and experienced warriors. The cover of soft dressed skin was generally made first. On it was painted a design different from that on the shield itself. This cover remained in place until the warrior went into battle. Then the face of the shield would be exposed with its full power directed at the enemy. The front of the shield was painted after the cover was made and the other decorations were attached to it. A sling of soft skin was fastened to the upper edges. With this it was slung from the left shoulder so that the left hand was free for grasping the bow. While the decorations were being applied, special songs were sung and *coups* were counted. The ceremony was concluded with a feast, after which the shield-makers entered the sweat lodge. The finished shield was hung in an honored place inside the lodge at night or in stormy weather, but on fair days it was set up on a tripod to the rear of the tipi to ward off danger or harm.

Making a Shield

A shield for use in dances and pageants can be easily made in a short time from old canvas or other heavy

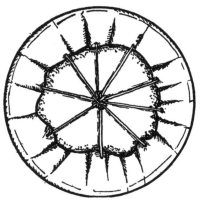

Fig. 93. Reverse Side of Canvas Shield

cloth and a barrel hoop. Cut the hoop down to half of its original thickness and smooth and sandpaper its rough edges. Then cut out a circular piece of canvas six inches greater in diameter than the hoop. Punch holes around the edges of the canvas, and with a piece of heavy cord lace it tightly over the hoop. Fig. 93 shows how the back of the shield should look when this work is finished.

Paint the canvas with a ground color of white or

buff, and when it dries apply your design. Sketch it on the canvas with pencil before you begin to paint. The design may be one of your own or you may copy one of those shown in the drawings. When your shield is decorated, sew a strip of cloth six inches wide, to which feathers have been attached, along its upper edge, and long enough to form two pendants on each side.

A covered shield may be made from a piece of wall board and covered with imitation buckskin or chamois on which designs are painted. Imitation buckskin for this purpose may be made by soaking canton flannel in a mixture of yellow ochre, glue, and water.

In Fig. 94 are shown some decorative and protective designs taken from old shields from different tribes. The first is that on a Dakota shield now in the American Museum of Natural History. According to Dr. Clark Wissler, the pattern shows the eagle which was the special protector of the owner. The four stars are each of a different color; yellow for the dawn, green for the sky, red for day, and black for night. The lightning shows the death-dealing power conferred on the owner. The red-striped shield on the eagle's breast represented the emblem of the United States and was supposed to be of help in contending with soldiers.

The next pattern commemorates a fight the shield's owner had with the Crows. He was completely surrounded, but he managed to escape because he was pro-

Fig. 94. Shield Decorations

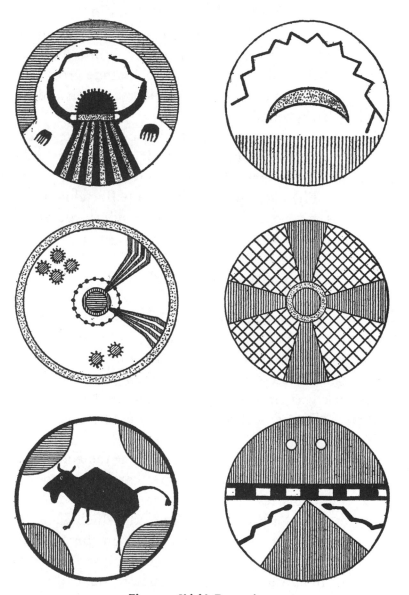

Fig. 94. Shield Decorations

tected on all sides by his helper, the bear. His position is indicated by the center of the shield, while the bear claws symbolize his protector. The Maltese cross represents the four quarters of the universe and is red on a yellow background.

The third pattern, which is blue on a white background, represents rain. Next to it on a white background is a buffalo skull pattern in red, yellow, green, and blue. The two lower designs symbolize clouds and mountains in blue and red, and the thunderbird, which is in red and yellow.

Lances and Coup Sticks

Lances and coup sticks were often carried in dances by some of the Plains Tribes and had an important part in certain ceremonies. Lances also formed a part of the insignia of certain of the warrior societies. The *coup* stick was similar to the lance except that it was without a flint or steel head. It was used for touching an enemy in battle.

Among the Kiowa, a society known as the Kaitsenko, made up of the bravest warriors, carried a crooked lance wrapped with otter skin as one of their emblems. They also wore a broad buckskin sash which came together at the waist, from which a pendant hung to the ground, Fig. 95. If a battle went against them they would dismount and drive the lance through the sash

Fig. 95. Sash and Lance of the Dog Soldiers
Fig. 96. Feather Banner (AMNH)

into the ground so that they were anchored in place. There they would stand and fight until they were killed or until one of their fellow members withdrew the lance and allowed them to escape. Under the rules of the society they could not free themselves and a man who did so would be dishonored and disgraced.

Nearly every Plains Tribe had a similar society, and in most cases they bore names that meant "brave dogs," "old dogs," "crazy dogs," or something of the same nature. This caused them to be known as "dog soldiers" to the soldiers and frontiersmen, who knew and respected their bravery and fighting qualities.

The lances were nearly always decorated with beaver, otter, mink, and weasel skins, or with feathers of different birds arranged in various ways. Each kind of feather had a meaning to the lance-bearer. Thus a Pawnee lance had a bunch of owl feathers at its top which represented the north star which watches over the people at night. The owls watched over the camp at night and warned the people of enemies prowling about. Crow feathers were attached first when the lance was made because the crows are always the first to find food and they helped the people find the buffalo. Swan feathers represented the thunderbird, which often brought thunderstorms to save the people when the enemy was on the point of attacking. The point of this lance was made of flint because that stone was believed to be related to the thunder and was supposed to be found wherever lightning strikes. Thus the stone lancehead symbolized the power to strike an enemy before he was aware of the danger.

To make a lance, cut a straight staff about three-quarters of an inch in diameter and from five to six feet long. Paint it or carve or burn decorations on it. If you want to make a feather banner, prepare your feathers as for a war bonnet trail and attach them to a strip of cloth six inches wide and a foot shorter than the length of the staff. The cloth is tied to the top of the staff and at intervals along its length. Lances of this style were popular with the Siouan tribes, Fig. 96. A decoration of feather clusters is easier to make and requires fewer feathers. The clusters are made of four feathers prepared with lacing loops as for use in a war bonnet. They are fastened in place by means of a thong passed through the loops and tied to a notch cut in the staff. Streamers of horsehair may be tied with the feathers. Another type of lance may be made by covering the stick with red flannel held in place by tacks and by a spiral wrapping of cord. The feather decorations are sewn direct to the flannel wrapping.

War Clubs

War clubs of many varieties were used by the different tribes. They were made of wood, stone, bone, antler, buffalo horn, and copper. One of the most common types was carved from a solid block of hardwood, with a ball at one end, usually fashioned of a knot. These clubs, like other Indian weapons, were supposed to possess supernatural power.

Another widely used type was the gun-shaped club made from a flat slab and resembling a gun butt in shape. These clubs often had flint or metal blades or spikes fastened in their lower edges.

Stone-headed Clubs of the Plains Tribes (BAE)

The Plains, Southwestern and Plateau Tribes used a club made by shrinking a rawhide wrapping around a smooth stone and fastening it to a wooden handle. In the Southwest wooden clubs, resembling a potato-masher, were used, and also a curved stick for killing rabbits, much like the Australian boomerang. Clubs made of whalebone, carved stone, and of beaten sheets of copper were used on the Northwest Coast.

You can make a club to carry in the war dance by

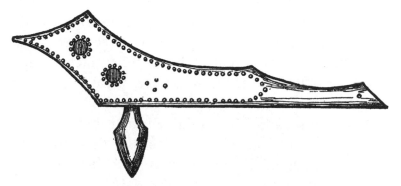

Fig. 97.   Gun-shaped Club

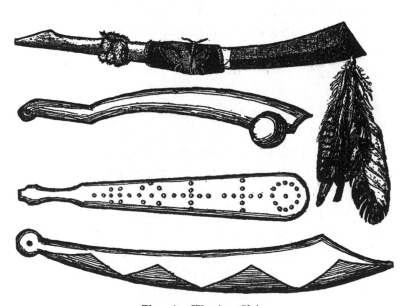

Fig. 98.   Wooden Clubs

uprooting a small dead sapling and carving and painting the roots to suit your fancy. A gun-shaped club, Fig. 97, can be made from a board three-quarters to one inch thick, and twenty-four to thirty inches long. Draw the outline of the club on the board and saw it out. Then with a knife shape the handle and edges and sandpaper it smooth. Then finish it by rubbing in two or three coats of linseed oil. Decorate the club with painted designs or by studding it with brass-headed tacks. Drill a small hole near the end through which a wrist thong may be tied. Knife-points for the lower edge of the club may be whittled from soft wood and painted with aluminum paint. These should be doweled into the club and glued in place. Patterns of other clubs, which can be made in this way, are shown in Fig. 98.

Why Indians Painted

While the Indians painted their bodies with special protective designs when they went to war, all Indian paint cannot properly be called "war paint," as it was often used for purposes in no way connected with war.

Indians painted their faces for decorative purposes and for protection against the wind, sun, snow and insects. Designs of various kinds were used to designate membership in certain societies, in ceremonies, as marks of achievement, and in mourning for the dead.

When used merely for personal ornamentation, there was no guide to the way it should be applied beyond the individual fancy of the wearer.

The colors used were made from minerals or vegetables. Red, which symbolized human life and which was perhaps the most popular color, was made from fine clays containing oxides or iron. Black, the color of death, was made from powdered charred wood. Green came from copper ores, and white was obtained by grinding down kaolin. Yellow was obtained from bull berries or the moss on pine trees. All these colors were mixed with fat before being applied. When painting for protection against the elements, the Indian rubbed grease made from buffalo-back fat into his palms and then rubbed it in on his face. Then he would put his greasy fingers into his bag of powdered paint and rub that which adhered to them evenly all over his face. When the whole body was painted the finger nails were frequently drawn over the paint, producing a peculiar barred appearance.

Among the Omaha, a leader of a war party painted diagonal lines on his face from the bottom of the eyes to the neck. These represented the path of his tears while crying for the success of his expedition. Returning warriors who had taken scalps painted their faces black before entering their home village. Pawnee scouts painted their faces white to symbolize the wolf whose medicine was considered to be of the greatest

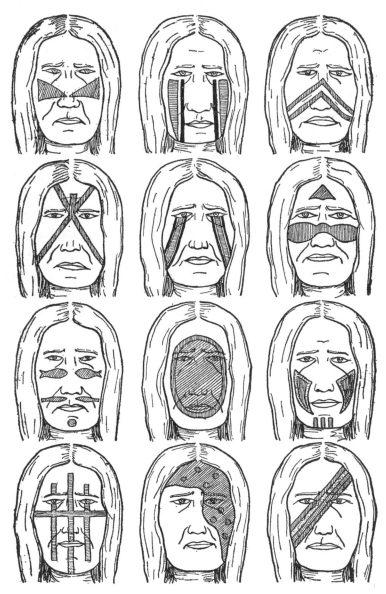

Fig. 99.   Facial Decorations

help in scouting. Red paint was generally applied to the face of persons taking part in ceremonies or who were being initiated into societies. Animal figures were sometimes drawn on the body to indicate the totem of the family to which the person belonged. A number of facial decorations which you may use are shown in Figure 99.

Indian Make-up

To make up as an Indian, you will first need a ground color to darken your skin. For this you can use regular theatrical grease paint which comes in a special Indian shade or a liquid make-up. The grease paint is best for stage work under heavy lights, but the liquid has some advantages over it for general use. It can be applied to all parts of the body and it will not come off on costumes as readily as the grease.

Liquid make-up can be bought all ready prepared or you can make it yourself from Indian theatrical powder. To do this, mix the powder with a small quantity of warm water to a pasty consistency. Then dissolve this paste in a larger quantity of water. It can then be applied with a soft sponge. Cocoa or powdered red cinchona, which you can purchase from the druggist, can be used in place of theatrical powder when the latter cannot be secured.

Your make-up outfit should include, in addition to

the ground color, a box of cold cream, red, yellow, black, white, and blue grease paint liners, and some of the small paper lining swabs used by actors. All of these can be purchased from drug stores that sell theatrical make-up.

Making-up should be carefully done if it is to add to the effect of your performance. A common fault is to apply the colors too thick, especially the war paint. These colors, standing out in a much too glaring way, make the actor look not only unnatural, but absurd. It should be borne in mind that Indian character varied as does the white man's, so that your character make-up can be coarse or fine, cruel or kindly, or however you decide to make it.

The first step in making up is to cover the face with cold cream. Spread it on thin with the fingers and then rub it off with a piece of cheese cloth. Apply the ground color and rub it in evenly with the tips of the fingers. A bit of yellow should now be rubbed on the cheek bones to bring them out. To do this successfully, place the ends of your fingers on the yellow spot and work outward so that the yellow gradually tones off into the brown background. To bring the cheek bones to still greater prominence, darken the cheeks with black under the inner part of the eyes so as to create the effect of a depression. Eyebrows may be omitted entirely or made straight and drawn well in toward the nose. Draw a thin black line all around the eye and bring it well in to the nose. From the outer corner of the eye draw a line down one inch long. Finish your make-up by applying the war paint or ceremonial design that you have chosen.

Wigs can be made or purchased from a theatrical wig-maker. Indian hair-dressing styles and costumes varied so that before you start to make up, study as many pictures as you can, of the type you wish to repre-

Fig. 100. An Eastern Indian

sent. Eastern Indians and some of those on the plains shaved off all of their hair except a narrow ridge in the middle that ran from the forehead to the neck and from which hung the scalp lock, Fig. 100. To represent this type, make a tight-fitting skullcap of white muslin and dye it in liquid make-up. Then sew a band of close-cropped fur down its center to represent the hair. A braid of horsehair may be added for a scalp lock. The Southwestern Indians wore their hair bobbed and wore a band around the head. Sometimes it was worn long in the back, and this part was done up in a tight knot on the back of the head. A specially made wig is needed if you wish to copy it exactly.

How to Make a Wig

A Plains wig can be made from black horsehair, hair which you may purchase from a hair-goods dealer or

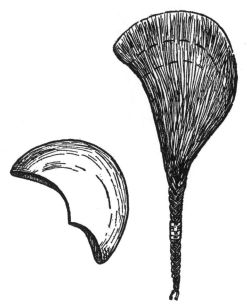

Fig. 101. Skull-cap and Side View of Wig

from common binding twine or hemp rope dyed black. To prepare the latter for use, cut it in three-foot lengths, unravel and soak it in warm water, which will soften it and help remove the kinks. Then dye it with household dyes according to the directions on the package.

Next make a close-fitting skull-cap of heavy black muslin according to the pattern in Fig. 101. With chalk mark a line along the cap's center to indicate the part line from front to back. Beginning at the front of

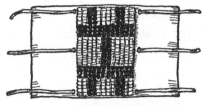

Fig. 102. Braid Wrapping

the cap, sew strands of hair to it so that the center of each strand comes on the white line. When the hair has all been stitched along the center, it should be taken up with other lines of stitches, so as to make it cover all parts of the cloth cap. The loose ends hanging down over the ears should now be combed out, divided into three parts, and braided. Into the ends of the braids pieces of red ribbon about nine inches long may be woven. Braid wrappings made of soft leather with beaded decorations were worn by the Plains Indians. These may be made from a piece of soft leather one and a half inches wide and two and a half inches long, as illustrated in Figure 102.

Chapter Nine

PIPES AND BAGS

THE pipe has always occupied a prominent place in Indian stories as an emblem of peace and friendship. That this is so is due to the fact that to the Indian, smoking was a religious ceremony to be indulged in only on solemn occasions, to bring good and to arrest evil. An Indian smoked to allay storms, to gain protection from his enemies, to bring game, and to invoke

A Calumet (USNM)

the blessing of supernatural powers on anything of importance that he was about to undertake. Ordinarily, young men did not smoke, as it made them short-winded. Certain pipes or pipe stems which were seldom made for actual smoking were supposed to be possessed of sacred power and are known to us as calumets. They get their name from a French word meaning reed or tube. Calumets were used by many of the tribes when peace treaties were made and it is from this custom that the term "pipe of peace" came into being. Such pipes were recognized as flags of

Blackfoot Medicine Pipe (AMNH)

truce between warring tribes and were used by messengers as a passport. Calumets also had an important part in adoption ceremonies and dances of the Omaha.

Medicine pipes kept in bundles, which were regarded as powerful medicines for use in curing the sick and for bringing success in war, were used by most of the Plains Tribes. These pipes could be unwrapped and used only by their owners, with elaborate ceremonies. When not in use they were wrapped in furs with rattles, paints, and other articles used in the pipe rituals. These bundles were hung inside the tipi at night over the owner's head, and in the daytime over the lodge door or on a tripod to the rear. The Blackfoot believe that these bundles were given to them by the thunder and speak of them as thunder's pipes.

The Meaning of a Cree Peace Pipe

A peace pipe belonging to a prairie Cree was found a few years ago by Mr. Donald Cadzow, and by him secured for the Museum of the American Indian, where it now is. Here is his description of this interesting old pipe.

"The stem, forty inches in length, is made of a green ash sprout; attached to it with sinew thongs are tufts of red horsehair, and the heads of six northern pileated woodpeckers with the mandibles turned back upon the red crests. This symbolizes the suppression of anger, for the red crest of this woodpecker always rises when the bird is

angry, and therefore is here held down. When
the tribe was at war the sinew was cut and the
crests allowed to rise. A similar symbol is used
by the Pawnee.

"The end of the pipe stem is covered by the
head and neck of a loon, in addition to the woodpecker mandibles referred to. The loon's head
symbolizes land, water, and sky, where the loon
is said to be at home. Near the base of the loon's
neck are little bunches of downy snow-owl feathers tied to the stem with sinews; these impart to
the stem the power of the owl, which sees and
hunts at night. Beneath the owl feathers and likewise attached to the stem are eight eagle plumes,
threaded to form a fan, to which are attached
small sticks upon which are woven porcupine
quills colored red, blue, and yellow, with native
dyes. At both ends of each of the sticks is a tuft
of green-dyed horsehair, symbolizing the color of
the earth."

Tobacco was the only crop cultivated by some of
the tribes. It was often mixed with sumach leaves,
the inner bark of dogwood or red willow, to make a
mixture known as kinnikinnick. The willow bark was
scraped off in long shavings, put on a piece of rawhide, and left to dry. Then with the hands greased
with buffalo fat, the bark would be crushed into small

particles. The grease which adhered to it helped to make it burn freely.

Seldom more than one pipe was used when it was smoked in council. The medicine man or host would light the pipe with a coal from the fire and, blowing a puff of smoke toward the sky, would point the pipe stem toward it as a prayer to Those Above. He would then point the stem toward the earth and to the four winds. He then passed the pipe to the man on his left who smoked in the same manner. The pipe went around until it reached the man seated at the door of the lodge. After he had smoked, it was passed back around the circle to the right until it reached the man on the other side of the door, for it was not permitted to pass the pipe across the doorway. It then was again passed to the left until it reached the medicine man or was smoked out. In this way the pipe was supposed to be following the path of the sun.

Pipes were of many different shapes and were made of various materials. Some were straight tubes, others were curved, and some had bowls at right angles to the stem. A T-shaped pipe made of the stone was the type most commonly used on the plains. Hardwood, bone, clay, and stone were used for making pipe bowls. Blocks of hard, tough clay were carved out as pipe bowls and rubbed with grease. These were hardened over a fire and by use. Steatite, serpentine slate, and catlinite were the stones principally used. The

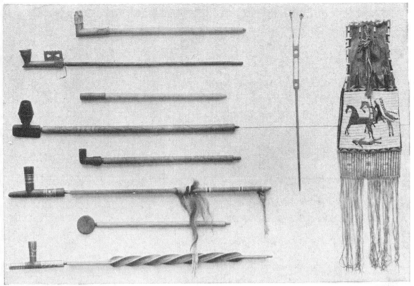

Indian Pipes

1-2. Pawnee Sacred Pipes; 3. Cheyenne Sun Dance Pipe; 4. Blackfoot Pipe;
5-7. Cheyenne Pipes; 6-8. Sioux Pipes; 9. Pipe Tamper, Sioux; 10. Pipe
Bag, Sioux.

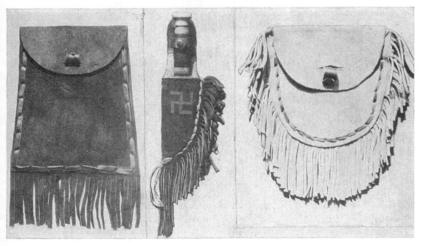

Square and Round Type Pouches and Knife Sheath

Dakota Knife Sheaths

Photo by Fay Welch

This Boy, aged 11, made his own Willow Bed and Tipi and Camped in it for Nine Weeks

last named is a soft red stone found in the famous pipe-stone quarries in Minnesota. These quarries have long been sacred to the Dakota and the tradition is that they were regarded as neutral ground by all of the tribes. This stone can easily be worked with a knife. White traders took advantage of this quality and turned out thousands of pipes on lathes for the Indian trade.

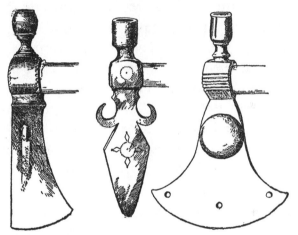

English, French and Spanish Tomahawk Pipes (USNM)

It gets its name from George Catlin, an artist who wrote one of the earliest accounts of the Western tribes and who was the first to describe it.

Pipe stems were nearly always made from ash, which has a soft pith in its center which can easily be removed. In the old days the stem was split, the pith scraped out, and the two pieces glued and bound together. The elaborate decorative wrapping of quillwork and fur helped to hold the two parts together. In modern times the pith has been removed with a red-hot iron. Another method of removing the pith, said to have been used in the old days, was to drill a small hole in the pith at one end of the stick in which a wood-boring grub was inserted and the end sealed. The stick was then heated over a fire and the grub, following the line of least resistance, would bore his way through the pith to make his escape.

The famous steel tomahawk pipes were, of course, made by white men. In most cases they were presented by the settlers to their Indian allies. Each nation used a different pattern. Thus the English resembled a straight ax, the French a fleur-de-lys, and the Spanish a broad-ax. "Bury the tomahawk," as an expression to indicate the making of peace, originated in the fact that when the blade of a pipe tomahawk was driven in the ground, it immediately became a peace pipe.

Making a Pipe

You can make a pipe for use in camp-fire ceremonials from clay or hardwood that, with a little care, can be made to look like a catlinite pipe from the Dakotas. If you can run a lathe it will be a fairly simple task for you to turn a pipe bowl out of cherry or mahogany in accordance with the drawings (Fig. 103). If you can't, carve the bowl from a clear piece of white pine or

other soft wood. In either case, finish it by staining
it a brick red and giving it a wax finish.

A pipe bowl may also be molded from blue clay or
potter's clay. Brick clay, which will burn red, is especially suitable. Mold your pipe to the shape shown in
the drawings and cut out the openings for the bowl and
stem with round sticks. Dry the pipe in the shade and

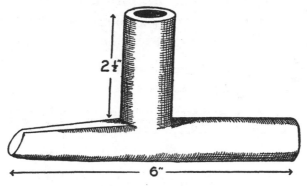

2⅟₄"

6"

Fig. 103.   Pipe Bowl

then in the oven of a stove. It may be fired in a wood
fire out-of-doors or better yet in a kitchen stove. Place
it directly in the coals and leave it there overnight or
until the fire burns out. Do not attempt to remove it
while it is warm or it may crack.

For the stem, nothing is better than an ash sapling
such as was used by the Indians. Cut a stick a little
larger than you want the finished stem to be and peel
off the outer bark. A good size is about one inch in
diameter and eighteen inches long. Dry this thor-

oughly and then smooth it by planing and with sand-paper. Now with a red-hot wire burn out the central pith. A piece of iron baling wire is just right for this purpose. Cut the mouthpiece and pipe insert on the ends as shown in Fig. 104.

The stem may be decorated by carving, painting, or burning designs on it or studding it with brass headed tacks. Or you may make a medicine pipe of it by decorating it with strips of fur, bunches of horsehair or feathers as shown in Fig. 105. The horsehair and fur

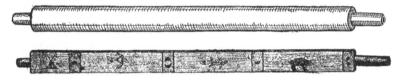

Fig. 104.   Pipe Stems

strips are bound to the stem with linen thread covered with water-proof cement and the feathers are laced to-gether with leather thongs drawn through their shafts.

The Pipe Bag

Pipes and tobacco were carried in long bags, heavily fringed, by the Dakota and most of their neighbors on the plains. A bag of this type can be made of split calfskin, sheepskin, or any other soft leather. The front and back of the bag are made from one piece of leather sixteen inches wide and twenty-four inches

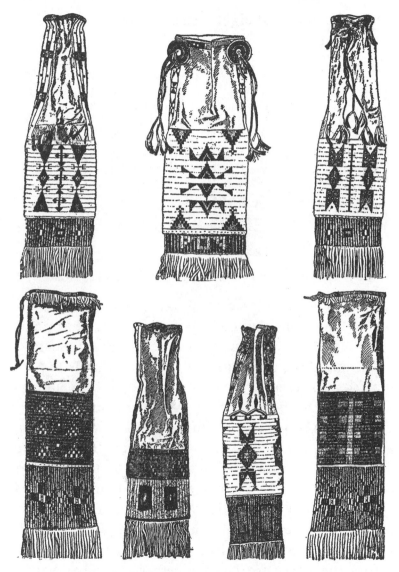

Pipe Bags with Bead and Quill Decorations (AMNH)

long. Another, cut eight inches square, is required foi the bottom fringe (Fig. 106).

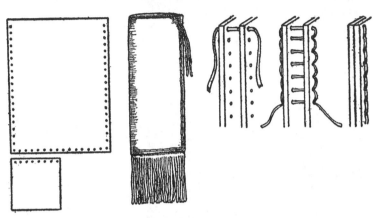

Fig. 106. Pipe Bag Pattern   Fig 107.   Thong Lacing Method

The bag may be sewed or laced together. If you use the latter method, make holes with a leather punch a half inch apart around the three sides of the large piece and along one edge of the leather that is to form the fringe. Then with a thong an eighth of an inch wide lace the bag together by the method shown in Fig. 107. The ends of the thong are tied with a square knot and cemented together with water-proof cement. The fringe piece is laced between the bottom edges of the bag and cut into a fringe when the lacing is finished. A thong, a half inch wide, should be laced around the top of the bag to be used as a drawstring for closing it. If the bag is to be beaded, this work should be done before the parts are laced together. A pipe bag of

this type is excellent for carrying a fire-by-friction outfit in.

Strike-a-light Pouches

After the introduction of flint and steel, the Indian
carried these implements on his belt in small bags
called strike-a-light pouches. These were of a variety
of shapes and sizes. They are easily made and are
attractive to wear with a full costume or with camp

Arapaho Strike-a-light Pouch (AMNH)

clothes. These small bags may be beaded and can be
laced or sewn together. The pattern for a round pouch
of this kind is shown in Fig. 108. The piece for the
outside of the pouch is five inches wide across the top
and five inches deep. The back piece, which includes
the flap and fringe, is nine inches wide at its greatest
width and ten inches at its extreme depth. The flap
is two and a half inches long. Belt loops are made in
the back by cutting slits two inches long and a half

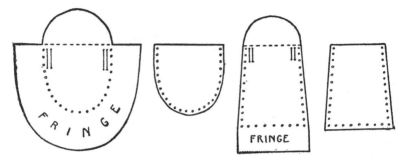

Fig. 108. Round Pouch Pattern   Fig. 110. Square Pouch Pattern

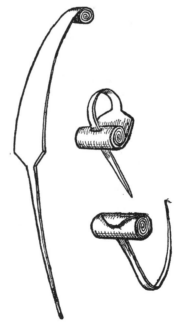

Fig. 109. Leather Pouch Button

inch apart as shown in the diagram. Lace the parts together by the same method as that used in the pipe bag. Pouches of this kind can be made very attractive by using a lacing thong of red, yellow, blue, or green calf or sheepskin. A button to hold them closed can be made of a half-inch thong by rolling it up tight. Then with a thin knife blade cut a slit through the center of the roll and draw the tapered end of the thong through it (Fig. 109).

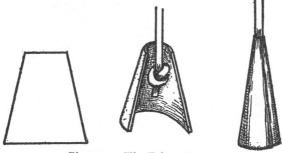

Fig. 111. Tin Fringe Rattle

Another type of strike-a-light pouch is shown in Figure 110. This is six inches long in front, four inches wide at the top of the flap, and five inches wide at the bottom. The fringe is an inch and half long and the flap is two inches deep. On the fringe may be fastened tin rattles, which were a common form of decoration on many articles. These are made from triangular-shaped pieces of tin cut from a can with tinners' shears and bent round the fringe by a pair of pliers (Fig. 111).

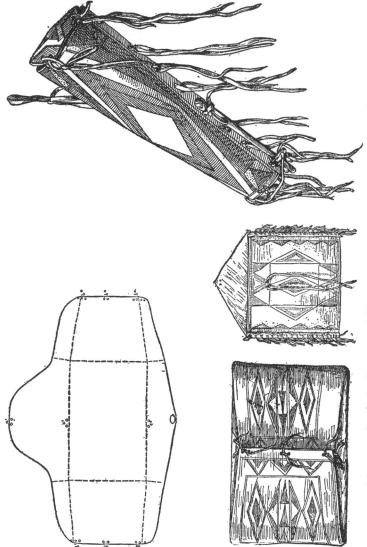

Fig. 112. Parfleche Pattern and Finished Case   Fig. 114.   Square Rawhide Bag
Fig. 115.   War Bonnet Case

Parfleches

Other bags used by the Plains Indians were made of rawhide. The flat rawhide clothes case, known as a parfleche, was made from a whole skin. A calfskin prepared according to the directions given in Chapter Four can be turned into a parfleche by cutting it to shape as shown in Fig. 112 and folding it while wet along the dotted lines. Dry it under pressure and insert laces in the holes, and it is ready for use. It should be decorated with painted designs such as those shown in Fig. 113. Parfleches of this kind were used to hold clothing, food, and any other articles that the Indian might care to pack in them. Another type of rawhide bag is shown in Fig. 114. This is cut from a single piece and laced up the sides. Short laces are used that are tied together after being drawn through each pair of holes. Their ends are left long to form a fringe.

Cylindrical parfleche cases were used as containers for war bonnets and other war paraphernalia. A case of this kind, as shown in Fig. 115, is made of three pieces of rawhide. The piece for the sides is an irregular rectangle eighteen inches long, twenty-two inches wide at the top, and sixteen inches wide at the bottom. The top and bottom are circular, seven and five inches in diameter, respectively. The case is laced together at the top, bottom, and sides with extra-long laces,

Fig. 113. Parfleche Decorations (AMNH)

the ends of which form a heavy fringe. The dimensions we have given are only approximate, as the case may be made any size. This and the other parfleche cases make attractive properties for use in plays and pageants. For this purpose they may be made of cardboard.

Knife Sheaths

Knife cases are also made of rawhide and can be decorated with painted decorations. More elaborate

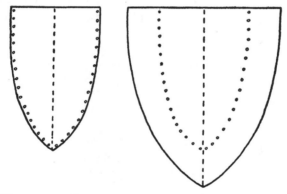

Fig. 116. Knife Case Pattern Without and With Fringe

ones can be made by sewing soft leather over a rawhide case and decorating it with beads. The pattern for a rawhide case is shown in Fig. 116. The soft leather pattern is the same except that an extra two inches may be allowed on the outer edges which can be cut into a fringe. If you own a hunting-knife, the factory-made sheath can be covered with a soft leather case made in this way and decorated with beadwork.

Chapter Ten

MUSICAL INSTRUMENTS

MUSIC was one of the greatest pleasures of the Indians and was so well developed by them that it could express every phase of their lives. Every tribe had songs for use in fasting and prayer, to bring good fortune in war or hunting, for games and dances, defying death and treating the sick. There were also lulla-

Pottery Drum

bys and children's songs, love songs, game songs, comic songs, and songs for work. Many of the songs were of a sacred character and were used as prayers to implore the help of supernatural power.

Songs came to men in dreams and were supposed to have medicine power. They were considered the personal property of individuals or societies, so that others

wishing to use them had to purchase the right from
the owners. Many had no words but were sung with
vocables, meaningless syllables like hi, ho, ah, or ay.

The instruments used by the Indians to accompany
their singing were simply made and few in number.
Drums, rattles, and whistles were used in dances and
ceremonies, and a flute for courting and sometimes in

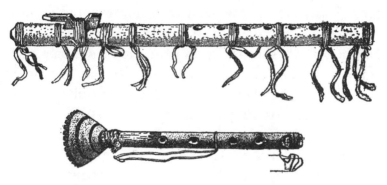

Kiowa Flute and Zuñi Flageolet (USNM)

giving war signals. The flute was generally made from
a piece of cedar or sumac split and hollowed out and
nicely fitted together. Drums, or tom-toms, were of
three main types: the single or double headed hand
drum, the large dance drum, played by several men,
and the water drum used mainly by the Woodland
Tribes. These were cylindrical in shape except in
northwestern California and on the Northwest Coast,
where square drums were also used. Clay pots and

baskets were sometimes used as drum frames, but generally they were made of wood.

How to Make a Drum

For a hand drum a cheese box is used for the frame. These have been used by the Indians for this purpose for as long as they could get them from the white man.   Rawhide for the heads can be prepared according to the directions in Chapter Four.   For small drumheads, use sheepskin, and for the larger ones calfskin.   Rawhides for this purpose can be purchased through your butcher or direct from an abbatoir.   If you do not care to prepare the hides yourself, you may purchase a clarified calfskin from a wholesale leather house or a dealer in craft-leather supplies.   Drumheads may also be used, but they are rather expensive.

To make the frame, take the cheese box apart, using pliers to pull the nails and staples that hold it together. This will minimize the danger of splitting the wood. Then with a knife and saw trim the wood down to the proper length and width for the size drum you intend to make.   The average size used by the Indians was about eighteen inches in diameter and from three to four inches thick.   A good size for a hand drum is fourteen inches in diameter and three inches deep. We will presume you are going to make one of this size. Cut two pieces of wood about forty-nine inches long

An Indian Drummer

Drums, Drum Frame and Rattles

In Council—Scout Leaders in Costume

and cut them down to the proper width. Round off all edges with a knife and sandpaper. We cut these the same size because we are going to make the frame double, which helps prevent warping and keeps it in shape.

Now with a red-hot iron make holes about a quarter of an inch in diameter in each piece, as shown in Fig. 117. Those in the center are made two inches apart and should be spaced so that the holes in the two pieces will correspond. Using a lace of wet rawhide and the double row of holes in the ends of one of the pieces of wood, it should be laced together. The other piece is now wrapped around the first piece and its ends are likewise bound together. Now with the joints of both hoops opposite each other they are laced together with a wet rawhide lace passed through the center holes (Fig. 118). As the rawhide dries, it shrinks and so binds the two pieces tightly together. The frame is now finished.

The drumhead should be soaked in lukewarm water and with it should be placed about six feet of rawhide thong about a quarter of an inch wide, to be used as lacing. Cut the head twenty-two inches in diameter and with a punch make one-eighth inch holes two inches apart all around the circumference, placing them a half inch from the edge. Through these holes lace a thong, drawing it up slightly. Fit the head over the frame and draw this lace up as tight as possible, and tie its ends together. Now, with a long thong, lace back and forth across the bottom of the drum, pass-

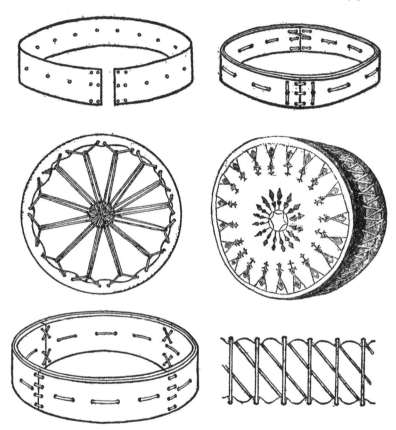

Fig. 117. Section of Drum Frame Fig. 118. Drum Frame Complete
Fig. 119. Lacing for Single Head Drum   Shoshone Drum (AMNH)
Fig. 120. Large Drum Frame   Fig. 121. Method of Lacing Large Drum

ing the thong over and under the inner lace until the head is drawn up as tight as possible (Fig. 119). Wrap a length of thong over the laces where they come together at the center, drawing them tighter still and at the same time forming a ball-shaped wrapping, which is used as a hand grip. Your drum is now finished. Set in in the shade and allow it to dry slowly. It will then be ready to use.

The Double-headed Drum

The large double-headed drums, made from hollow cottonwood or pine logs, by the Indians of the Southwest, were generally twice as deep as the diameter of their heads, while those of the Plains and Woodland Indians were of directly opposite proportions. For the frames of the latter, discarded bass-drum shells have been used in recent times, and it may be that you can secure one for this purpose. A frame for a large drum of this type may also be made from four cheese boxes laced together so that the joints are overlapped, as shown in Fig. 120. Bend each box into a semicircle after soaking it in boiling water, which will soften it and make it easy to bend. Lace the ends of the two boxes that are to form the inside of the frame together first, and then lace the two for the outside around them. The inner and outer frames are then lashed together in the same manner as that described for the smaller drum. An excellent frame for a large drum of the Pueblo type can be made by simply removing the heads from a nail keg or wooden container, such as bulk cocoa comes in. Ask your grocer to save one for you.

For a drum thirty inches in diameter and twelve inches deep both heads should be cut so as to lap over the frame by at least two inches. For a larger drum the heads should be cut from six to eight inches larger than the diameter of the drum. Punch holes one inch from the edge of the heads and three inches apart around their circumferences. Two laces are used to lace the heads on. The method of lacing is shown in Fig. 121. Care should be used in drawing the laces up tight, or they will tear through the edges of the heads. Do this work gradually as the head dries, working round and round the drum so as to draw the heads up evenly. Rawhide handles should be attached to the laces on each side of the drum. The drum frame may be painted before or after the heads are in place. The latter method is followed by the Pueblos, who get some interesting effects by alternating two colors in painting the spaces between the laces.

A Water Drum

The water drum is the most resonant and pleasantly toned Indian drum. It can be heard great distances. In the old days it was made by hollowing out a basswood log and closing one end with a water-tight

wooden plug. A small hole with a wooden stopper
was made in the lower section, through which water
could be added or drawn off. The head was detach-
able and was held in place by a wooden hoop. When
in use the drum was filled about one-third of its capa-
city with water. Its tone could be changed by splash-
ing the water against the head and then partially
drying it before the fire. Water drums were usually
made small enough to be held in the hand, but larger

Fig. 122. Water Drum Fig. 123. Hard and Soft Drum Sticks

ones about eighteen inches high and twelve inches in
diameter were used in ceremonies (Fig. 122).

To make a drum of this type we may use a small
wooden keg. The one-gallon size is about right for a
hand drum, and the five-gallon for a large one. Kegs
of this kind can be purchased from the large mail-order
houses. Remove the upper head and make a new and
longer bung plug than the one that comes with the
keg, as it is generally too short to be easily removed

once the drum is in use. From cheese-box wood make a hoop an inch wide that fits loosely around the top of the keg. Wrap it to a thickness of about one half inch with strips of soft leather until it fits snugly over the top. The drumhead is now cut out so that it laps over the top by at least four inches. Soak it and put it in place by slipping the hoop over the top of the keg. The head may be tightened by pushing the hoop down. Fill the keg a little less than half full of water and it is ready for use.

Drum Sticks and Decorations

Drumsticks are easily made. A stick twelve to fifteen inches long and about a quarter of an inch in diameter is about the right size. The end of the stick should be padded and the pad may be made hard or soft, according to the tone desired. To make a hard pad in the simplest way, wrap a few thicknesses of ordinary gauze bandage around the end of the stick and cover it with adhesive tape. For a soft pad, wrap enough cotton batting around the end to form a ball about an inch and a half in diameter and cover it with adhesive tape. Tape an inch wide is best for this purpose. The tape covering may be painted or covered with soft leather for a more Indian-like effect (Fig. 123). Two notches may be cut in opposite sides of the stick about three inches from the end, which are used for a grip for the thumb and forefinger. These are useful when learning to drum, but they are not necessary after you have become an expert Indian drummer.

The heads of the drums were almost always painted with decorative or symbolic designs. A number of these taken from old Indian drums are shown in Fig. 124. Colored water-proof draughtmen's ink should be used for painting drumheads, as ordinary house paint will spoil their tone. Artists' colors may be used if thinned down, but they have the disadvantage of taking rather long to dry. Drumsticks should be painted, too. Banded designs were often used on them.

Large drums were generally suspended on four poles stuck in the ground when in use. A stand adapted from the Indian style may be made from two pieces of "two-by-four" and four saplings, four feet long and about an inch in diameter. Make a cross of the "two-by-fours" similar to a Christmas-tree stand. The size of this will depend on the diameter of your drum. Then peel the saplings, thin down their upper ends, and whittle them flat. Tie a string similar to a bow string to the ends of the sapling after bending the upper part and allow them to dry. Bore holes large enough for the ends of the saplings six inches in from the ends of the cross frame and set them in so that they stand upright. The drum is held in place by thongs tied

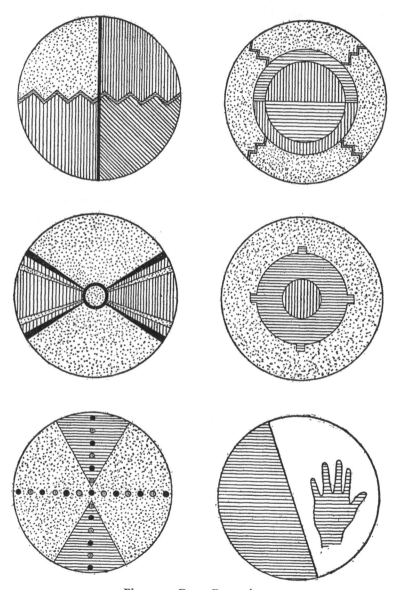

Fig. 124. Drum Decorations

from its handles to the poles. Fasten feathers and ribbon streamers to the ends of the poles and paint them. When finished the drum stand should appear as in Fig. 125.

The drum rhythm ordinarily used is made up of a loud beat followed by a soft one in four-four time.

Fig. 125. Drum on Stand (BAE)

More will be said about drumming later on. The Indian says that the tom-tom does not sing in rainy weather. By this he means that the drumheads soften when they are damp and so do not give a clear, sharp tone. The drum can always be tuned, however, by warming it before the fire. Care should be used in doing this not to draw the heads too tight.

Making Rattles

Rattles used by the Indians were of several different types.   Gourds, tortoise shells, elm bark, horn, and rawhide were used as the containers for pebbles.   Other

Fig. 126.   Can Rattle
Fig. 127.   Gourd Rattle
Fig. 128.   Cow Horn Rattle

rattles were made by suspending bits of bone, dew-claws, or deer hoof, loosely on a long stick.

Baking-powder cans have been used for making rattles by the Plains Indians for the past fifty years. To make a rattle of this kind, simply pierce holes through the center of the cover and the bottom of the can and push a stick about a foot long and a quarter of an inch in diameter through them. The stick should extend through the top for two inches. A shoulder, cut around the stick where it enters the bottom of the can, will help hold it in place and a small brad driven through the stick over the cover will keep the can closed. A few pebbles placed inside will complete the rattle, which should be decorated with painted designs (Fig. 126). A few downy turkey feathers and some ribbon streamers may be fastened to the end of the stick as an additional decoration.

Dried gourds, if you can get them, make excellent rattles. Cut the neck of the gourd off close to the globe and cut out the blossom end, making a small hole there. Then with a piece of wire remove the seeds and the dried pith from the inside. Now cut a stick long enough to go through the gourd and to allow for a comfortable hand grip. Drill small holes through this above and below the gourd and run wooden pegs through them to hold it in place. Put a few pebbles inside, decorate it with painted designs, and it is ready for use (Fig. 127). Another type of rattle can be made from a piece of cow horn as shown in Fig. 128. Cut a section off the wide end of the horn and make two wioden plugs to fit the openings. Fasten these in place with brass-headed tacks and bore a hole through the small end in which the handle is fitted. Then put a few small pebbles inside and nail the handle in place with finishing nails.

Rawhide rattles can be made in a variety of shapes and sizes. Calfskin prepared as for a drumhead is best for this purpose. To make a round rattle cut out two circular pieces of hide five inches in diameter. Sew the edges of these together for half the distance around their circumferences. Now with a mixture of wet sand and clay make a ball-shaped mold. Fit the hide over this and increase the size of the mold, if necessary, until it fits tightly. Now resume the sewing, leaving an open space about a half inch wide on each side. These openings are for the handle. When the sewing is finished, set the hide and mold in the sun to dry. When thoroughly dry the hide may be gently pounded against a hard surface and the mold broken and removed through the handle openings. The rattle is finished by inserting a handle and pebbles in the same way as that described for the gourd rattle.

Deer hoofs and dew-claws are practically impossible to secure these days, but a good rattle of the dew-claw type can be made from chicken wing and leg bones. At least thirty of them will be needed and they should be cut to uniform length of two inches. For the handle cut a knife-shaped piece of soft wood fourteen inches long, an inch wide, and a half inch thick. String each bone on a soft leather thong about a quarter of an inch wide. Knot it at the bottom and cut it long enough so that at least an inch protrudes from the top. With large brass-headed upholsterer's tacks fasten the thongs to both sides of the handle as close together as possible. Paint the handle before putting the bone rattlers in place (Fig. 129).

A rattle of this type was also made by the Indians with tin rattlers similar to those used in decorating pouches, but larger in size. To make them, cut tri-angular-shaped pieces of tin two inches long and wrap and pound them around knotted thongs as described in Chapter Nine. These may be fastened to a wooden handle with tacks, or holes may be drilled in it through which the thongs can be drawn and knotted on the other side.

Turtle-shell Rattles

Rattles made of tortoise and turtle shells were used by many of the tribes. The large shells were used as containers for pebbles, with the skull forming part of the handle. Smaller shells were used as leg rattles. To make the first type a shell of any size may be used. Clean it out thoroughly and sprinkle the inside with alum and allow it to cure in the sun. From soft wood cut a paddle-shaped piece to form a plug for the smaller opening of the shell and also the handle. Slip this in place through the opening in the opposite end of the shell, nicely fitting it by careful whittling. When it is in place burn two holes on each side through the upper and lower shells and through the handle. A thong is passed through these and tied underneath to hold the handle in place. The other end of the shell is closed with a strip of rawhide, cut to fit, and sewn in place by means of small holes burned in its edges and those of the upper and lower levels. Pebbles or

Fig. 130. Turtle-shell Rattle

shot are used as rattlers. The Iroquois, who used rattles of this type, made them differently from the method we have described, but we believe our method is the simplest (Fig. 130).

For a turtle leg rattle, which is worn above the calf of the leg, a turtle shell from four to six inches long is used. Holes are made in the center of one side of the shell, on both the upper and under sides, spaced an

inch and a half apart. A stout thong, such as a rawhide shoelace, is drawn through these holes and knotted
on the under side to prevent its slipping through. The
ends of the lace should be long enough to go around

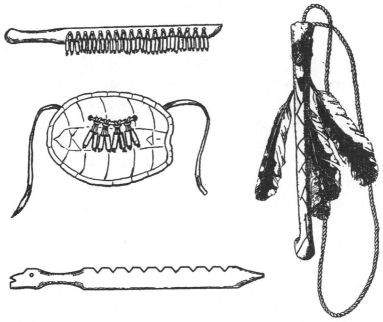

Fig. 129. Wood and Bone Rattle Fig. 131. Turtle Leg Rattle
Fig. 132. Morache Fig. 133. Eagle Bone Whistle (AMNH)

the leg, as they are used to hold the rattle in place.
Prepare six or eight chicken bones, one inch long, as
described for the stick rattle, except that they should
be fastened in pairs to a thong about four inches long.
These thongs are looped over the rawhide lace on the
front of the rattle, as shown in Fig. 131. Strings of

sleigh bells are also used by Indians for leg rattles nowadays. These can be bought from mail-order houses or from your local hardware dealer.

The Morache

A morache, or notched-stick time-beater, may be made from a piece of wood of medium hardness two feet long, two or three inches wide, and a half inch thick. The end of the handle may be plain or carved with a snake or animal head, as shown in Fig. 132. The notches are spaced a half inch apart and are about a half inch deep. Their edges should be slightly rounded. The rubbing stick should be round and about nine inches long. A piece of broom handle or a flat bone answers the purpose well. In using the morache the musician kneels and, resting one end of it on a resonator, rubs the stick back and forth in time with the drum-beat. A small wooden box or the bottom of a tin or galvanized iron water pail will make an excellent resonator in case you cannot get the dried-out gourd of the Pueblos, or a folded piece of rawhide such as the Plains Tribes use for this purpose.

War Whistles

Whistles made from the wing bones of the eagle, crane, swan, and goose had a prominent place in ceremonies and were used by warriors and medicine men. The eagle-bone whistle was used in the sun dance, where it was blown by dancers to simulate the cry of the eagle as they faced the sun (Fig. 133). Whistles made from crane bones were blown by men riding into battle. The whooping crane is a bird of great courage, very difficult to kill, and if wounded will attack anyone who comes near it. This fighting power and strong medicine in war was believed to come to the man who used such a whistle. Larger whistles were made from a bamboo-like reed. Often two of different tones were bound together. Reed whistles sometimes had a bird quill split and bound upon the vent hole of the tube to serve for what we call a reed or sounding tongue to vibrate by the passage of air through the vent.

To make a bone whistle use a turkey or chicken-leg bone. Saw off the ends and clean out the marrow. Cut a triangular opening in the upper side of the bone with a nail file and, by dropping sealing wax through it, make the stop. The latter may be shaped with a thin knife blade until the whistle makes the desired sound. The stop should be about a quarter of an inch wide at the bottom and its upper edge should be sharp and parallel with the upper edge of the opening. It will probably require a bit of experimentation before you get your whistle to blow properly. A reed whistle can be made from a piece of bamboo about three quarters of an inch in diameter and twelve to fourteen inches long. A wooden or sealing-wax stop may be used in it.

A thong, a quarter of an inch wide and two feet long, is fastened to the bone whistle for use as a neck cord. The ends of the thong should be cemented to the sides of the whistle with water-proof cement. A piece of soft leather an inch wide is then cemented over them. This may be decorated with beads, and pendants of fluffy turkey feathers may be attached to it. The bone itself may be decorated by scratching a design in it with a nail file or knife blade and then rubbing colored crayon into the scratches.

Chapter Eleven

FIRE-MAKING AND COOKING

MAKING fire by rubbing two sticks together as the Indians did is not so difficult a feat as most people imagine. With apparatus made of the right kind of wood almost anyone can produce fire with a little practice. A knife and ax are the only tools required to make a fire-making set. A good wood for this purpose can be found in almost any part of our country. The best is probably yucca, which grows in the Southwest and on the plains. The sticks are cut from its tall, central flower-bearing stalk. This wood was known to many of the tribes, and fire sets made from it were often carried by war parties even after notches had been introduced. According to Dr. Gilmore, fire drills were also made of yucca leaves on the treeless prairies. The hard, sharp-pointed blades were tightly bound together with sinew to form the drill, and the stem, peeled and dried, was used as a hearth. Other good woods, in addition to yucca are balsam, fir, basswood, cottonwood, red cedar, white cedar, cypress, elm, poplar, redwood, sycamore, white pine, and willow.

Making Fire with the Bow-drill

There were different ways of making and using the fire-making apparatus, but in all methods a drill and fire-board, or hearth, was used. Three ways that you can copy we will describe here. The first method, and perhaps the easiest, is known as the "bow-drill," and was used by the Eskimos, some of the Canadian tribes, and those in the northern part of the United States. To this apparatus there are four main parts besides the tinder. They are the fire-board, the drill, the hand socket, and the bow. The fire-board may be from a foot to eighteen inches long, from one to three inches wide, and from a quarter to seven-eighths of inch thick. These dimensions are not arbitrary, but have been found best after much experimentation. The drill may be made from the same kind of woods as the fire-board, or it may be of harder or softer material. It should be between twelve and fifteen inches long and from a half to three-quarters of an inch in diameter. Its sides are roughly rounded and its upper end is tapered like a lead pencil. The lower end is bluntly pointed (Fig. 134).

Hand sockets may be made from a block of hardwood or from a piece of softwood in which a socket of stone or other hard material has been set. If hardwood is used, whittle out a block that comfortably fits the hand and bore a hole a quarter of an inch deep in its under side. Smooth off the edges of this pit with a knife. A more elaborate and perhaps more effective socket can be made from a block of white pine and a

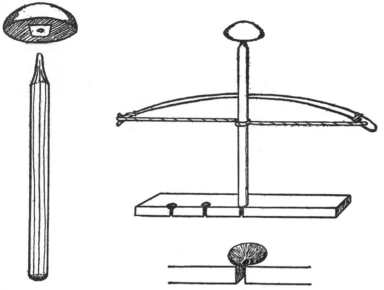

Fig. 134. Hand Socket and Fire-drill Fig. 135. Bow-drill Set Ready for Use Fig. 136. Notch in Fire-board

small piece of soapstone such as is used for washtubs. Cut the wood roughly half egg-shaped, so that when finished it will be about an inch thick in the center. Then inlay the soapstone in the under side of the block. A pit can now be drilled in the stone similar to the one described above. It will help if the pits are greased when the socket is used.

The bow may be pliant or rigid. Hickory, ash, and

blue beech or hornbeam all make excellent bows. A good bow should be between eighteen and twenty-four inches long and about a half inch in diameter. Sometimes a branch can be found naturally shaped for the purpose with a fork at one end. If you can get a stick like this, there is little to do to convert it into a bow. Peel off the bark, cut the fork down so its ends are an inch long, and in the opposite end drill two one-eighth-inch holes a half inch apart. These are for the thong. For the latter there is nothing better than a strip of real buckskin. A hide of this can be bought from a wholesale leather dealer who knows it by its trade name—"natural jack buck." Such a hide may be cut into many half-inch-wide thongs, and so their cost will not be so high as the price of the hide may cause you to imagine them to be. Ooze split cowhide is also good, but it lacks the strength of the buckskin and so will not last so long. Fasten one end of the thong to the forked end of the bow and twist it spirally so that it forms a tight round cord. The other end is led up through one hole at the end of the bow and down through the other. This makes an adjustable fastening, as it is often necessary to increase or decrease the tightness of the thong. The end of the thong should be long enough to be wrapped and firmly tied around the end of the bow.

The best natural tinder is that used by the Indians— shredded cedar bark mixed with pounded dried grass.

The long shreds of red cedar bark are rubbed between the hands or pounded between stones until they are reduced to a fluffy mass. The grass is then mixed with it. The tinder may be baked in an oven and should then be kept in a water-proof bag until it is used. For this purpose the Indians also used fungi and punky cottonwood.

Before making a fire it is necessary to drill a small pit in the fire-board. Twist the bow string once around the drill, fit the socket over the top of it, and rest its other end close to the edge of the fire-board (Fig. 135). To do this you will have to kneel on the right knee, place the socket in your left hand and the bow in your right. The fire-board should be directly in front of you and it is held in place by putting your left foot on it. The left arm is braced around the left knee so that the drill may be held firmly. Take a few even strokes and press firmly on the socket until smoke appears. Now with a knife cut a notch in the edge of the fire-board until it reaches the center of the pit you have drilled (Fig. 136). This pit catches the fine powder ground off by the drill, and when as a result of the friction it becomes hot enough it forms a spark.

Getting the Spark

You are now ready to make a fire. If in the outdoors, you make a depression in the earth under the fire-board where a handful of tinder can be placed to catch the spark. Indoors it is best to put a piece of cardboard under the pit to catch the spark and from which it may be lifted on the tinder. Take the same position as you did in drilling the pit and with long even strokes slowly revolve the drill. Be careful to keep your bow parallel with the ground so that the thong will not work its way down the drill. Gradually increase the pressure on the socket until smoke appears. Do not rush or hurry. At the same time increase the rhythm of your bow strokes, and when the smoke gets heavy and the ground-off powder appears to be very black, the chances are that you have a spark.

Drop the bow and drill and tap the fire-board lightly to loosen the spark and to cause it to drop on the tinder. Fan the spark with the palm of your hand until it begins to glow. Now pick up the tinder and press it tightly about the spark. Hold it high to keep the smoke out of your eyes and gently blow on it with short puffs that are gradually increased in strength. If the spark is big enough it will burst into a flame almost immediately and your fire is made.

The Hand-drill Method

Not all of the Indians used the bow in making fire with the rubbing sticks. The drill was twirled between the hands while the fire-board was held in place on the ground with the knees. When you have mastered the art of fire-making with a bow you may wish to try this more difficult method. Your tinder and fire-board will be the same as before, but the drill should be at least eighteen inches long, with a slight taper from the base toward its upper end. The set should be made from a piece of yucca that has been well dried in an oven. No socket is used.

Practice at first with a friend, as two persons can produce fire in this way quite easily. Sit or kneel facing each other, holding the board firmly in place with the feet or the knees. Then place the palms of the hands together at the top of the drill, with it between them. Arch the hands out stiffly and rub them together, causing the stick to twirl. Bear down at the same time. The hands will gradually work down to the bottom of the drill. When they do this, return them quickly to the top. Repeat until the spark is formed. With two persons the hands of one reach the bottom as those of the other are halfway down, so that the drill is kept in constant motion. Considerable practice is necessary to master this most interesting and spectacular method of making fire.

Iroquois Pump-drill Method

The Iroquois, Delaware, Pueblo and central-California tribes used the pump-drill method for making fire. A set of this kind is made exactly like the bow-drill set, except that there is no bow and the drill is quite different. Balsam, fir, and red cedar are the best woods, for a set of this kind.

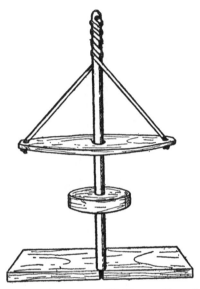

Fig. 137. Iroquois Pump-drill Fire-making Apparatus

Make the drill two and a half feet long and three-quarters of an inch in diameter. Next make the fly-wheel, preferably from a piece of hardwood. This wheel is an inch and half to two inches thick and seven inches in diameter. The hole in the center of it is just large enough to force the drill through, so that the wheel will stay in place without the use of nails or glue. The cross-bar is fourteen inches long, a half inch thick, three inches wide at the center, and an inch wide at its ends. Its edges are rounded. The hole in the cross-bar's center is an inch and a quarter in diameter.

Now cut a hole through the drill an inch from its top. The cross-bar is then slipped over the drill, and the thong, which is approximately four feet long, is fastened to its ends after being passed through the hole in the top of the drill. The fly-wheel is pushed in place so that it is about six inches above the bottom of the drill. The set is now ready for use (Fig. 137).

While it can be operated by one person, two can do it more easily. In this case one manipulates the drill while the other holds the fire-board in place and takes care of the tinder. Start the drill by turning the wheel with the hand so that the thong coils about the drill and draws the cross-bar up. Then grasp the cross-bar close to the drill and push it down quickly. By the momentum given to the fly-wheel the bar is again drawn up. Continue pumping until a spark is formed and make fire as described before.

Indian Food

Once the Indian had his fire he had quite a variety of food he could prepare on it. His larder was not as limited as we may have imagined nor was it confined entirely to fish and game. By slow experimentation he had learned the use of the native plants and had succeeded in cultivating and developing some of them. In every tribe there were certain people who knew the uses of the wild plants in the region in which the tribe lived. These persons who knew more than others about plants and animals were the botanists and geologists to whom people went whenever they needed to know what material was best for a certain purpose.

Food was cooked in many different ways. Boiling was done in pottery vessels or by the hot-stone method in wooden boxes, bark pails, water-tight baskets, or in a rawhide suspended on stakes or used to line a hole in the ground. Baking was done in the ground, in ovens, or on flat stones. Meat and fish were roasted before the fire, in the ashes, or by incasing in clay, and broiled in the coals, on a stick, or on a grid of wood or stones.

Maize, or corn, as we call it, was the most important of Indian foods and there were numerous ways of preparing it, including such well-known ones as corn bread, popcorn, samp, hominy, and succotash. In addition, many other vegetable foods, wild and cultivated, were known to the Indian. The early white settlers learned of these and found them good, so that today they are some of our most popular dishes. There are many others equally good, but not so well known, so we are setting down the recipes for some of them.

Pemmican

Pemmican, which was an important winter food of the Plains Tribes, was made in the old days of dried buffalo meat, pounded up with dried berries and mixed

Drying Meat and Making Pemmican. *Courtesy Fleming H. Revell & Co.*

with melted marrow fat. It was packed in rawhide bags until used. A good pemmican can be made from dried beef cut fine by running it through a meat-chopper with a half cup of raisins to each pound of beef. Put the ground meat and raisins in a shallow pan and pour melted suet over it, thoroughly mixing it in. Allow it to cool and set so that a rectangular cake resembling sausage is formed. Pemmican made in this way will keep indefinitely.

The Pit Oven

A favorite method of baking meat and vegetables used by many tribes was by use of a pit oven. This is the method used in the outdoor clam-bake, which is another cooking method we have learned from the Indians. A hole was dug some three feet deep and closely lined with stones. A fire was started in it, and when the rocks were thoroughly heated the fire was raked out. The meat wrapped in leaves was placed in the hole with or without vegetables, and hot rocks were placed over it. Leaves and earth were heaped over the hole and after an hour or two the meal was nicely baked.

Zuñi Succotash

Succotash as made by the Zuñi was a most appetizing dish. To make it, prepare some beef cut in small squares as for an ordinary stew. When the meat is tender, green corn, which forms the main part of the dish, is added, together with a quantity of string beans. Sunflower seeds are used to thicken the stew, and salt for seasoning. It should be cooked until it is quite thick.

The Mohegan made succotash by boiling the beans two hours with a lump of fat (pork will do). The green corn was then scraped off the cob and added to the beans, the cobs being put in, too, to add their milk to the whole. It was then allowed to boil for just twenty minutes more, when the seasoning was added and it was ready to serve.

Chippewa Stew

The Chippewa made a fish-and-vegetable stew from wild rice, dried corn, wild onions, and fish. The corn, rice, and onions were cooked together first, and the fish added when they were done. Fresh salmon was often prepared in this way.

Corn Roast

Corn roasted in the husk was one of the Indians' favorite ways of preparing it. The coals of a bright fire were raked away and the green ears laid in rows on the hot ground. They were then covered with cold ashes and hot coals raked over. A hot fire was built and kept up until the ears were thoroughly roasted. Another way was to build the fire between two logs and lay the ears across them.

Parched Corn

Parched corn was used by Indian hunters and warriors because it could, when ground to a flour, be made into a gruel without cooking, that was capable of sus-

Pueblo Women Grinding Corn (JRCN)

taining life on long journeys when it was necessary to travel light. To parch corn, strip it from the cob and place it in a frying-pan that has been filled with salt. Stir the corn under the salt and hold the pan over a hot fire. The corn will swell in the heat and gradually roast. When it is well browned it is done. Gently shaking the frying-pan will bring it to the top. The corn is then pounded to a rather fine meal, when it is

A Fire Making Contest between an Indian and a Boy Scout

A Californian Indian Making Fire by the Hand Drill Method

Cooking by the Hot Stone Method

Bread Baking in a Pueblo Oven

ready for use. The Iroquois sometimes mixed it with dried cherries or maple sugar. Sugar, though, was not used when the corn was intended for the use of hunters or athletes. The branches of the maple sway about in the wind, so that the Indians thought that those who ate the sugar would likely get dizzy.

Hominy

Hominy may be made from dry white field corn by removing the hulls with a lye of wood ashes. The corn is placed in a gallon of water with a half pint of wood ashes and boiled until the hulls come off easily. It is then washed in clear water. The hominy is boiled in water and seasoned to taste. It is excellent when eaten with milk.

Corn Cakes

Green corn scraped from the cob can be baked into delicious corn cakes. Mash the corn up, shape it into oblong cakes, and dust them with fine corn meal. Place these cakes in a fresh corn husk and bake in the ashes the same as roasting ears.

Baked Squash

Squash was baked whole in the ashes and every part of it, including the shell and seeds, was eaten.

Wild-rice Soup

Wild rice found around the Great Lakes was prepared by the Chippewa and Pottawatomi in a number of ways. Mixed with blueberries it was made into a delicious soup. When cooked plain or with sugar, it was prepared in much the same way as we cook our rice. To get the best results with it it must be washed three or four times before it is cooked. When boiling it use twice as much water as rice.

Acorn Mush

Acorns were used for food by the Dakota, Iroquois, and Californian Tribes, and those who lived wherever oak trees grew. Those of the sweet varieties, such as the white and chestnut oaks, being preferred. To prepare acorns for use it is necessary to leach the tannin from them. Remove the shells and dry the meats by splitting them and placing them in the sun. Then grind them to a flour by running them through a meat-chopper and pounding them up finely. Place the flour in a fine strainer and pour warm water over it. Gradually increase the heat of the water until finally boiling water is used. Taste the flour from time to time until it is found to be sweet. This is the method used by the California tribes. Others boiled them in a lye of wood ashes, preferably the ashes from basswood. To make a soup from the flour it is seasoned with salt, put in a kettle and brought to a boil. Two quarts of dough to three gallons of water is the correct proportion. For acorn mush less water is used.

Acorn Bread

Acorn bread can be made from the same dough used as it is or mixed with wheat flour. The dough is shaped into a flat loaf about six inches in diameter. A hot rock rolled in oak leaves is placed in the center of the dough, which is then folded and wrapped around it. The whole mass is then wrapped in a covering of oak leaves and placed in hot ashes to bake. Horse chestnuts or buckeyes were used in the same way as acorns. The poison in them was dissolved out by steaming them in an underground pit oven for two or three days. Another method was to break the nuts and soak them in water for a day. The kernels were then crushed to a powder and the poison removed by the acorn-leaching process.

Corn Bread

Corn bread was made by mixing the meal with water to form a stiff dough. Salt was added, and the dough, formed in thick cakes, was baked in the coals. In the

Southwest a wafer-like corn bread, known to the Hopi as piki, is baked on smooth, flat griddle stones that have been well greased with salted suet. Two kinds of batter are used in making these cakes—a thin paste mixed in hot water and a thicker paste mixed with cold water. A spoonful of the hot batter is placed on

Pueblo Oven   Baking Piki Bread (JRCN)

the stove first, and the same quantity of the cold batter is immediately poured over it. These cakes bake in about thirty seconds, and so can be peeled off the baking stone almost as soon as the batter has been spread on it.

Zuñi Bread

A true wheat bread is baked by the Zuñi in their beehive-shaped adobe ovens. The dough is prepared with yeast in practically the same manner that we use. A small quantity of it is then molded into a small round loaf that is well greased and sprinkled with flour. It is then pricked full of holes with a grass straw and set aside until ready to be baked. A great fire is built in the oven and kept up until the latter is thoroughly heated. The fire is then raked out, the loaves placed inside, and the vent hole at the top and the oven door are sealed up with mud. In twenty or thirty minutes the bread is well baked. These methods were probably learned from the Spaniards.

Indian Potatoes

Many roots were prepared in the same ways that we use with potatoes. Cat-tail roots were eaten raw, boiled, or pounded into a flour from which bread could be made. Camas roots found in the Northwest were a favorite food of some of the Plains Tribes. They were generally baked in a pit oven and then dried for future use. The groundnut, or wild potato (*apios tuberosa*), and pomme blanche (*psoralea esculenta*) were other varieties of Indian potatoes.

Puddings

A pudding was sometimes made of pumpkin or squash pared and quartered and boiled with apples and maple sugar. Another was made from popped corn and chestnuts pounded together and boiled with maple sugar.

In the spring all of the Northern tribes made quantities of maple sugar. The sap was collected in bark buckets and boiled down in the way now used by the white men. Sugar-making time was a happy one for all the people, but it was especially looked forward to by the children, who were always allowed to boil candy and pour it on the snow to cool.

Nut-meat Gravy

Nuts, seeds, berries, and wild fruits of many varieties were gathered for food. A nut-meat gravy was made by boiling the pounded meats of hickory, walnut, or other nuts until the oil floated to the top. It was then skimmed off, boiled again, and seasoned with salt. This was used with bread, potatoes, pumpkin, squash, and other foods. The meats left after skimming off the oil were often seasoned and mixed with mashed potatoes. Nut meats were also crushed and added to hominy and corn soup to make it rich.

Birch Tea

Beverages were made by boiling sassafras roots, sweet-birch twigs, wintergreen leaves, and other plants, much in the same way that we make tea. Young leaves of the strawberry were also used in this **way.**

An Indian Garden

In camp an Indian garden may be planted, and occasionally Indian meals may be served in which its products are used. Sweet corn, flour corn, flint corn, popcorn, kidney beans, lima beans, squash, pumpkins, white potatoes, sweet potatoes, tomatoes, sunflowers, gourds, cotton, and tobacco are some of the things which might be planted in a garden of this kind. In addition to the things grown, such things as chocolate, pineapple, tapioca, and peanuts that we got from the Mexican and South American Indians can be included in our Indian meals. Here are a few menus. Others can easily be worked out.

Tomato soup

Roast turkey

Sweet potatoes   Squash

Corn bread

Pumpkin pie

Chocolate

Bean soup

Stewed rabbit

Baked potatoes   Succotash

Tapioca pudding

Cocoa

Baked clams

Sweet potatoes   Roast corn

Piki bread

Sliced pineapple

Peanuts

Cold chocolate

Broiled salmon

Boiled nuts and potatoes   Baked squash

Acorn biscuits

Baked apples

Birch tea

Chapter Twelve

GAMES

NEARLY all of the Indian tribes played a great variety of games. Some of them were quite simple, in which two or three players would take part, while others with hundreds of players in them resembled sham battles. Many games were of a sacred character and were played for other reasons than pure amusement. They were used to heal the sick, to bring rain, to increase the fertility of animals and plants, to avert disaster, or as part of the ceremonials to amuse and entertain distinguished guests. Others trained men in the use of weapons and the strategy of war. Certain games were played at set times and seasons as necessary religious ceremonies. In connection with practically all of them there was considerable gambling.

The Indian had many games and amusements which we have not space to describe here. Games similar to our own, such as battledore and shuttlecock, quoits, cat's cradle, and the street game called cat or tipcat, were all played by them. They also had a great variety of dice and guessing games which were very popular. Children amused themselves with tops, stilts, and popguns made of ash and elder, from which they used to shoot wads of chewed elm bark. In winter they coasted on sleds of buffalo ribs or rawhide.   According to Dr. Grinnell, Cheyenne mothers encouraged their children to use the hides, as it was a convenient and labor-saving method of wearing the hair off the hides that were to be used for moccasin soles.

Like the games themselves, the implements with which they were played were considered sacred and could not be sold.   They were often decorated with sacred symbols that were supposed to bring luck to the player.   All the players made their own gaming equipment.   This was not difficult, for every adult Indian was more or less of a craftsman.   Some of their methods that you can copy we will describe later.

Lacrosse

The best-known of Indian games, and one that was played in one form or other by most of the tribes, is lacrosse.   It gets its name from the "crosse," or racket-like stick, carried by each player which the early French colonists likened to a bishop's crozier.   The game has been adopted by us and is one of our popular college sports.   It is the fastest as well as the oldest of the games we know.   Played under the simple Indian rules, it is an excellent camp game.

To the Indian the game offered excellent training for war.   It developed team work, gave practice in fast running and in warding off the blows of an adver-

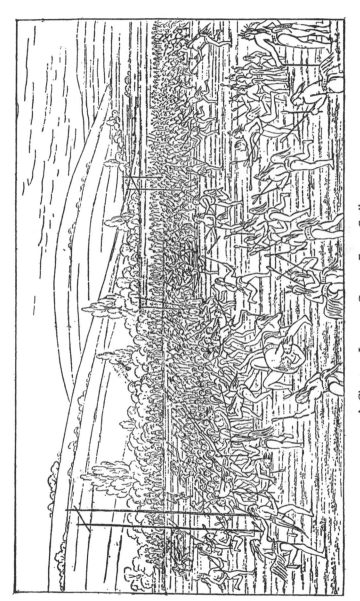

A Choctaw Lacrosse Game. *From Catlin*

sary. A skilled player knew how to use the racket, to run rapidly, to pass the ball when surrounded by opponents, to stop a player on the other side in possession of the ball, and to avoid the other team when he had the ball. Play was rough and any tactics were allowed. Rackets were often used as clubs and at times groups of players would engage in fist fights. It was for this reason that players and spectators left all weapons behind when they went out to the game. Even without them serious injuries were often suffered and it was not unusual for players to have arms or legs broken in the rough and tumble of the game.

Preparations for a big game were often carried on for months before it took place. Teams were trained almost as systematically as those of our colleges. Bathing, exercise, and diet were prescribed by custom and a man almost never broke the training program. A good part of it was governed by religious beliefs and superstitions. Thus a Cherokee player was very careful not to eat frogs' legs before a game because they are brittle and break easily, but he would rub his legs with those of turtles, for he knew they were very strong. In this way he hoped to avoid the bad qualities of the one and to get the power of the other. Likewise, he would not eat rabbit, for that animal is timid and likely to lose its wits when pursued by its enemies. Before the game, dances and ceremonies were held that were supposed to bring strength and success to the team.

The game was played on a field from five hundred feet to a mile and a half long. At each end a goal, generally consisting of two posts set several feet apart, were erected. The object of the game was for one

A Choctaw Lacrosse Player. *From Catlin*

team to drive a wooden or buckskin ball between their opponents' goal posts. The ball could be thrown or carried in the racket, but at no time could it be touched with the hand.

As it is played under modern rules the game has some points in common with football and hockey. The stick used is modeled after that of the Iroquois, but it is so different that early Indian players would hardly recognize it. The ball is now of solid but resilient rubber. Netted goals on iron frames six feet square are set one hundred and ten yards apart. Around each goal is a lined-off box twelve feet square, known as "the crease," into which a player may not go under penalty of a foul. Off-side, cross-checking, and tripping rules have made the game less dangerous to the players than it was in the old Indian days.

Camp Lacrosse Rules

For camp use the game can be played with equipment made after the Indian patterns and with very simple rules that the players may make to settle any disputes which may arise. A field fifty to seventy-five yards square may be used, depending on the age and strength of the players. For small children a tennis court is large enough. Poles set in the ground six feet apart are used to indicate the goals. It will add to the interest if these poles are decorated with Indian symbols. Any number may form a team.

Teams line up in two columns facing the center of the field. There the ball is put into play by the umpire, who tosses it into the air between the two team captains.

The ball may be tossed or carried in the racket, but at no time must it be touched by the hand or kicked along. If it goes out of bounds it is put in play by the umpire at the point where it left the field. As in hockey and basketball, the opposing team gets the ball. Fouls may be penalized by advancing the ball toward the goal of the guilty side, the distance depending on the gravity of the offence. A game may be played in four quarters of ten minutes each. Goals are changed at the end of each quarter.

Making a Racket

Rackets may be made in a number of ways and some patterns are given in Fig. 138. They are from three to five feet long, ordinarily, but they should be made of a length convenient to the player. All are made from hickory or ash or some other tough, pliant wood. Heavy cord may be used in place of the rawhide that the Indians used for netting. The wood should first be whittled to its proper pattern and then bent to its final shape.

The Seminole racket is made of a single stick bent double and whittled flat on the side where the parts forming the handle are lashed together. The netted part of this racket, like that of all the others except the Iroquois, is about the size of a man's open hand. The Iroquois stick is held in shape by a heavy cord that

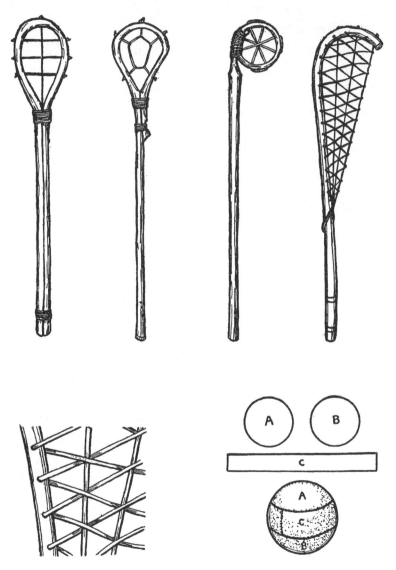

Fig. 138.   Seminole, Choctaw, Ojibwa, and Iroquois Lacrosse Sticks
Fig. 139.   Detail of Iroquois Lacing
Fig. 140.   Indian Ball Pattern

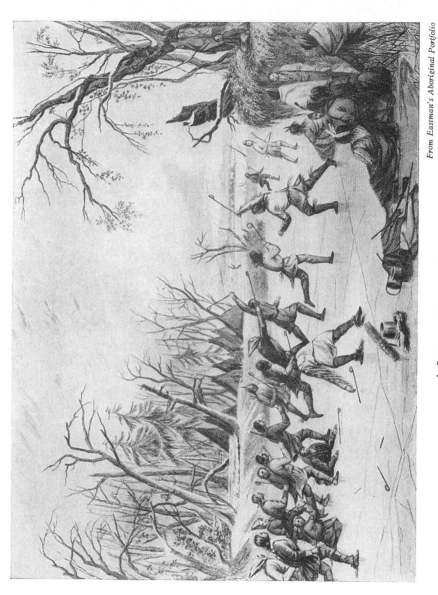

From Eastman's Aboriginal Portfolio

A Lacrosse Game on the Ice

Hoop and Pole Game in a Mandan Village

goes from the curved end to a point two-thirds of the
distance up the handle. At its lower end it is from
six to ten inches wide. The stick may be bent while
the wood is green or by steaming it later on. In the
other sticks the curved portion is whittled flat and
thinner than the rest of the wood, so that it may easily
be bent when green. Holes for the net lacing are
burned through the center of the stick after it is shaped.

Heavy white carpenter's cord or fish line makes excellent netting, although ordinary heavy string will do.
The vertical laces on the Iroquois net are put in place
first. The three laces that form the cross netting are
started at the top and are laced diagonally back and
forth between the frame and the outer cord until they
reach the bottom. The laces are looped about each
other where they meet, as shown in Fig. 139. The lacing for the other types of stick is much simpler. The
cords are knotted on the outside edge of the frame and
tied about each other where they meet in the center.
Rackets of different styles may be used in the same
game, according to the choice of the player.

Wooden balls are not recommended, as they are
likely to injure the players. A copy of the buckskin
ball can be made from any soft leather. When finished
it should be about three inches in diameter. As shown
in Fig. 140, the ball is made from two circular and one
rectangular pieces of leather. It may be stuffed with
upholsterer's hair, cotton, or hay. Another Indian way

of making a ball was to make a round leather bag with a draw string on top, which was stuffed with deer hair. A tennis ball, especially a "dead" one that has lost its resilience, is an almost ideal substitute for the Indian's ball of buckskin.

Hoop and Spear

Even more popular than lacrosse among the Indian tribes of this country was the game of hoop and spear. It is an excellent game, but, unlike lacrosse, it has been practically never played by white men. It is played, as its name indicates, with a wooden spear which is hurled at a rolling hoop, the object being to spear the hoop while it is in motion. According to Dr. Stewart Culin, the authority on Indian games, the hoop and spear symbolize the shields and bows of the twin war gods. The game was a test of fleetness, eyesight, and skill in throwing the spear. Among the Choctaw, who used a round stone disk instead of a hoop, it was known as chungke, which meant "running hard labor."

The Indian hoops were of many different types and sizes. Some, but a few inches in diameter, were made of stone. Others were as large as eighteen inches and had an elaborate rawhide network woven on them (Fig. 141). The spears varied as much as the hoops, from small darts and arrows to poles fifteen feet long. The game was played with small-sized implements inside a lodge, but it was primarily for the outdoors. There a smooth, level course was built.

For our purpose a hoop twelve inches in diameter is a good size. To make it, cut a pliable stick about a half inch in diameter, peel it and bend it in the form of a hoop. Whittle the ends down flat where they join and bind them together by closely wrapping them with

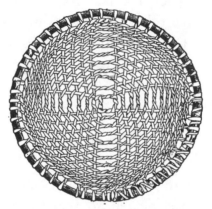

Fig. 141.   Indian Netted Hoop

heavy cord. Tie two cords from rim to rim so that they cross in the center, and divide the ring into four equal parts (Fig. 142). Paint each quarter of the rim, a different color so that one will be red, the next yellow, the third blue, and the other green.

The spear may be made of a straight stick five feet long and from three-quarters to an inch in diameter. Willow, ash, and oak were favorite woods of the Indian for this purpose. The butt end should be sharpened for a distance of six inches from the tip. This point should be painted red. Three bands of color, one above the other and each six inches wide, are painted round the stick, beginning at the edge of the red tip. The second band is yellow, the third blue, and the fourth green. The entire spear should be decorated as shown in Fig. 143. An Indian method for making these decorations was to peel a spiral band of bark from the stick and to carve other designs in it. The stick was then held over a fire just long enough to burn the ex-

Figs. 142 and 143. Hoop and Spear

posed inner wood to a dark-brown color. The rest of the bark was then peeled so that the brown designs stood out against the white background. Coup sticks, war clubs, and pipe stems were also decorated in this way.

The game may be played by two players or by teams. When two play, one carries the hoop as well as his spear. At an agreed signal, both run side by side. The man with the hoop rolls it and as soon as it hits the ground both men may try to hurl their spears through it. The object is to stop the hoop by casting the spear through for as little distance as possible. On both hoop and spear the red counts ten, the yellow five, the blue three, and the green one. Thus if the point of the pole and the red quadrant touch, the player's score is twenty; or if the blue band of the pole and the yellow quadrant are touching, the score is eight. If the pole goes through beyond its colored bands the points indicated by the color of the part of the hoop it touches are added to the player's score.

The player making the highest score rolls the hoop in the next try. In case neither spear touches the hoop the player whose spear is nearest the hoop has the privilege of rolling it. When more than two play, they may divide in teams and pool their scores or play as individuals. Games between two players are usually for fifty points, while teams play for one hundred or more, depending on their skill. Where the game is played often a flat piece of ground at least fifty yards long should be prepared for it.

Football Race

The Indians had football games somewhat similar to our own in which teams kicked balls between goals. Most of these resembled soccer, as the players were not allowed to touch the ball. They also had stick and football races, which helped to train them as runners. One of these as played by the Maidu, a California tribe, you may care to try.

Two goal posts are set up at one end of the field about thirty feet apart. The two teams of from four to six players form two long parallel lines facing the goal, beginning at the opposite end of the field. Each player stands from thirty to fifty yards from his team mate. The two men farthest from the goal each have a ball. This may be a football or one of any type suitable. The Indians used a buckskin one made like a lacrosse ball but about nine inches in diameter. At a signal each man kicks his ball and follows it up until it reaches the second man. The second man up the line chases and kicks it on farther to the third, who in turn kicks it to the fourth. Thus it is passed from one to the other, that side being the winner whose ball first touches the goal post.

Shinny

The game which we know as shinny was another favorite Indian sport. It was played with sticks with curved ends and a small ball somewhat similar to the one used in lacrosse. Two posts or stakes set three feet apart at the ends of the field served as goals. Any number played on a team.

To play, the ball is placed in a shallow pit in the center of the field by the umpire while the teams line up just inside the goal posts. At a signal, both teams or chosen members of it rush to the hole, secure the

ball and drive it toward their opponents' goal. The
ball may not be touched with the hand or foot, or, in
fact, with any part of the body.

The sticks are three or four feet long, curved at one
end (Fig. 144). This curve may be made in a straight
stick or a stick with a natural bend in it may be used.
An excellent stick may be made from a piece of hickory
or ash about an inch in diameter. The part to be bent
may be flattened as shown in the drawing. When the

Fig. 144.   Shinny Stick

stick is finished it should be decorated with painted
colored bands or other patterns.

Another way of playing shinny, which might be
called "Indian golf," was for the two teams to form
parallel lines as for the football race. The players are
spaced a hundred feet apart along a piece of smooth
ground and the ball is driven from one to the other.
The first man attempts to drive it to the point where
the second is stationed. If it falls short, he takes additional strokes until it reaches his team mate. The second man drives it to the third, and so on until the goal
at the end of the line is reached. The smallest number
of aggregate strokes on a side wins.

Double Ball

The game of double ball was generally played by women and only occasionally by the men. It is, however, an excellent game for both girls and boys. It gets its name from the two balls or wooden billets tied together with which it is played. Teams of equal strength play on an open field of any length at the ends of which goal posts similar to those used in football have been erected. The posts may be about six feet apart and the cross-arm about that distance from the ground. The goal is made when the balls or billets are hung across the arm. This may be too difficult for beginners, so a score may be allowed when the ball is driven between the posts.

The ball may be made of two balls three inches in diameter, fastened together with a rawhide thong a foot long. For these the lacrosse pattern can be used. The wooden billets, which were more commonly used, are made from two sticks six inches long and about an inch or inch and a half in diameter. Holes are bored through them two inches from one end, through which a foot-long rawhide lace is passed to tie the two pieces together (Fig. 145). The billets should be painted some bright color so that they may be easily located in case they fall in deep grass or brush.

The players each carry a stick three feet long that

has been smoothed off and tapered gradually from an inch in diameter at the handle end to a half inch at the other end. With a little skill these can be used to throw the billets or balls great distances with a fair degree of accuracy. At the start of the play the teams line up in center field, facing each other and about twenty feet apart. The captain of each team stands in

Fig. 145. Double Ball Billets and Stick

the center between the umpire, who tosses the ball in the air between them. Each tries to catch it on his stick and toss it to his own team. In a moment there is a lively scramble and the ball is on its way to one goal or another.

Toss and Catch

A game different from any of these was toss and catch, which was played in one form or other by Indians from Alaska to Mexico. In the latter country I have seen Indians play the game with a small barrel-shaped block that was caught on a wooden pin. Our own Indians used a thin bone awl on which they caught hollow bones. These were strung very loosely on a buckskin thong tied to the end of the awl. The string of bones is swung in the air and an attempt is made to catch them on the awl. To do the trick requires skill that only comes with practice.

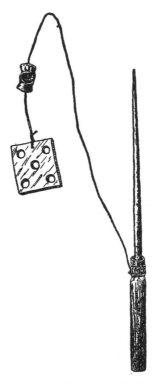

Fig. 146. Toss and Catch

A game of this kind can be made from materials that your butcher will gladly give you. A wooden pin or an iron meat skewer is used for the pin, and four sec-

tions of marrow bone, each a half inch wide, are used
for the targets. Sections of chicken or turkey leg bones
an inch long can be used after you have learned to
catch the larger beef bones. To make the set, string
the bones on a thong twelve to fourteen inches long and
tie one end of it to the loop in the skewer. On the
other end a square piece of heavy leather, large enough
to prevent the bones slipping over it, may be tied. In
this three or four holes a quarter of an inch in diameter
may be made. The leather forms an additional target.
The bone nearest the skewer should be painted red
with water-proof draughtsmen's ink, the one next to it
blue, the next yellow, and the fourth black. When
finished the game should appear as in Fig. 146.

If caught, the red bone counts twenty-five, the blue
twenty, the yellow fifteen, and the black ten. Each
hole in the leather counts five. A game is for two hundred and fifty. The players toss in turn.

Snow Snake

With the growing popularity of winter camping the
game of snow snake, one of the best of Indian winter
sports, should be revived. The game is played with
specially shaped spears or poles which are made to
glide along the snow or ice. The snakes are thrown
along the surface of the snow or in straight, smooth,

shallow grooves made by drawing a log through the snow. In the contest the players cast for distance and

Blackfoot Method of Throwing the Snow Snake

the snake which went the farthest won a point for its owner. In team games six generally played on each side. In addition to the point given for the snake that

went farthest, an additional point was given if a second
snake went farther than all of those on the other team.
Single points were also awarded in this way for each
snake which had passed all of the ones belonging to
the other team. A game was usually for ten points.

Indian snow snakes were as long as ten feet, but for
the average boy or girl a good size is from four to six
feet. For them cut a straight stick of hickory or ash
about an inch to two inches in diameter. Remove the
bark and with a plane carefully smooth the stick off.
Then curve the head as shown in Fig. 147. It should
be rounded and turned up slightly on the under side.

Fig. 147. Snow Snake

The plane is used again to trim the stick down to half
of its original thickness, except at the head. The bottom surface may be left round or slightly flattened.
The head may be inlaid with lead to give it extra
weight. When finished it should be decorated and the
snake's head painted on the front.

In throwing the snake, the index finger is placed
against the tail end, with the thumb away from the
body and the three remaining fingers opposite (Fig.
148). The player stoops over, holding the snake parallel with the ground, and hurls the stick forward with
a long sweeping throw.

Seal-spearing

An Eskimo game which may be played indoors on rainy days, for which I am indebted to Mr. Arthur Woodward, is called seal-spearing. For it a piece of cloth two feet square is required, which represents the

Fig. 148. Iroquois Throwing the Snow Snake. From an Indian Drawing. *Courtesy of the New York State Museum*

ice. Irregular or round holes are cut in it at odd intervals. These are the breathing-holes. The seal is made from a piece of thin leather or wood three inches long. Holes about a quarter of an inch in diameter are made in its head and body to represent vital spots. A string by which it may be pulled about is attached to the head. A small harpoon about six inches long is also required.

One player manipulates the seal beneath the "ice" and now and then the animal is made to come up to one of the holes to breathe. The object of the game is to see who can harpoon the seal in vital spots the most times in a given number of chances.

Chapter Thirteen

DANCE STEPS AND MUSIC

DANCING played a much more important part in the Indian's life than it does in ours. Instead of being a social affair to be indulged in occasionally for exercise and amusement, it was associated with the more serious things in life and was used as a means to express every emotion. Many of the dances were really religious ceremonials whose purpose was to influence the supernatural powers. Others were associated with war and were held before a war party started out and on its victorious return. There were comic dances, dances for curing the sick, peace dances, planting and harvest dances, mourning dances, hunting dances, as well as dances of a purely social type. Some dances were performed solely by men or by women, while in others they danced together. Dances were held in which anyone might take part and others were performed by a single dancer. Dances, like songs, were private property and could only be performed by their rightful owners. Thus, though the Pueblo Indians performed the dances of their neighbors, they did not do so before they had obtained the right to use them by trade or purchase. Many of the Plains Indian dances that have to do with mystery and war belong to the warrior societies. In

these the performers are often disguised as the animals
which had given their power to the societies' founders.
Somewhat similar dances used in curing the sick were
owned by societies of medicine men. The word
"dance" has often been wrongly applied by white men
to great Indian rituals and ceremonials in which dancing plays but a small part. This is true of what we
know as the calumet dance, the ghost dance, the snake
dance, and the sun dance.

Indian dances were not merely haphazard jumpings
up and down and posturings, but, on the other hand,
followed set forms that had become more or less con-
ventionalized and were in some cases handed down
through generations. Every song, prayer, and dance
connected with a ceremony had to be performed correctly, for it was believed that misfortune and divinely
inflicted punishment would follow any failure to give
a strictly accurate performance. Because of this belief
the dances and songs were as well known and as invari-
able as if they had been printed and the form of the
dances was well defined. Only in the dances where
personal experiences were portrayed was the dancer
allowed a freedom of invention, but even here he was
compelled to follow conventional forms or his story
would not be understood. This tendency to keep the
ceremonies from changing did not interfere with the
development of new dances or prevent the spread of a
dance from tribe to tribe.

As in nearly everything else, the different tribes varied in their ways of dancing. Thus, dances bearing the same name might be entirely unlike one another when performed by different tribes. In the ceremonies of the Northwest Coast Indians, the Iroquois of the woodlands, and the Pueblos, Navajos, and Apaches of the Southwest, dancers were dressed and masked to represent sacred beings, who acted out parts of the ritual. This, however, was seldom done in the religious ceremonies of the plains. The Pueblo dances were largely dramatic representations of myths in which song and musical accompaniment took the place of dialogue. These dances were mostly concerned with rain, fruitful harvests, and abundant supplies of game. The public dances held on the plaza were generally processional in form, which was another way in which they were distinguished from those of the Plains Indians. Clowns or delight-makers relieved the seriousness of the Pueblo ceremonies by making merry and doing what mischief they could while the dance was in progress. They also had a more serious part to play because they were believed to be the only persons who could conduct the gods of rain and fruitfulness into the village. The Pueblos have succeeded in preserving their dances better than any of the other Indians in the country, so that so far as the steps, songs, regalia, and general idea are concerned, there has been little change during the three hundred and sixty years since the Spaniards came.

How Indians Danced

The Indian dancer saw, heard, and felt the story he was trying to portray, so that it was not difficult for his audience to catch the meaning of his every motion. In the Pueblo dances the degree of acting was so intense that the masked dancers seemed to become the divine beings they were impersonating. The Indian danced with a great freedom of movement, using every part of his body. The amount of activity varied according to the character of the dances, some dances requiring violent action, while in others the people danced simply by flexing their knees and taking short shuffling steps. The men's dances were more strenuous and required greater activity than those of the women. In many of the dances the dancers moved in a circle from right to left or from left to right. In others they stood in long lines facing, or alongside one another. In these dances all would generally use the same step and execute the same figures, but there were others where each man danced by himself without regard to a general form or to the other dancers.

Music for the dances was furnished by the singing of the dancers and the playing of the instruments they carried, or by a separate chorus and orchestra, or by both. If a chorus was used the singers generally gathered around the drum and either stood or sat to one side, or sometimes in the center of the circle of dancers. There were times in some dances when the music of the orchestra would stop while the dancers provided their own, after which the process was reversed or the two would combine. In other dances the music was provided solely by the orchestra. Drums and rattles were the principal instruments used to accompany the singing. Time was generally marked by the drum.

Several pieces of Indian music suitable for use in dances are given at the end of this chapter. There is also a list of phonograph records, and of instrumental music based on Indian themes. The latter will be found helpful in large pageants, where a band or orchestra is used to create atmosphere, or to supplement Indian instruments and singing. Additional music will be found in the books on Indian music listed in the Bibliography.

The Dance Steps

Dance steps in great variety were used, but most of them were of remarkable simplicity. We are going to describe in detail a few of the more common ones that are easy to learn and that may be used in a great variety of dances. Different tribes knew these steps by different names. We have made no attempt to use the Indian names for the steps described here, but have simply assigned names to them which we think describes them best. The first group of steps, numbers one to fourteen, are all done to a LOUD, soft, LOUD, soft, beat on the drum.

1. Toe-heel step.—The weight of the body is shifted to one foot and the other is advanced so that the heel is lifted and the toe just touches the ground. The heel is

then brought down sharply with a good deal of force. These movements are then repeated with the other foot. The toe is brought down on the loud drum-beat and the heel on the soft one. This step may be done fast or slow.

2. Toe-heel-drag step.—This is a slow forward step in which one foot is advanced with the toe-heel step, while the other is dragged behind. The dragging foot slides on the ball of the foot as the heel is lifted slightly. In some dances a few steps will be taken with first one foot in advance and then the other. The change from right to left, or *vice versa,* is made by doing a toe-heel step with each foot.

3. Side step.—The side step consists of exactly the same movements as a soldier performs as he executes right or left step. At the start the feet are together. When done to the right, the right foot is lifted about four inches off the ground and placed about eighteen inches to the right, with the foot pointing straight down and the toe touching the ground. The heel is brought down sharply, and at the same time the left foot slides on the ball of the foot and takes its position alongside the right. To do the step to the left the movements are reversed. In moving around in a circle a change of direction may be made by executing a toe-heel step on each foot. An extra-long step of this kind is sometimes used. When doing it, it is necessary to extend the arms to the side to preserve balance.

Side Cross Step

4. Side-cross step.—This step, like the ordinary side step, is used in circle dances. The foot movements are like the side step except that one foot is crossed in front of the other and the foot that does the crossing does the toe-heel. Thus in moving to the right, the left foot is crossed in front of the right and does the toe-heel. The right foot then slides around behind the left to its position alongside of it.

5. Toe-heel grape-vine step.—The grape-vine may be done backward or forward, using an ordinary toe-heel step. In doing it the feet are crossed over one another alternately.

6. Scrape step.—This is another modified toe-heel step. The foot is advanced as far as possible, so that the toe just touches the ground. It is then dragged

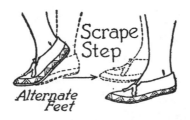

back and the heel is brought down. This movement is repeated alternately with each foot. The dancer either remains in place or makes a slight advance forward at each step.

7. Hop step.—Next to the toe-heel this is one of the commonest steps used in Indian dances. It is a skipping step with a double hop on each foot. The movement is on the ball of the foot, with the knees lifted fairly high. The heel does not touch the ground.

Hop-Step

8. Flat-foot step.—The leg motions in this step are exactly the same as in the hop step, but the entire foot is brought flat to the ground. When the foot is lifted the movement is sharp and sudden and the foot is kept absolutely parallel with the ground. When this step is used the upper part of the body is often kept absolutely rigid, with the arms slightly flexed and the fists clenched.

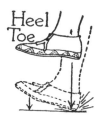

Heel
Toe

9. Heel-toe step.—This step, as its name indicates, is exactly the opposite of the toe-heel. Each foot in succession is raised from two to eight inches from the ground and the heel is brought down with great force, the toe following.

10. Double-side-hop step.—The feet are spread slightly apart and short jumps to the right or left are made on the balls of the feet. The body and legs are held almost perfectly rigid. This same step may be done forward or backward.

Flat-foot Step

11. Woman's double step.—This common form of dancing by Plains Indian women can hardly be properly called a step, as it consists of only raising the body on the toes and letting it drop in time with the music. The body moves freely and the arms hang loosely from the shoulders.

Elk-leap Step

12. Double-jump step.—The feet are held together and double jumps are taken much in the same manner as girls jump rope.

13. Gallop step.—A short fast galloping step in which the right foot is advanced and brought down with more emphasis than the left.

14. Run step.—This is a short rapid step in which a slight advance forward is made which is exactly like the exercise, "running in place." It may be done forward or backward or in place.

15. Squat step.—This is a single jump step in which the dancer keeps a squatting position and does a single jump, holding both feet together.

16. Elk-leap step.—A high leaping step done on single beats of the drum. The dancer leaps in the air, thrusting one foot forward, taking as long a step as possible.

17. Trot step.—This is also a single-beat step, but much faster than the elk leap. It is simply a short running step a bit slower than the double time of the soldier.

18. Stamp-five-toe step.—This step is done to music written in six-eight time or to a LOUD, soft, soft, soft, soft, soft drum-beat. In it one foot is brought down flat with a stamp. With the other, five light taps with the toe are made on the ground. In making them the toe describes an arc from back to front. After the fifth tap the foot is brought down with a stamp and the other foot repeats the taps. This step may be varied so as to have two, three, or four toe taps instead of five.

19. Southwestern stamp step.—This is the step commonly used in most of the elaborate ceremonies of the

Southwestern Stamp Step

Southwestern tribes. It is done to a LOUD, soft, soft beat on the drum in three-four time. The right foot, held horizontally, is raised about six inches off the ground, takes a short step forward, and is brought down with a stamp. The left foot follows behind, but is hardly raised from the ground, and the left knee is therefore kept almost stiff. The dancers using this step usually have a tortoise rattle fastened below the right knee and carry gourd rattles in their right hands. The right forearm moves up and down, in time with the right foot, and the left arm hangs inactive.

Indian Music

OMAHA MUSIC

The Omaha songs that follow are from the 27th Annual Report of the Bureau of American Ethnology, "The Omaha Tribe," by Alice C. Fletcher and Frances La Flesche, and are reproduced by special permission of the Bureau.

No. 1   SHUPEDA

THAE THA AE THAE HE THAE AE HAE! HUAH - TA

NA-ZHIN THAE AE THAE THA AE THAE HE THAE.

No. 2   **GRASS DANCE**

Mysteriously ♩. 188
Double beat=

NUN-G'THAE THAE-TAE   HE-THA-KE-UN   TAE

THUNAH-HE DAE   NUN-G'THAE THAE-TAE HE-THA-KE-UN- TAE

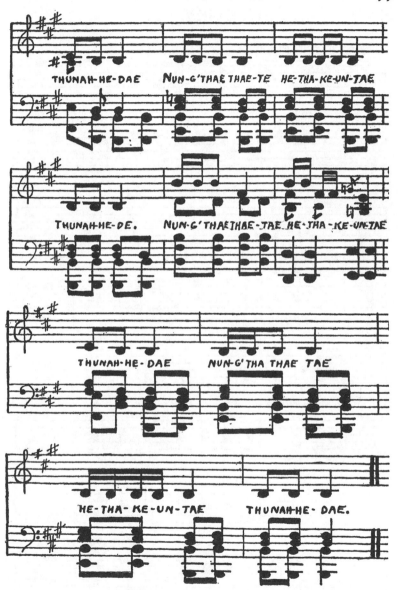

BLUE SKY SONG

YA AH HUN-GA   KAE-THA HUN-

GA EEN-TUN-EE-NAE THAE HUN-GA.

No. 4   OMAHA PEACE CHORUS

with religious feeling

THAE AH-WA-KAE-DEA HEA-OO-THA HEA-OO-THA

THA — KAE-DAE-HEAH-OO-THA THAE AH-WA KAE-DAE

HEAH-THAE HAE HEAH-OO-THA AH - KAE-DAE

HEAH - OO THA AH-WA KAE-DAE HEAH-THAE HAE.

No. 5 OMAHA TRIBAL PRAYER

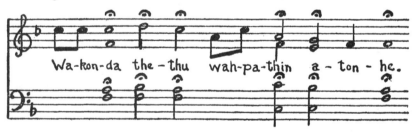

Wa-kon-da the-thu wah-pa-thin a - ton - he.

Wa-kon-da the-thu wah-pa-thin a -ton-he.

No. 6 WAR HONOR SONG

No. 7   CALUMET SONG

THAE-NAN HO— DAN   THA   HAE

THAE-NAN HO-   THAE NAN HO— DAN

THAE-NAN HO— DAN   HUN— GA.

No. 8   CALUMET DANCE

Smoothly

Repeat ad lib.

No. 9 ARAPAHO GHOST-DANCE SONG

This song and the one that follows are from the 14th Annual Report of the Bureau of American Ethnology, "The Ghost-Dance Religion," by James Mooney, and are used by special permission of the Bureau.

No. 10 CADDO GHOST-DANCE SONG

Ha'i-wi'-o'-wi' ta' ; na'i-wi'-o-wi'-ta;

do'-hya-di-wa bon na' na'i-wi'-o'-wi ta',

do'-hya-di-wa bon na' na'i-wi'-o'-wi ta;

na' ha' na'da ka' a',na' ha' na'da ka' a'.

CHIPPEWA MUSIC

No. 11   OJIBWA DEATH SONG

From Frederic Burton's "American Primitive Music." Special arrangement by Rev. William Brewster Humphrey. Used by permission of The American Indian League.

MAH-NOO NE-NAH NIN-GA MAH-JAH, MAH-NOO NE-NAH,

NIN-GA-MAH-JAH, A-O-DA-NA WIN-E' NIN-GA-DE-

JAH MAH-NOO NE-NAH NIN GA MAH-JAH-NEEN,

A-O-DA-HA-WIN-E' NIN-GA DE JAH.

The Chippewa (Ojibwa), Teton-Sioux, Ute, and Mandan songs on the following pages are from bulletins of the Bureau of American Ethnology, by Frances Densmore, and are reproduced here by special permission of the Bureau. In all cases where words are not given, vocables such as ho, ho, ho, or he, he, he, he, may be used instead.

No. 12   SCALP-DANCE SONG

No. 13   SONG OF THE PEACE PACT

E huñ - ga   e huñ - ga

Ga-ga-gins o - gi ma   e - huñ - ga

e huñ - ga   e huñ ga.

No. 14   DANCE OF THE DOG FEAST

Drum:

No. 15 SONG OF THE DEER DANCING

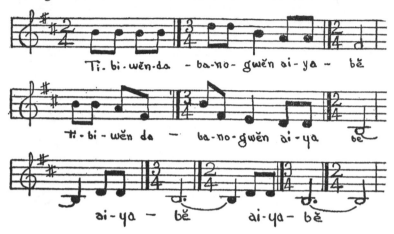

Ti - bi - wĕn - da - ba - no - gwĕn ai - ya - bĕ

ti - bi - wĕn da - ba - no - gwĕn ai - ya bĕ

ai - ya - bĕ   ai - ya - bĕ

TETON SIOUX MUSIC

No. 16   SONG OF THE ELKS

No. 17   DANCING SONG

No. 18   DANCING SONG

No. 19   DANCING SONG

No. 20   WEAPON SONG

No. 21   SONG OF SITTING BULL

A Plains Dancer

Blackfoot "Dog Soldier" Dancing

Hopi Snake Dance

I=hi-ei-ze wa-on kon he wa-

na he-na-la ye lo he i-yo ti-

ye ki - ya wa-on

No. 22 OPENING SONG OF THE SUN DANCE

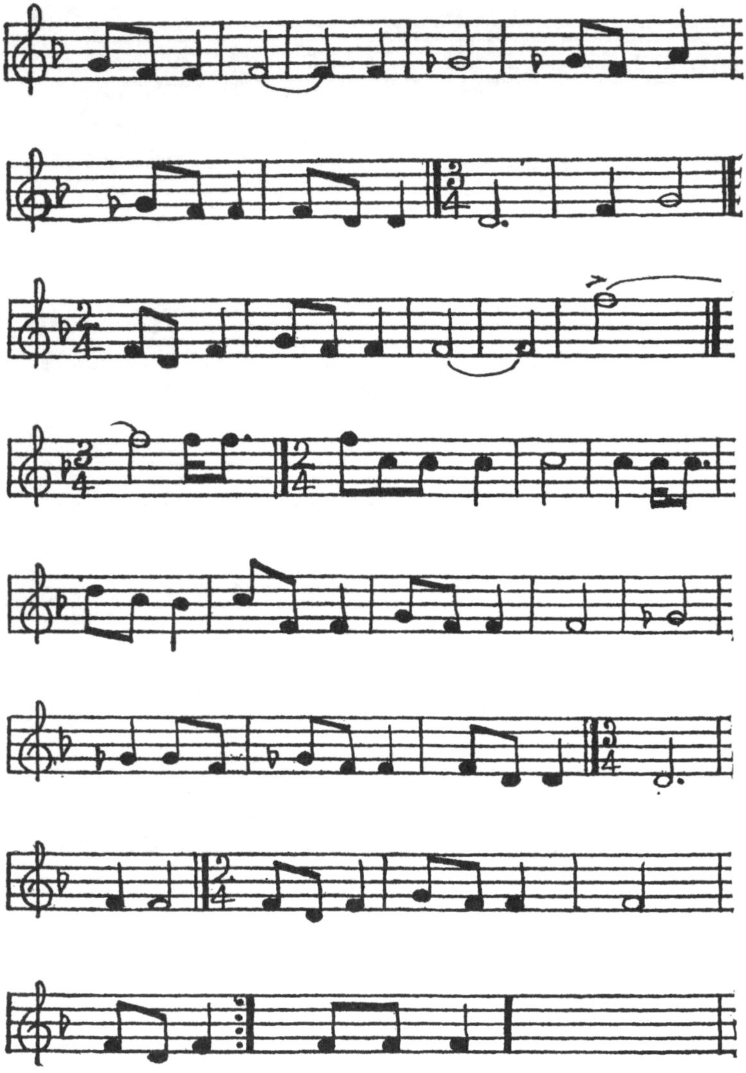

UTE MUSIC

No. 23   SUN DANCE SONG

No. 24   SUN DANCE SONG

No. 25   WOMAN'S DANCE SONG

No. 26 BEAR DANCE SONG

No. 27 BEAR DANCE SONG

MANDAN MUSIC

No. 28   SONG OF THE BEAR

No. 29 BUFFALO SOCIETY SERENADE

MUSIC FROM OTHER TRIBES

No. 30 IROQUOIS FALSE-FACE DANCE

No. 31 KWAKIUTL SOCIAL DANCE

No. 32   DAKOTA SUN DANCE

No. 33   NAVAHO DANCE SONG

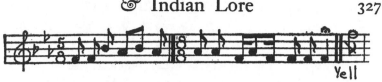

Yell

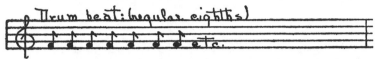

No. 34 SANTO DOMINGO CORN AND FEATHER DANCE

No. 35   ZUÑI RAIN DANCE

Phonograph Records of Indian Music

V = Victor Record   C = Columbia Record

INDIAN SONGS

Medicine Song, White Dog Song, Grass Dance Song (Blackfoot).
   V. 17611
Eagle Dance and Snake Dance Songs (Hopi). **V.** 20043
Penobscot Tribal Songs and Papupooh. **V.** 18444
Children's Chorus and Funeral Chant (Seneca). **C.** A3057
Omaha Dance Song, Dakota Flute Melody, and⎫
   "Shuffling Feet"   ⎬ **C.** A3162
Omaha Tribal Prayer and Mohawk Songs   ⎭

ADAPTATIONS OF INDIAN THEMES

Deer Dance and War Dance—Skilton. C. A6131
From the Land of the Sky-blue Water—Cadman. V. 1115, 1140
By the Waters of Minnetonka—Lieurance. V. 1198, 1228, 19829
From an Indian Lodge—MacDowell. V. 19460
Sioux Flute Serenade and Kickapoo Social Dance. C. A3106
Dagger Dance (From "Natoma")—Herbert. V. 55200
Indian Lament—Dvořák—Kreisler. V. 6186

Sheet Music

BAND MUSIC

Indian War Dance—Bellstedt. Carl Fischer
Chant from the Great Plains—Busch. Carl Fischer
Sun Dance—Friedman. Carl Fischer
Dagger Dance—Herbert. Carl Fischer
Scalp Dance—Lake. Carl Fischer
Two Indian Dances—Skilton. Carl Fischer

Powhatan's Daughter—Sousa. The John Church Company
The Red Man—Sousa. The John Church Company

VOCAL AND INSTRUMENTAL MUSIC

Songs of the American Indians—Bimboni. G. Schirmer, Inc.
An Indian Dance—Browne. J. Fischer & Brothers
Intermezzo (From "Shanewis")—Cadman. White-Smith Company
Prelude (From "Shanewis")—Cadman. White-Smith Company
The Thunderbird—Cadman. White-Smith Company
Wah-wah-tay-see—Cadman. White-Smith Company
To a Vanishing Race—Cadman. The John Church Company
From the Land of the Sky-blue Water—Cadman. White-Smith Company
Indian Action Songs—Densmore. C. C. Birchard & Company
American Indian Melodies—Farwell. G. Schirmer, Inc.
From Mesa and Plain—Farwell. G. Schirmer, Inc.
Impressions of the Wa-Wan Ceremony of the Omahas. G. Schirmer, Inc.
Tales of the Red Man—Grant-Schaeffer. Arthur P. Schmidt Co.
Desert Suite—Grunn. Carl Fischer
Tomahawk Dance—Herman. Carl Fischer
Indian Song Book—Jeancon. Denver Allied Arts
Five American Dances—Lane. J. Fischer & Brothers
By the Waters of Minnetonka—Lieurance. Theodore Presser Company
Four Indian Melodies—Lieurance. Theodore Presser Company
Lyrics of the Red Man—Loomis. G. Schirmer, Inc.
From an Indian Lodge—MacDowell. Breitkoff & Hartel
Indian Suite—MacDowell. Breitkoff & Hartel
Indian Papoose—Mueller. The John Church Company
Indian Suite—Pabst. The John Church Company
The Fire Dance—Rochelle. The John Church Company
Moccasin Game—Rochelle. The John Church Company
The Red Man—Sousa. The John Church Company

Powhatan's Daughter—Sousa. The John Church Company
Primitive American Suite—Skilton. Carl Fischer
Kiowa—Apache War Dance—Troyer. Theodore Presser Company
Zuñian Clown Dance—Troyer. Theodore Presser Company
Ghost Dances of the Zuñi—Troyer. Theodore Presser Company
Suite Aboriginal—Wheelock. Carl Fischer

Chapter Fourteen

DANCES AND CEREMONIES

IT IS virtually impossible to describe Indian dances exactly as the Indians gave them so that they may be reproduced for the entertainment of white audiences. Often an Indian dance will consist of the same step and series of figures repeated over and over again. This was true of a rain dance I witnessed at Zuñi a few years ago. It was made up of a series of three simple

Menomini Dance Ground (BAE)

movements in which the same step was used, yet it lasted from nine o'clock in the morning until four o'clock in the afternoon. Such a dance performed by white dancers would hold little interest for either the dancers or their audience. All of the dances described

here are based on Indian themes taken from many different tribes. An attempt has been made to keep each
dance as nearly like the one on which it is based and
at the same time to make it interesting and its meaning intelligible to a white audience.

While the dances are suitable for use on a stage they
are at their best when given in their native element—

Northwest Coast Wooden Masks (AMNH)

the out-of-doors. Many of the tribes had special dance
grounds or buildings in which the dances were held.
Most of these were circular in form and had a place
for a fire in the center. In summer camps such a place
may be made by smoothing out a piece of ground and
placing seats around it. A good size is about thirty
feet in diameter. Such a ring is ideal for Indian dancing. If dances are given at night in a ring of this kind

Dakota Medicine Man

Hopi Katchina Dancer

you may use the same device for "changing scenes" as do the Hopi in their underground kivas. When they present a drama dance in two or more scenes, the fire-keepers hold their robes before the fire so as to shut out all light while scene-shifting is under way. When everything is ready a signal is given and the robes are dropped.

The dances requiring masked characters may be given without the masks, but, of course, they are much

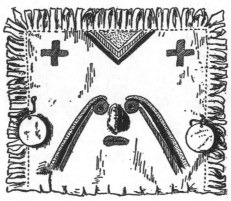

Assiniboine Clown's Canvas Mask (AMNH)

more effective if the masks are used. Southwestern masks can be made from rawhide, cardboard, or stiff felt from a man's derby hat. Iroquois masks can be carved from white pine or other soft wood. Balsa, a very light soft wood used in airplane construction, is excellent material for masks when it can be obtained. Cloth masks can be made from canvas or sacking.

Medicine Pipe Ceremony

This dance is based on an ancient Blackfoot ceremony used in curing the sick.   The medicine pipes
carried in the dance were beautifully decorated with
feathers, skins, and painted designs and were supposed

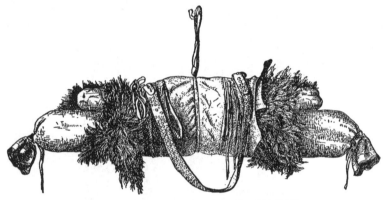

Blackfoot Medicine Pipe Bundle (AMNH)

to have come to the people as a gift from the Sun.
When not in use they were rolled in bundles of many
thicknesses of fur, together with rattles, tobacco, sweet
grass, and other things used in the ceremony.   These
sacred pipes were only unrolled for the benefit of the
sick, for parties going to war, or for prayers for the
general good and prosperity of the people.

The dance may be done as a solo or by a group of
four medicine men.   A person to act as patient and
two drummers who bring the patient in are needed in

addition to the dancers. The properties required are a decorated pipe in several wrappings of fur or cloth, a rattle for each dancer, and some red grease paint. The ceremony is supposed to take place inside a tipi. In the description we presume it is being given around a camp council ring.

The two drummers enter first, carrying their instruments and supporting the patient between them. They place the patient halfway between the fire and the edge of the ring and cover him with a blanket. They then seat themselves to one side and begin to drum with a slow, soft, single beat. The four medicine men then enter in single file and walk slowly around the ring. The first one carries the bundle containing the pipe, which he places on the ground between the patient and the fire. After he lays down the bundle he takes his place alongside the others, who are standing facing the fire on one side of the ring. All then seat themselves.

The drummers now change their beat to two-four time and all sing the Sioux dancing song. Medicine man number two gets up after a moment and, using the toe-heel step, dances slowly around the ring until he reaches the pipe bundle. There he stops and stoops down as if to open the bundle, but just as his hands are about to touch it he suddenly leaps back. He does this twice again before he finally touches the bundle and begins to carefully unwrap it. This is in accordance with the ceremonial custom of making three feints or four movements before touching sacred objects. When the pipe is unwrapped it is placed on top of the wrappings or it may be set up against a rack of sticks as shown in the diagram. The medicine man then dances to his place and sits down. The second medicine man gets up at once and dances to the patient. He paints the patient's face with sacred red paint and, standing, says this prayer to the Sun:

"Ho, Sun! Ho, Thunder! Ho, Napi! Bless our children and may our paths be straight. Look down

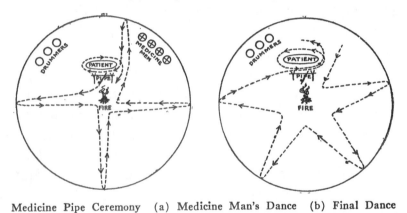

Medicine Pipe Ceremony (a) Medicine Man's Dance (b) Final Dance

on all of us and pity us. Let us all reach old age. Let our lives be complete. You will smoke. We fill the sacred pipe."

The drummers now beat a bit faster as the medicine man picks up the pipe and dances with it to the four quarters of the circle. He uses the toe-heel step. He carries the pipe in both hands and his arms are stretched out straight from the shoulder. His gaze is fixed on the pipe. In a straight line he dances first to the west, then to the south, east, and north. There he dances round the patient, passing the pipe over his body. He then places the pipe back on the rack or bundle and returns to his seat.

Once more the drummers beat faster. All four of the medicine men, carrying rattles in their right hands, now dance with the hop step in a zigzag pattern around the ring. They keep in single file as they dance from the fire to the edge of the circle. When they reach the patient the drum time is again increased. With a fast hop step the medicine men separate and dance about the patient. They are driving spirits from his body with their rattles, so they shake their rattles at him and suddenly leap away. This continues for a minute or so, when the drum-beat slows down. The four medicine men stand side by side and with the side step move once around the patient. They hold their rattles high overhead, and as a roll on the drum is given bring them down until they touch the patient's body. This is repeated four times. The second time the rattles come down the patient is seen to move. The third time he sits up, and the fourth time he is helped to his feet by two of the medicine men. Medicine man number one then ends the ceremony by stepping to the center and saying:

"Ho! Ho! Our brother is cured! Great is the power of the Thunder Pipe!"

Buffalo Dance

The buffalo dance was performed by the Mandan and other Siouan tribes. It was thought to have the power of bringing game when food was scarce, but it was primarily a ceremony belonging to the Buffalo Society, which was made up entirely of chiefs or tried warriors. The dancers carried lances, shields, and clubs and wore horned head-dresses or masks made from the head of a buffalo.

Any number may take part in the dance. All of the dancers should carry shields and clubs or lances. If possible, there should be at least six in the orchestra, four with drums and two with rattles. They enter first. They form a single line, face the audience, and sing "Shupeda," the Omaha buffalo-dance song. They then sit down in a row and begin to drum a slow loud-soft beat in two-four time.

The buffalo enter in an irregular procession, dancing slowly with the flat-foot step. They stamp heavily on the loud beat of the drum and sway their bodies slowly as they move about. In this way they move around the circle once. They then kneel, facing the fire or center of the circle, keeping up a dancing motion with their bodies. After a moment of this they rise to their feet,

one at a time, and begin the scrape step without moving
from their places. At the same time they start to snort
and sway their heads from side to side, simulating the
pawing of a buffalo about to charge. This is done to
show that the dancers are as bravely defiant as a buffalo
bull. The snorts stop and the dancers again shout out
the buffalo-dance song, "Shupeda."

When the song is over the drum-beat becomes more
rapid and the buffalo break into a wild dance, using a
rapid toe-heel and hop step. At times their bodies are
bent double; at others they leap up suddenly with both
feet off the ground. They threaten the audience with
their lances and clubs. Finally they imitate buffalo
fighting. They charge and attempt to hook each other
with their horns. While the fight is at its height the
music begins to slow down. With it the noise of the
fight dies down and the buffalo, using the same slow
step as when they entered, follow their leader out of
the ring. The drummers beat a final roll and retire.
This ends the dance.

Social Dance

For this dance those taking part form two circles,
one inside the other. The inner and smaller circle
moves "with the sun"—that is, from right to left. The
outer goes in the opposite direction. Both circles use

the side step. The singers form a line to one side, the ones with drums being in the center.

The circles move completely around three times. Then at a signal on the drums the dancers, using the toe-heel step, close in toward the center, where they form a compact mass. There they stop, bend down, and give a long-drawn-out wolf howl. They then turn

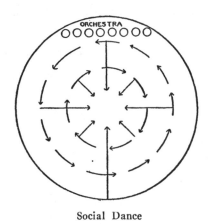

Social Dance

and dance back to their original positions, where at another drum signal they move about as before. After repeating these movements three times the dance is ended.

Ghost Dance

From 1888 to 1890 a religious revival known as the ghost dance spread over the plains. It owed its origin to Wovoka, a Piute, who taught that if the tribes would follow ways of peace and abandon the customs they had adopted from white men, an Indian Messiah would appear, who would destroy the white race, restore the buffalo and the old ways of life. In the dance white cotton shirts decorated with painted sacred symbols

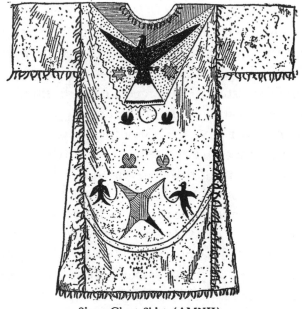

Sioux Ghost Shirt (AMNH)

were worn that were supposed to protect the wearer from all harm. It was usual in this dance for many of the dancers to dance themselves into a hypnotic trance, during which they believed their spirits wandered to the Spirit Land where dwelt the ghosts of their dead relatives.

This dance is most effective when performed by a large number of dancers. In an outdoor pageant where a band furnishes the music, "The Dagger Dance" from "Natoma" is an excellent piece for this dance. The Arapaho and Caddo ghost-dance songs and the Omaha Peace Chorus may be sung by the dancers when band music is not used.

The dance begins with the entry of the drummers, who seat themselves to one side of the space where the dance is to take place and begin to drum softly in time for a slow drag step. The dancers enter in small groups and sit down on the edges of the dance ground. Some carry blankets or have them wrapped about their shoulders, while others are wearing ghost shirts. When all are seated a warning roll is given on the drums and the drum-beats become louder. A few dancers get up, take hold of hands, and dance in a circle, using a dragging side step as they move from right to left. They sing as they dance. The others gradually join them until all have formed a great circle. Four medicine men dance in the center. They carry short feathered wands that they occasionally wave over the heads of the other dancers.

At a signal roll on the drums the dancers sit down where they are and the medicine men dance by themselves in the center of the circle. They begin with the same slow drag step the other dancers have been using, but gradually work into a rapid hop step, the drums keeping time accordingly. From the fastest step the dance quickly slows down again to the drag step and the medicine men sit down.

Another signal roll and the large circle moves about again as it did at first, but this time the step gradually gets faster. The medicine men get up and dart in and out among the dancers, waving their wands in the faces of those who they think are weakening. When such a person is found, he or she follows the medicine man in toward the center of the ring. The medicine man whirls his feathered wand rapidly in the face of the dancer in an effort to bring on a hypnotic trance. Suddenly the dancer falters, totters, and falls face downward and the medicine man searches out a new subject.

In the meantime the big circle moves about, singing. After it has circled about four times the dancers still standing stop, shake out their blankets to drive away the spirits, and then walk off the field. The dreamers gradually awaken, draw their hands across their eyes, slowly get up, and with faltering steps leave the dance ground. The drummers give a final roll which marks the end of the dance.

Elk Mystery

The Elk Mystery was performed by men who had had visions of the elk and who belonged to the Elk

Society.   They wore triangular masks made of thin skins stretched on willow frames to which were fastened forked boughs as antlers.   In their dance they acted out the life of the elk.

Any number of dancers may perform this dance. With twenty or more taking part, it is most effective.

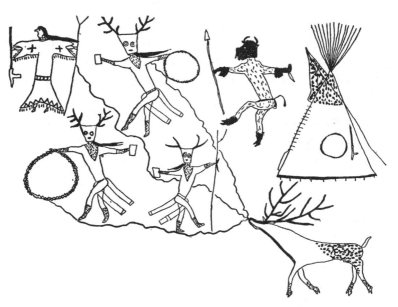

Elk and Buffalo Dancers.   From an Indian Drawing   (AMNH)

An orchestra at one side of the dance ground provides the music.   The elk, carrying forked boughs as antlers in their right hands, which are held against the forehead, enter in two lines from opposite ends of the field. They use a slow toe-heel step, taking attitudes of caution, as the elk might do when stepping forth from cover to look about them. The line on the right moves farther forward than the other and turns to the left. The left line turns to the right as it enters, so that both lines are parallel and about twenty feet apart.

When the two lines are opposite they stop and face each other. The drummers begin a slow single beat,

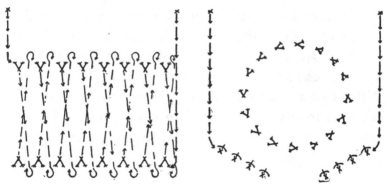

Elk Mystery   (a) Entrance of the Elk   (b) Hunters Ready to Shoot

and with a high elk leap step both lines dance toward and through each other. They then turn and return to their original positions. Next at a signal on the drums they lower their heads and horns and with a rapid scrape step the lines charge each other. They meet in the center, pair off, lock horns, and swing round each other two or three times. With the same step they once more return to their places in line. Another drum signal is given and the elk resume the high leaping step. With the man at the left end of the rear line leading off, the two lines form a single circle that moves from left to right.

At the same time as the circle is formed, two lines of hunters enter from either side. Each hunter carries a bow and arrow. They use the toe-heel step, although the drummers are playing a single beat for the elk step. The hunters move in front of the circle and form a line facing the elk on either side. At a signal from their leader, they fit an arrow in their bows and raise them overhead. They then bring the bow down. This is repeated three times. The third time the hunters drop to one knee and take aim. A loud drum-beat is given. With a shout the hunters let their arrows fly and the elk rush madly off in the directions from which they came. The hunters, yelling, rush after them and the dance is ended.

Iroquois False Face Dance

According to Iroquois belief there are certain evil spirits who have the power to inflict injuries and spread disease among the people. These spirits hide in dark corners, among rocks and in hollow trees. To protect the people against these evil ones, societies known as the "False Faces" were organized. These societies also had the power to drive away disease and to cure certain illnesses. At certain times of the year the members of the False Face Society appeared in public and gave

a dance. The dancers wore masks carved from basswood or woven from corn husks, ragged clothing, and
carried tortoise shell rattles.

Any number of dancers may take part. There is no
orchestra, the music being furnished by the rattles and
the singing of the dancers.

Iroquois Wooden Masks

The dancers enter, using a slow toe-heel step with
their bodies bent low. As they circle around the fire
they shake their rattles gently over the ground with
long sweeping motions. At intervals they grunt and
make other noises. In this way they circle twice and
then sit down facing the fire. Their leader now stands
up and walks about the circle once, scattering wood
ashes from a bag he carries, over the heads of each

dancer. When he reaches his original position he gives
a signal for all to rise.

The dancers get up and sing the False-Face dance
song once and then begin to dance, using the hop step

Iroquois False-Face Dancer. *Courtesy of the New
York State Museum*

in slow time. With this step they circle about, singing
as they dance. After two rounds they increase the time
of their step and stop singing. They next break their
circle formation and dash up to persons in the audience,

From Maximilian's Atlas

Mandan Buffalo Dance

Masked Dancer of the Northwest Coast

Pueblo Buffalo Dancers

at whom they shake their rattles. With them they also
strike at the fire and at anything else that may be within
reach. About three rounds about the circle are done
in this way and then the dancers form a single line
behind their leader, using the heel-toe step in slow
time. He leads the line about in a spiral that finally
winds up tight about him on one side of the ring. Then
all dancing stops and for a moment rattles are shaken
vigorously. There is a chorus of grunts from the
dancers and the spiral breaks. The dancers run about
the ring singly, as if chasing some object which leads
them out of the ring. One by one they leave and their
dance is ended.

Wolf Dance

Among the Dakota all who had dreamed of wolves
must give a feast and go through the dance in order to
become members of the Wolf Society. The regalia
which was worn in the dance consisted of a wolf mask
and wolfskins which were worn on the backs, on the
arms and legs. The members were supposed to have
power to cure the sick and to withdraw arrows from
wounds. They also made war medicines, especially
shields. Because of their wolf-like power they acted as
scouts for war parties.

The wolf dance described here may be done as a solo
or by a number of dancers. To make the movements

clear we will assume that twelve dancers are taking part. The orchestra is seated to one side.

The wolves enter at a slow walk. Their bodies are bent far forward and they turn from side to side as if sniffing at and following a trail. In this way they go around in a circle once and then bunch tightly together, facing the center. They then bend their heads forward

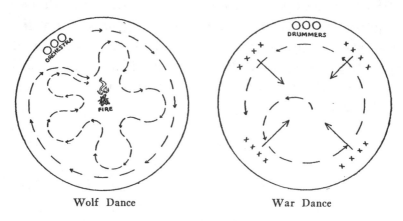

Wolf Dance   War Dance

and give a long howl. Next they stand and sing a wolf song. At the end of the song the orchestra sings a wolf dance song and beats time for the trot step. Using it, the wolves form a circle and follow their leader around the ring. After describing a circle the leader winds in and out, as if following a trail, and the others follow him. In this way the dancers circle about the ring about three times. In this part of the dance they mimic wolves on the trail, picking up the trail, losing it, sniffing the ground, and going forward or to the right or left in sudden leaps. At intervals they bark and howl.

At a signal from the leader the drum-beat is changed for the hop step. It is begun rather slowly, but it gradually increases in time until the dancers are going at top speed. Then it gradually slows down, and as it does so the dancers shift to the toe-heel step. They circle around once with this step, and then turn toward the center. They sing a short wolf song until they reach the center, where they give another howl which ends the dance.

War Dance

Before war parties started out they would gather to sing, dance, and perform religious ceremonies which were supposed to insure success to their expedition. The dances had as their object the arousal of courage and enthusiasm for war.

The dancers are divided into four groups, who seat themselves, facing the center, in the four corners of the dance ground. They carry clubs, bows or lances, and shields. The orchestra is seated in the rear. A roll on the drums followed by three sharp beats is the signal for the dance to begin. At the third beat the dancers rise and dance with a rapid hop step toward the center. Lances are extended, clubs raised as if to strike, and it appears as if the opposite groups are about to attack each other. They come together with a yell. The drum-time becomes slower and the step changes to a slow toe-heel. The dancers form an irregular circle and begin acting out war experiences.

At first their movements are slow and stealthy. By their gestures they show the way of advancing on an enemy, by hunting out and following up the track, discovering the enemy, and preparing for the attack. This takes three rounds. Then with a double drum-beat as a signal the time and step change again to a rapid hop. Arms and legs are now lifted at sharp angles; the body is bent and raised with sudden and varied movements, as in a charge, or as if dodging arrows or warding off blows of weapons. All this is done in time with the music. Each dancer acts out his story without regard to what the others are doing, so that at the same instant one might be seen in an attitude of attack, another of defense, drawing the bow, striking with the war club, some listening or waiting an opportunity, and others of striking a foe. This action takes place while the dancers circle around four times. Then the drum-time changes for the rapid flat-foot step. With this step the dancers divide into groups of three and not more than four. In each group one dancer takes an attitude of defense, while the others attack him. He swings his shield from face to face and thrusts his lance, all in time with the music. The attackers pretend to snatch at his weapons and fight him off. Clubs are struck together and lances and bows are struck on the shields. The lone fighter gradually drives the others back.

Once more the drummers increase their beat to rapid hop-step time. At first it is rather slow, but the time increases, reaching its climax as the dance ends. The dancers again take fighting attitudes, making sudden rushes and charges as they shout war cries. Finally they gather in a compact group in the center, hold their weapons high overhead, and together give a loud yell. They then break into their original groups and dash out.

Bear Dance

Among the Cree, the bear dance was performed to obtain the good will of the bears and as a prayer for their assistance in obtaining long life. The Iowa gave it when a party was about to hunt the bear, as an appeal to the bear spirit. The Ute bear dance, different from either of these, was a social dance held in the early spring, about the time the bear comes forth from his hibernation. The morache is used as a musical instrument in this dance because the Utes say its sound is like the noise made by a bear. In the Dakota bear dance some of the dancers dressed in bearskins and others wore masks made from bear's heads.

In the dance six dancers appear as bears and two as hunters. The orchestra consists of two drummers, two with rattles, and four playing moraches. The orchestra enters first and takes its place to one side. The drummers begin with a soft, rapid single beat. A warning shout is heard off stage and the two hunters dash in, hotly pursued by the bears, all running around in a wide circle. The hunters use a short running step. The bears, who appear to be very ferocious, run with a waddling step and hold their closed fists to their heads to imitate the bears' ears. At times they growl and pretend to scratch the hunters. The chase goes around the ring three times, when the hunters make their escape. As they leave, the drumming ceases and the moraches begin to keep time for a slow toe-heel step. At the same time the bear dance songs are sung.

The bears now form a small circle and drop to their knees. Their arms are bent and extended forward and their hands hang as do a bear's paws when he is sitting up. In this position they sway their bodies in time with the music. One by one they get up and begin to dance slowly around the ring, using a step that consists of a slow alternate lifting of the feet. They grunt and growl, smell the palms of their hands, and lean forward, holding their heads out as bears do. The time of the music increases slightly and the rattles and drums join the moraches.

The two hunters reappear, creeping stealthily around the bears, who dance about without noticing them. As the hunters reach the opposite side of the dance ground

Sioux Bear Dance *(From Catlin.)*

from which they entered, they are discovered by the leader of the bears. The bears at first appear frightened and huddle in a compact group, while the hunters stand up and using a rapid toe-heel step, approach the bears, and swing their lances at them. The bears growl and suddenly turn and charge in a group. The hunters turn and run off stage.

The drum-beat becomes faster now, and the bears, using a high flat-foot step, dance triumphantly. The hunters, using the same step as the bears, reappear again without weapons, but carrying a pipe. This they offer to the leader of the bears, who dances to the front and faces the hunters. The other bears form a semicircle in back of the hunters and the bear chief and keep up the dance step. With apparent feeling and fear the bear chief takes a puff at the pipe and emits a groan of anguish; his power is broken. With the other bears he creeps out weakly, followed by the hunters.

Scalp Dance

A dance of this kind was held after a war party had returned with scalps. Among the Cheyenne it was a social as well as a triumph dance in which both men and women took part. The scalps taken in battle were tied to poles carried in the dance.

The dancers form in four separate lines, facing the fire or the center of the dance ground. Some carry

Scalp Dance (*From Catlin.*)

clubs and every other dancer has a rattle. The drummers stand in the center of one row of dancers. In each line at least one scalp pole is carried. These may be made by tying a tuft of horsehair, or frayed rope

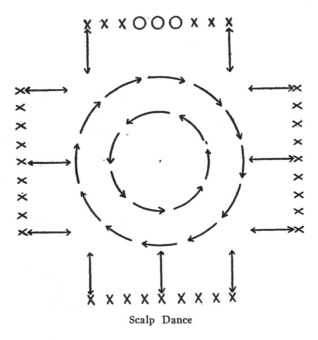

Scalp Dance

dyed black, to a five-foot sapling. The lines move forward four steps with a toe-heel grape-vine step and then with the backward grape-vine return to their original position. This is repeated five times, when the drumming stops. The rattle-bearers, using the stamp drag step, advance the left foot and vigorously shake their rattles. They form in a single column and dance once about in a circle, when they return to their original positions.

The drummers now take a position on one side and beat time for the stamp-three toe step. Using this, the rattle-bearers form a circle and move toward the right. The other dancers form a circle inside the other and dance in a circle in the opposite direction. Though both circles move in their original directions, the dancers face now to the rear and then to the front. Those carrying clubs swing their weapons in a threatening manner as they turn about. The drum-time becomes faster and the dancers gradually break into a rapid side hop. The circles break after one round of this step and the dancers, without regard to a regular formation, dance with a rapid toe-heel. The scalp-bearers gather in the center, facing outward, where they mark time while holding their scalp poles high. The dancers shout war cries as they dance, and with a final yell given in chorus rush madly off the dance ground.

Zuñi Rain Dance

The Zuñi, a pueblo tribe, have many ceremonial dances which are intended to bring rain, so that the crops may be successful and the general happiness of the people insured. The rain priests who took part in the ceremonies I have seen wore turquoise-colored masks to which were attached long black beards of horsehair. Around their waists were kilts of white cotton cloth embroidered with colored yarns on the edges, and broad sashes of the same material. Their moccasins had high tops and were painted red, blue, and yellow. Each dancer's body was painted with designs in color. In their right hands they carried gourd rattles, and in the other a bunch of spruce twigs. Sprigs of spruce were also tucked in the armbands they wore above their elbows, in their moccasins, and in the sashes about their waists. On the left leg each man wore a turtle-shell rattle. They also wore silver ornaments and many strings of beads which rattled and jingled as they danced.

The Koyemshi, "delight-makers," or clowns, called "mud heads" by the whites, provided fun at intervals throughout the ceremony, to relieve the tedium of the performance. They were naked except for a black kilt and black neckerchief. Their heads were covered with bag-like masks of sacking painted a brownish-pink color. These had large lumps on the top and sides of the head and doughnut-like projections around the eye and mouth openings. In all, forty rain priests and nine "mud heads" took part in the performance, which began early in the morning and ended at sundown.

In our dance any number of dancers from nine to fifty may take part. As a rule there should be one clown to eight rain priests.

The dancers enter in procession, single file, using the Southwestern stamp step and singing the rain-dance song. The head priest walks in front of the line, sprinkling cornmeal in the path of the dancers. This he carries in a bowl. The dancers move rather quietly, softly shaking their rattles and singing in a low tone. In this way they move in column across the dance ground. On the other side each man does an about face, keeping up the dance step as he does so. They

Zuñi Clown's Mask

then dance to their original position. This movement is repeated twice.

When the dancers return the second time they stop singing and mark time in place. The head priest walks down the line and scatters cornmeal up the right arm, over the forehead, and down the left arm of each dancer. As this ceremony is finished the clowns enter, rushing and whooping. They stay until the dance ends. All through the dance they carry on their activities according to their own desires. They get in the way of the dancers and dance out of order and out of turn. They sit on the ground with hands clasped across their knees and rock their bodies to and fro. They carry foxskins or pieces of fur; drop them on the ground; walk away as if unconscious of their loss; pretend to miss them; act as if searching anxiously for the skin which lies in plain sight; screen their eyes with their hands and crouch low to look; pretend, at last, to find the lost skin; jump on it as if it were a live animal they were killing; shoulder it and carry it off as if it were a heavy burden, and fall under it. They come and go irregularly and endeavor in all ways to amuse the audience.

The rain priests sing their chorus again louder and a bit faster. They advance in single file, first turning halfway to the left and then to the right at regular intervals. To execute this movement three steps are taken forward, three to make the turn, three to turn back, and three forward again. In this way the procession moves about in the form of a square. At the end of this figure the rain priests retire and the clowns take the floor. Each carries a bunch of light switches, which at the end of the dance they use on one another. In a clumsy fashion they attempt to imitate the dance the priests have just performed. One clown continually remains behind the others, and at the close of the clowns' dance he remains going through the steps, pretending to be

Dance of the Zuñi Clowns. *Courtesy of the Peabody Museum*

oblivious of the fact that they have stopped; then feigning to discover the fact, he follows them at a full run.

Once more the rain priests enter doing the Southwestern stamp step, and singing their song. They line up facing the audience and stop singing. They now advance the left foot, bend their bodies to the right, shout, shake their rattles, dip them with a long sweep of the arm as if dipping water, and bring them up to their mouths. They almost touch the ground in doing this. This movement is repeated, and then the dancers face about and dance to the back of the dance ground with the stamp step. There they face the audience again and repeat the dipping movement twice again.

The head rain priest takes the lead, as he did at the beginning, and sprinkles cornmeal in the path of the dancers. Singing loudly and using the stamp stej, they move twice around the dance ground. On each side they stop, mark time, and then each dancer turns around in place. When they come to the front they dance in a lock-step, packed as closely together as dancing will allow. There they halt, give a prolonged shake of their rattles, shout, and move away at an ordinary walk, in silence. This ends the dance.

Sir Robert S. S. Baden-Powell, Chief Scout of the World, with American
Scouts who took part in the London Jamboree Pageant of 1920

The Pony War Dance from the Culver Pageant

An Indian Dance in a Boy Scout Camp

Chapter Fifteen

PRODUCING AN INDIAN PAGEANT

THERE is no better way to end a season of work in Indian crafts in school or camp than with the production of an Indian pageant. It is a project that if carefully planned is not at all difficult to successfully carry out. In the pageant all of the articles which have been made may be put to practical use in reproducing the life of an Indian tribe or group of tribes. The natural setting for a pageant of this kind is the out-of-doors, so that if given in town a park or playground should be used in preference to a stage, if it is at all possible. This permits the use of many properties and a larger cast than on an ordinary stage. Plays with authentic backgrounds are also worth while doing, but the pageant has two main advantages over them in that it permits the entire group to take part and has few speaking parts to be learned.

A story of some kind is needed on which the pageant's action is to be based. There is no need for an elaborate plot, but there should be some connection, however loose, between the various episodes of which it is made up. The story may be based on some local Indian legend or historical event, or it may aim to tell in a simple way what the life of the Indians was like.

Good material for pageant plots can be found in the books listed under "Stories of Indian Life" in the Bibliography at the end of this book. Dances and ceremonies, because they are spectacular, will have a large part in a pageant program, but one should not neglect the opportunity to demonstrate handicrafts, cooking methods, and games which will be equally interesting to the audience and at the same time give it a more fully rounded picture of Indian life. By no means should the element of humor be entirely left out. The Indians were not the stoics that fiction has made them, so that we can, by introducing clowns and practical jokes, show this side of their life. If spoken parts are written in verse, avoid the monotonous "Hiawatha" meter, which is not Indian, and use instead an Indian rhythm which may be selected from one of the modern collections of Indian poetry.

Music is next in importance to the story. For a large pageant a band is needed to supplement the Indian instruments, although they should be used alone in some episodes. An orchestra is next best, if a band cannot be secured, or even two or three musicians will add a lot to the effectiveness of the performance. A hidden flutist in a tipi, or in a canoe far out on a lake in a pageant given on the shore, can be used with beautiful effect. Shore pageants also permit singers to be heard in the distance, first as they slowly approach the scene, and the opposite effect of having their song gradually fade out as they paddle off. An appropriate piece of music played just before the action begins gives the audience an emotional key to the action.

Proper organization is essential to a successful performance. Whether the group is large or small, strong organization is needed to insure that the performance will begin on time and move smoothly without the breaks and delays that soon tire an audience and lose its interest. In control of all the elements of the pageant is the director who coaches the various episodes and directs the performance. If the number taking part is small the director may work alone, but where large numbers are involved he will need several assistants to coach the various episodes. A musical director selects the music and makes the necessary arrangements with the band or orchestra leader. Costumes are made and cared for under the direction of the costume director. It is his duty also to see that those taking part are properly costumed and ready on time for dress rehearsals and performances. Working with him is the make-up director, who purchases make-up supplies and with his assistants "makes up" the cast. He will find handy large colored charts showing various face-paint patterns. These can be hung on the wall, facing those who are applying the make-up. Another member of the director's staff is the stage manager, who is in charge of all properties and the preparation of the setting. All properties are made under his direction and carefully stored until ready for use. He also has charge of scene-shifting, if any is done. If tickets are sold and programs and seats for the audience need to be provided, these matters are handled by the business manager. If horses and dogs are used, as they should be whenever possible because of their spectacular effect, an assistant director should be put in charge of them. He arranges for their care and feeding, for the erection of picket lines, and for the construction of travois and other properties used with them. The actors themselves are best organized in groups of six or eight, each of which is in charge of a group leader or "dog soldier." In large pageants three or four groups may be organized into a "band" in charge of a "band chief." All the members of a group have similar parts—that is, they may be "squaws," "old men," "children," "young men," or "warriors."

The number of rehearsals necessary for each episode should be determined and a detailed schedule for them prepared. This schedule should show exactly what is to be done on each day until the performance takes place. It should also include postponement dates in case rain prevents the performance from taking place on the original dates set. All rehearsals should be so managed that they are not too long and exhausting to the boys or girls who are taking part. The rehearsals, like the performance itself, should start and end exactly on time. Unless the director is familiar with the

accomplishments of all the members of the cast, the
first few rehearsals should be in the nature of "try-
outs." In these the dance steps and songs are practiced,
so that the best dancers and natural leaders may be
singled out and selected as dance and group leaders.
The less desirable parts should not be arbitrarily assigned, but should be filled before any others by volun-
teers. A little skillful leadership on the part of the
director may sometimes easily accomplish this seem-
ingly difficult task. Horses, if used, need rehearsal as
much as do the human actors. Even though trained
for cavalry drills, horses may fail in the close formations of an Indian dance or shy at things as unfamiliar
as war bonnets and feathered coup sticks.

The organization and direction of an Indian pageant
can, perhaps, best be explained through the story of a
successful pageant which is based on one produced a
few years ago by the author at the Culver Woodcraft
School. The action was supposed to take place on the
plains at the time when the ghost-dance religion was
spreading from tribe to tribe. The setting was a semicircle of tipis that faced the audience. Six tipis were
in place when the pageant began, and a seventh was
erected during the action, in order that the audience
might see how a tipi was set up. About the tipis were
all of the things one might find in a Plains Indian village. In back of the lodges were tripods on which
hung medicine bundles, shields, and bonnets. Hides

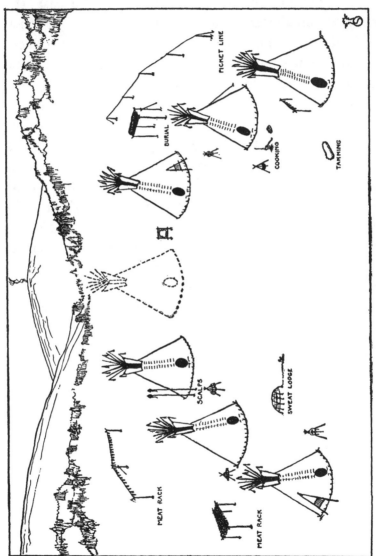

Fig. 149. Setting for the Culver Pageant

were stretched on frames or staked on the ground for tanning.   There were places for cooking and drying meat where stone-boiling and pemmican-making methods were demonstrated.   Parfleche food bundles

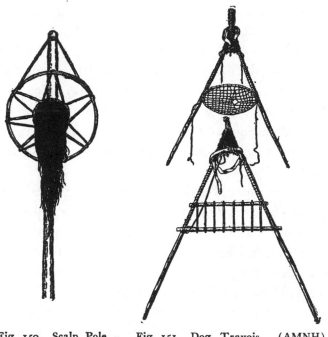

Fig. 150.   Scalp Pole   Fig. 151.   Dog Travois   (AMNH)

were hung from tripods and stored on platforms.   A windbreak of brush on one side acted as a partial screen for the picket line, and beyond it were scaffold burials and sweat lodges.   Travois leaned against the tipis or were stacked together.   A sweat lodge or two and some scalps drying on high poles completed the set. What it looked like can be seen from Fig. 149.

The meat used on the drying racks was made from strips of old canvas painted dark red. The scalps were pieces of canvas about four inches in diameter, to which had been sewn strands of dyed binding twine and which were laced on hoops made of a bent branch, as shown in Fig. 150. The parfleche bundles were for the most part made of paper painted with parfleche designs. The burials were cylindrical rolls of paper and brush covered over with canvas. Travois used in the setting and those actually drawn by the horses and dogs were made direct from the Indian patterns shown in Fig. 151.

Four groups representing women, old men, young men, and children took their places in the tipis before the audience was seated and remained out of sight until the band had finished playing the introductory number. It was then supposed to be dawn and signs of life gradually showed themselves about the camp. Women started to prepare the morning meal and soon smoke was curling from the lodge tops and from fires in the open. Old men and children came from the tipis and went toward a nearby stream for a morning bath. The regular tasks of the day were soon begun by the women. One or two started tanning hides, others pounded meat and berries together to make pemmican and placed meat on the drying racks. The children imitated the lives of their parents in their play. In one place a group of girls and boys were playing at moving camp, pulling a small travois on which was loaded a miniature tipi which they finally set up. Near the center of the camp, boys were practicing with bows and arrows. The lively hoop-and-pole game was being played by older boys. Toward the side of the camp old men gathered to gamble at dice. Others were making bows and arrows, and one was painting a shield. Off on the sky line of a distant hill a sentry sat wrapped in a blanket.

Suddenly this watcher sent up a smoke signal (by throwing flashlight powder on a small fire). A war party was returning! The signal was answered by a blanket waved from the camp. At once there was great excitement. All left their work and play and watched the returning war party that rode silhouetted on the sky line and then slowly down to the camp. At almost the same time a hunting party came on the scene from the left, and a third procession, that of a visiting delegation from other tribes, appeared on the right. The horses and dogs of both hunters and visitors were carrying packs or drawing travois heavy laden with game and presents.

The war party reached the camp first and was greeted by the women, children and old men, who ran out to meet it. Some of its members had their faces painted black to show that scalps had been taken. The

Horse Travois

party entered the camp and rode around the circle past the audience and out to the picket line in slow procession. It was followed closely by the hunting party and the visitors. Horses were picketed while the women of the hunting party unloaded the animals and erected their tipi in the center opening through which the procession had come. A herald then rode about the camp and announced that a council would be held to greet the visitors, and that a scalp dance would take place to celebrate the victory.

The entire cast was now seated in a semicircle facing the audience. In the front center a fire had been laid. The fire was lit by a medicine man, who used the old Indian method. In the lighting of the fire he recited this ritual, which is taken from a Pawnee ceremony called the Hako:

"I know not if the voice of man can reach the sky;
I know not if the Mighty One will hear us pray;
I know not if the gifts I ask will all be granted;
I know not if the word of old hath been received;
I know not what will come to pass in days to be.
I hope that only good will come, my children, unto you."

He then makes the fire and when the flame comes, says:

"Now I know that the voice of man can reach unto the heaven;
Now I know that the Mighty One hath heard me when I prayed;
Now I know that the word of old—we have truly heard it;
Now I know that Tirawa Atius, Heaven, our Father, hearkeneth
unto man's prayer;

I know that good, and good alone, hath come, my children, unto
you."

When he had finished a chief bearing a pipe stepped
forward, lit his pipe at the fire, and began the pipe
ceremony, which was used in various forms by most of
the Plains Indians. Blowing a puff toward the sky
and pointing the pipe stem upward, he says:

"I offer this to Wakantanka for all the good that
comes from above." Then with a puff toward the
earth, "I offer this to Maka-kin, the earth, whence come
all good gifts." Then a puff of smoke is blown and the
pipe pointed to each of the cardinal points, starting at
the west and going to the north, east, and south as he
says to each in turn:

"To you, Wiyo peyata, who dwells where the sun
falls, help us with the strength of the thunder.

"To you, Wazi yata, who dwells whence comes the
cold, send us the cold winds and let the tribe live."

"To you, Wiyo hinyanpata, who dwells where the
sun continually returns, send us good days and let the
tribe live.

"To you, Ito Kagata, who dwell in the direction we
face with outstretched arms, may the sun shine out in
full to us and let the tribe live."

When the ceremony was finished all stood, and with
outstretched arms sang the Omaha Tribal Prayer. The
chief then welcomed the visitors and announced that

the rest of the day would be given over to entertainment.

The scalp dance was given first. When horses are used in this dance, four mounted groups ride into the village in a simulated attack and then circle around in single file. They dismount, do the rest of the dance on foot, and when it is finished ride off. Following the scalp dance came a social dance in which the entire camp joined. At its end a short game of lacrosse was played by two fair-sized teams. All those not taking part in the events were seated about, looking on, or were engaged in real or imaginary tasks about the camp.

The field was now cleared for a group of medicine men, who put on the Medicine-Pipe Ceremony. This was followed by the Elk Mystery enacted by forty-eight dancers. Next the visitors gave a pony war dance, or horse dance, as it was called by the Blackfoot. This is a war dance performed by a group of mounted warriors who ride on the camp as if to make an attack, and then in a close group ride rapidly around inside the camp circle, describing a series of loops, figure eights, and straight-line formations. Twice they stop, dismount, and dance on foot while their horses are held by others. Finally with a shout, they remount and dash off the scene.

A bear dance was given next by two groups, and then the ghost dance, in which all but three groups joined

These were busy making necessary preparations for the closing scene.

The buffalo dance given by two groups of chief, followed immediately after the close of the bear dance. As it ends a mounted scout rides in and excitedly tells the people that soldiers are on their way to attack the camp. Preparations for war began at once. Men helped the women dismantle the camp, and while this was being done the war dance was begun. All the men joined in the dance, which ended with a rush off, leaving the stage entirely cleared.

To create the desired effect the ending had to be carefully organized and rehearsed. Each person was assigned to a definite task and was given charge of a certain piece of equipment. Contests were held between the tipi crews which developed speed in setting them up and taking them down. Similar contests were used to train the travois crews in loading the tipis and other equipment. As a result the scene was cleared with a suddenness and smoothness of action that took the audience completely by surprise.

This outline presents one plan for weaving the dances and ceremonies we have described into a somewhat connected story. There are many other ways in which it might be done and other elements that could be introduced. The important thing is to keep the background of your story as authentic as possible and to avoid the burlesque type of Indian pageantry that has too often taken place in the past.

Chapter Sixteen

INDIAN NAMES

As a high honor to one who has distinguished himself in his work in camp or at home, an Indian name may be given. In bestowing Indian names in this way, instead of assuming them without good cause, we will follow the custom of the Indians themselves, to whom personal names were generally sacred marks of honor that were treated reverently. An Indian would seldom, if ever, mention his own name, because it stood for something intimately connected with his life, such as a brave deed which modesty forbade him to mention. He believed that if he mentioned it he would become unfortunate in his undertakings. However, if he were pressed to tell his name he might get some one else to speak it for him.

Tribal customs in giving names, and the names themselves, differed widely. In some tribes clan names were given that referred to the totem, animal, plant, or object. These names were kept through life by the individual. In other tribes a man or woman might bear different names at different periods of life. Thus a boy might at first be known by a baby pet name which he would retain until he was about five or six years old. At that time he might be given the name of his uncle or grandfather. This he would keep until he went to war and won a name of honor. After that his name might be changed on special occasions. To assume a new name in some tribes it was necessary for a man to go through elaborate ceremonies. In others, all that was required was to hire a crier who would proclaim the new name throughout the camp.

On the eighth day after an Omaha child was born, and before it has received a name, a priest was sent for who introduced the child to the cosmos by reciting the following ritual:

"Ho! Ye Sun, Moon, Stars, all ye that move in the heavens; I bid you hear me!
    Into your midst hath come a new life. Consent ye, I implore!
        Make smooth its path, that it may reach the brow of the first hill!
Ho! Ye Winds, Clouds, Rain, Mist, all ye that move in the air; I bid you hear me!
    Into your midst hath come a new life. Consent ye, I implore!
        Make smooth its path, that it may reach the brow of the second hill!
Ho! Ye Hills, Valleys, Rivers, Lakes, Trees, Grasses, all ye of the earth; I bid you hear me!
    Into your midst hath come a new life. Consent ye, I implore!
        Make smooth its path, that it may reach the brow of the third hill!
Ho! Ye Birds, great and small, that fly in the air;
Ho! Ye Animals, great and small, that dwell in the forest;
Ho! Ye Insects that creep among the grasses and burrow in the ground—I bid you hear me!
    Into your midst hath come a new life. Consent ye, I implore!

Make smooth its path, that it may reach the brow of the
  fourth hill!
Ho! All ye of the heavens, all ye of the air, all ye of the earth;
  I bid you hear me!
    Into your midst hath come a new life. Consent ye, consent ye
    all, I implore! Make smooth its path, then shall it travel
    on even beyond the four hills."

This ritual was a prayer to the powers of the heavens,
the air, and the earth for the safety of the infant from
birth to old age. The four hills are those of infancy,
youth, manhood, and old age, to be crossed on the journey along the rugged road of life. As soon as the child
was able to walk about by itself it went through another
ceremony, at which time its baby name was discarded
and it received the clan name which it bore all through
life.

Men were sometimes known by nicknames because
of some absurd saying, ludicrous circumstances, or personal peculiarity. I first discovered a name of this kind
in a visit to the Blackfoot, where I met a man known as
"Butchers-with-his-head-down." The name was so
peculiar that I tried to learn its meaning and I finally
succeeded in getting its story from Curly Bear. It
seems that in the old days it was the custom of the older
and poorer members of the tribe to go out among the
men and women who were cutting up meat after a hunt,
and, by helping with the butchering, earn a share of the
meat. Nearly everyone was glad to help these people

in this way. But one man was so mean and stingy that, whenever he saw the old people coming toward him, he would bend way down and cut up his meat with his head close to the ground, pretending in this way not to see the needy ones who came to ask his assistance. This habit was soon noticed by the other members of the tribe, and some one in derision gave him the name "Butchers-with-his-head-down." In time he changed his ways, but the name he had received stuck to him all through life.

White men known to the Indians were often given names referring to some physical peculiarity. Thus their names when translated often meant such things as Long Neck, Fish Eyes, Old Crane, and Long Beard. Nowadays, few white people receive true Indian names. Indians are often hired, though, to give names to tourists or prominent people and sometimes also to make them "chiefs." In return for the money, a group of grinning Indians dance about the candidate and sometimes give names that no Indian could translate. The fact that one has received a name, even though it be a true one given by the tribe as a great honor, does not imply that the person has been adopted into a tribe. Such adoptions are very rare and can only be made by the entire tribe or its high council.

An Indian name won in camp should be awarded with proper ceremony. This should take place, if possible, around the camp fire and should include a recital of the facts in connection with which the award is being made. The old name of the candidate may be written on a piece of birch bark and dropped in the fire. The candidate's face may then be painted with the sacred red paint and his new name proclaimed. As part of the ceremony a dance may be performed in the candidate's honor.

On the following pages are lists of Indian names from many different tribes. We have included with personal and place names, the names of animals, birds, trees, common things the Indians made, and natural objects. These are given in the languages of tribes living in different sections of the country, so that you may adopt those that come from the section in which you happen to live. Many of the names are suitable for camps, buildings, and boats.

Unless otherwise indicated, vowels are pronounced as follows: *a* as in father, *e* as in they, *i* as in marine, *o* as in note, and *u* as in flute. Consonants are pronounced as in English. *Ai* is pronounced as the *i* in fire and *au* as *ow* in now.

Indian Names

Natick—Massachusetts

PERSONAL NAMES

Black Bird	—Cho'gan	Keeper	—Wad cha' mik
Camp	—Tup puk'sin nook	Medicine Man	—Pau'wau
Captain	—Mug'womp	Morning Star	—Mish an' nock
Chief	—Keh'chē		
Dancer	—Pum'muk onat	Rising Sun	—Ne'pauz Pash'pish au
Fishermen	—Omaen		
Founder	—Quen oh'tan	Runner	—Quog'quish
Guide	—Mon'cha tea	Sachem	—Sāchim

ANIMALS AND BIRDS

Bear	—mosq	Owl	—oh o' mons
Beaver	—tum'munk	Partridge	—poh poh' kussu
Crow	—kon'kon tu		
Deer	—ah'tuk	Rabbit	—tup'saas
Eagle	—womp sik' kuck	Skunk	—au'sonnch
		Squirrel	—ane'qus
Fox	—wonk'sis	Weasel	—am'ucksh
Moose	—moos	Wildcat	—pus'sough
Muskrat	—mŭsquash	Wolf	—mŭk'quo shim

TREES

Ash	—mo'nŭnks	Oak	—noo ti'mis
Cedar	—chik'kup	Pine	—co'waw

NATURE

Cloud	—ma'toqs	Night	—nu'kon
Day	—ke'sŭk	Rain	—so kan'on
Earth	—oh'-ke	River	—se'pu ash
Fire	—noo'tau	Rock	—qus'sŭk
Forest	—tou'oh ko muk	Sky	—ke'sŭk
		Snow	—ko'ŏn
Ice	—kup'padt	Star	—an'ogqs
Island	—mŭn'noh han	Sun	—ne'pauz
Lake	—nip'pis se	Thunder	—pad toh'quoh han
Lightning	—uk ku tshau' mŭn	Water	—nip'pe
Moon	—mun nan' nock	Waterfall	—paw'tuck
		Wind	—wa'ban
Mountain	—wad'chu		

HANDICRAFT

Arrow	—konh'quodt	Pipe	—ho pu'ŏnck
Bow	—ah'tomp	Quiver	—pe'tan
Canoe	—mish'oon	Wigwam	—we'tu
Moccasins	—mok'kus sin		

Iroquois—New York

PERSONAL AND PLACE NAMES

Among-the-pines	—Kah-ne do' go nah	Bright Sky	—De or oun' yathe
Beautiful Lake	—Skah nyah tei'hyuh	Burning Sky	—Or on hia tek'ha
		Dawn	—Tai'or hen sere
Beautiful Mountain	—On'on tiio	Dropping Snow	—Ga'neh yehs

Early Day	—A wen de'a
Energetic Man	—Ro'heh hon
Flying Messenger	—Daka rih' hon tye
Flying Sun	—Ka ra kon' dye
Good News	—Ka'ri wi yo
Great Night	—So son do' wah
Great Tree Top	—Sha renh ho wa'ne
Growing Flower	—A we'ont
Handsome Lake	—Ga'ne o di yo
Inexhaustible	—Da go no'we da
In the Forest	—Ka ha'gon
In the Pine Woods	—O tah'na gon
Man Who Combs	—Ha yo'went ha
Large Mouth	—Ho'sa ho ho
Leader	—Kon'wa hen deks
Long Feather	—Sa'ha whe
Looks Both Ways	—Tah kah'enh yunk
Mossy Place	—Tya wen'hen thon
Moving Flowers	—A we i'non
Music-maker	—Ha'ie no nis
On the Watch	—Da at'ga dose
Open Door	—Do ne ho'ga' weh
Opening Through the Woods	—Da yo ha gwen'da
Over the Creek	—Ska-no'-wun-de
Place of the Echo	—Da wa'da o da yo
Resting on It	—Tesh kah' hea
She Is Alert	—Ga nonk we' non
She Shakes the Trees	—Ga on da'was
Small Speech	—So a e wa'ah
Watcher	—Ya le wah noh
Wearing a Hatchet on His Belt	—Sah ha'hih
Woodsman	—Hoh squa sa ga'dah

ANIMALS AND BIRDS

Bear	—ya'o gah	Owl	—o ho'wa
Beaver	—jon i'to	Panther	—ha'ace
Crow	—ga'ga	Partridge	—kwa e'sea
Deer	—ska non'do	Robin	—jis ko'ko
Duck	—so'ra	Squirrel	—ar o se'a
Eagle	—otc an'yca	Turkey	—so'hont
Fox	—jit'so	Turtle	—ha nu'na
Moose	—o yan do'ne	Wolf	—hy ty o'ne
Muskrat	—no'ji	Woodpecker	—kwaa

NATURE

Day	—an'da	Sky	—ot sha'ta
Earth	—o eh'da	Snow	—o'kah
Fire	—o gis'ta	Star	—o jish an'da
Forest	—ga'ha da	Sun	—An da'Ka ga' gwa
Ice	—o we'za		
Moon	—So a'Ka ga' gwa	Water	—o na ga'nose
		Wind	—ga'-o
Mountain	—ga a nun'da	Winter	—ko sa'ge
Night	—so'a		

TREES

Oak	—ki-on da'ga	Pine	—o'staa

HANDICRAFT

Bow	—wa a'no	Moccasins	—ah'ta qua o weh
Canoe	—ga o'wo		
Head-dress	—gus'to weh	Pipe	—ah so qua'ta
Longhouse	—ga'no sote	Wampum	—ote ko'a
		War club	—ka ja'wa

Lenape or Delaware—Pennsylvania, New Jersey, New York, and Delaware

PERSONAL NAMES

Bird	—Cho'le na	Medicine	
Flower	—Woa'twēs	Man	—Quecksa'piet
Good; Hand-		Sachem	—Sa ki'ma
some	—Wu lis'so	White Sun-	
		shine	—Woa pa'sum

BIRDS AND ANIMALS

Bluebird	—chi ma'lus	Muskrat	—chu as'kwis
Buffalo	—si'si li ti	Rabbit	—wa'pach
Cricket	—ze'lo ze los		tques
Eagle	—who a pah	Red squirrel	—wis'a wa nik
	lan'ne	Weasel	—to hum'mish
Lizard	—mok do'mus	Woodchuck	—mon'ach gen

HANDICRAFT

Arrow	—al'lunth	Wampum	—keekq
Canoe	—am o'chol	Wigwam	—wik'wam

Cherokee—Virginia, North and South Carolina, Georgia Alabama, Kentucky, and Tennessee

PERSONAL AND PLACE NAMES

Amiable; gen-		Bear Place	—Ya'na hi
tle; attrac-		Beautiful	
tive	—Ga li'la hi	Place	—Wa lu hi'yi
Bear	—Ya'na	Bird Place	—Tsis kwa'hi

Black Fox	—I na'li	In the Woods	—A da'hi
Blossom	—Ad si'la	Lookout Place	—A ha hi'na
Butterfly	—Ka ma'ma	Midday Sun	—Nun-da ye'li
Council Place	—Uni la wi' sti	My Home	—Ah we na'sa
		Peacemaker	—Ga hi sti'ski
Eagle Place	—Wa hi li'yi	Place of	
Enchanted Lake	—A ta ga'hi	Friends	—Un a li'yi
		Rock Ledge	—Us ta wa'li
Excels All Others	—Tsun ga'ni	Squirrel	—Sa la'li
		Star	—Na'kwi si
Expert	—Si na'sta	They Run to	
First in the Dance	—A yun'li	Her	—Ga ti'tla
		Town House	—Ga ti'yi
Forest Water	—A ma da'hi	Water Side	—Am ai yul'ti
In the Oaks	—Ta la'hi	Young Beaver	—Ta yan i'ta
In the Pines	—Na tsi'hi	Young Deer	—Awi ni'tä

Choctaw—Mississippi and Alabama

PERSONAL NAMES

Blue-eyed	—Ok'ta lon li	Echo	—Ho'ba chee
Careful	—A'hah ah ni	Helper	—A pe la'chi
Curly-headed	—Yush'bo nu li	Perseverance	—A'chun an chi
		Merry	—Yuk'pa
Eagle-eyed	—Nish'kin ha lu pa		

ANIMALS AND BIRDS

Bear	—ni'ta	Deer	—i'si
Beaver	—kin'ta	Duck	—han'kho bak
Buffalo	—yan'nash	Eagle	—ta la'ko
Chipmunk	—chin'i sa	Elk	—i si'chi to
Crow	—fa'la	Fox	—chu'la

Opossum	—shu'ka ta	Raccoon	—shau'i
Owl	—o'pa	Skunk	—ko'ni
Panther	—ko'i	Wolf	—na sho'ba
Rabbit	—chuk'fi		

HANDICRAFT

Arrow	—os'ki	Moccasins	—shu'lush
Bow	—po lo'ma	Pipe	—os ku'la
Canoe	—i ti ku'la	Wigwam	—a te'pa

NATURE

Cloud	—a ho shon'ti	Rain	—um'ba
Day	—ni'tak	River	—chu'li
Earth	—yak'ni	Rock	—ta'li
Fire	—lu'ak	Sky	—shu'tik
Forest	—i ti a nun'ka	Snow	—ok tu'sha
Ice	—ok'ti	Star	—fi'chik
Lake	—hai'yih	Sun	—ha'shi
Mountain	—na'nih	Thunder	—hi'lo ha
Night	—ni'nak	Water	—fi'chak
Noon	—ha'shi	Wind	—fi o'pa

TREES

Ash	—shi-nap	Hickory	—uk sak'a pi
Birch	—o pah ak'sun	Oak	—chi'sha
Cedar	—chu'a la	Pine	—ti'ak
Cottonwood	—ash um ba'la	Willow	—ta ko in'sha

Ojibwa (Chippewa)—Illinois, Michigan, Minnesota and Canada

PERSONAL AND PLACE NAMES

At the Foot of the Mountain	—Ni'sa tin	In the Middle of the Forest	—Na'wa kwa
Butterfly	—Mem'en gwa	Island Forest	—Mi ni'tik
By the Lake	—Chick'a ga mi	It Begins to Dawn	—Bid'a ban
Dancer	—Na'mid	Little Star	—A nou gons'
Dreamer	—En a ban' dang	Lodge	—Wig'i wam
Eagle	—Mi gi si'	Log House	—Wa kai gan'
Eastern or Morning Star	—Wa'ba nang	Maple Forest	—Ma'na ki ki
		Near the Forest	—Chi ga kwa'
Fire Fly	—Wah'wah tas see	On the Shore	—A ga ming'
In a Forest	—No pim ing'	Red Cedar	—Mish'wa wak
		Rest	—An'web e win
		Star	—A nang'
		Woods	—Mi'tig wa ki

ANIMALS AND BIRDS

Bear	—nah'hak	Panther	—ke'che kak' shu gans
Beaver	—ah'mik		
Duck	—she'sheeb	Otter	—nee'gig
Crow	—abn'dak	Owl	—koo koo ku' hoo
Deer	—wa waush ka'she		
		Rabbit	—wah'boos
Eagle	—me'gee see	Skunk	—zhe'gaug
Elk	—ah'tik	Weasel	—shin'goos
Fox	—wah'goosh	Wolf	—ma'heen gun
Moose	—moons		

TREES

Ash	—ah ge'mauk	Oak	—me ti goo'
Cedar	—kee'zhik		meezh
Birch	—wig'wahs	Pine	—shing'wauk
Hickory	—me tig wau' bank	Spruce	—shing'oob

Dakota (Sioux)—Minnesota, Montana, Nebraska, North Dakota, South Dakota and Wyoming

PERSONAL AND PLACE NAMES

A Leader	—Wa ki con'za
At the River	—Wa zi ya'ta
At the Woods	—Chan ya'ta
Back from a River	—He ya'ta
Bear with a Big Voice	—Ma'to po tan' ka
Black Buffalo	—Ta'tan ka
Black Crow	—Kan'gi sha pa
Black Eye	—I sta'sha pa
Blue Jay	—Te'te ni ca
Blue Sky	—Makh pe'ya to
By the Side of a Stream	—Wa'kpi ca da
Dewdrops	—Chu'ma ni
Flute Player	—Cho'tan ka shka ta
Little Big Man	—Cha sa ton'ga
Marksman	—Wa o'ka

Medicine Bear	—Ma'to wa kan
Medicine Lodge	—Ti'pi wa kan
One Who Helps	—Wa wo'ki ye
One Who Is Skillful	—A khi ko'ka
Pretty Rock	—In yan was'te
Red Cloud	—Ma hpi ya' ni ta
Red Dog	—Shun'ka lu ta
Red Fox	—To'ka la lu ta
Red Lodge	—Ti'pi sa
Red Plume	—Wi'ya ka sha
Running Antelope	—Ta to'ka in yan'ka
Shooter	—Wa ku'ta

Pictographs of Dakota Names.

Sitting Crow —Kan gi i'ys tan'ka
Soft Snow —Wa'hi hi
Story-teller —Wa wo ya'ka
Teacher —Wa on spe'ki ya
Trustworthy —Zon'ta
Two Strikes —Nom'pa ap a

Where the Sun Sets —Wi'yo pi ya ta
White Hawk —Che tan'ska
Worker —Wo wa'shi
Yellow Bear —Ma to'zi
Yellow Hair —Pa'hi win
Yellow Hawk—Che tan'zhi

ANIMALS AND BIRDS

Antelope —ta to'ka dan
Beaver —cha'pa
Buffalo —pte
Buffalo Bull —ta tan'ka
Coyote —ma shle'cha
Deer —ta'hcha
Eagle, golden —wan bu li'
Elk —he ha'ka
Fox —shon ghi'la
Grizzly Bear —ma to'
Moose —ta

Mountain Lion —i gumu'tan ka
Owl —hin han'
Rabbit —ma shtin'shka
Rabbit, Jack —ma stin'ca
Skunk —man ka'
Weasel —ka za'za pi
Wildcat —i gumu'gule za
Wolf —shon zuma' ni tu

HANDICRAFT

Arrow —wa hin'kpe
Arrow point —wi suma'hi
Bow —i ta'zi pa
Moccasins —han'pa

Parfleche —wi zi'pan
Pipe —chan'non pa
Quiver —wan'zhu
Tent —ti'pi

NATURE

Cloud —ma'hpi ya
Day —an pe'tu
Earth —ma'ka

Fire —pe'ta
Forest —chon wo he shma

Ice	—cha'gha	Sky	—ma'hpi ya
Lake	—hule	Snow	—wa
Moon	—han he'pi wi	Star	—wi cha'hpi
Mountain	—pa ha'	Sun	—wi
Night	—han he'pi	Thunder	—wa'kin yan
Rain	—man gha'zhu	Water	—mi ni'
River	—wa kpa'la	Wind	—ta te'
Rock	—in'yan		

TREES

Ash	—pse'htin	Oak	—u'ta hu
Cedar	—han te'	Pine	—wa zi'
Cottonwood	—wa'gha chan	Willow	—wa hpe'po pa

Omaha—Iowa, Kansas, Missouri and Nebraska

PERSONAL AND PLACE NAMES

Among the Elms	—E'zhon ut	Eagle Chief	—Zi tha'ga ni ge
Arrow Chief	—Mon e'ga hi	Eagle Person	—Ai tha'ni ka
Bear	—Mon'chu	Elk	—O'pa
Big Little Sister	—Wihe'ton ga	Facing the Wind	—Ki mon'hon
Black Elk	—On pon'sa he	Fire Chief	—Pe de'ga he
Black Wolf	—Shon ga'sab he	Graceful Walker	—Mon'ke ne
Brown Hair	—Hin'zega	Gray Owl	—Wa po'ga
By the Brook	—Wa shid'ka ata	Gray Wolf	—Shon'ton ga
		Green Leaf	—A bey'tu
By the Lake	—Ney'a ti	He Who Is Feared	—Non pe wa' tha
Chief	—Ga'ne ge		
Coyote	—Mi'ka si	Home Builder	—I'ni a bi

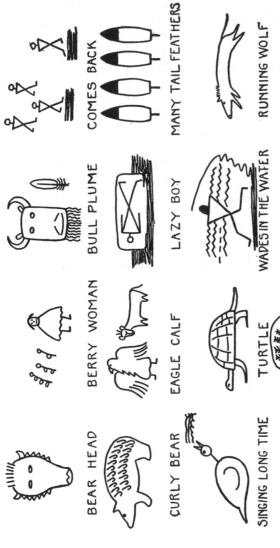

COMES BACK

MANY TAIL FEATHERS

RUNNING WOLF

YELLOW HEAD

BULL PLUME

LAZY BOY

WADES IN THE WATER

WOLF ROBE

BERRY WOMAN

EAGLE CALF

TURTLE

WHITE QUIVER

BEAR HEAD

CURLY BEAR

SINGING LONG TIME

WHITE GRASS

Pictographs of Blackfoot Names

Horse Leader—Shon ge hon'
    ga
Little Brother—Ka'ge zhin ga
Little Cook —Whon'zhin
    ga
Little Eagle —Zitha'zhin
    ga
Lone Cedar
 Tree —Ma si'ton
One Who Is
 Loved —Thae ge tha'
    bi

One Who
 Shoots —Wa ke'da
South Wind —A ka'wi
Sun Woman —Mi'he wi
Thunder Bird—Wa gi'on
Traveler or
 Wanderer —Uga shon'ton
Victory
 Woman —Wa'te win
Wind Maiden—Ta'de win
Wisdom —Wa zhin'ska
White Buffalo—Te'thon
White Eagle —Zitha'ska

Blackfoot—Montana

PERSONAL NAMES

Barred Eagle —Kik'si pa pe'
    ta
Bear's Head —Caw yu'to
    con
Berry Woman—Mi na'ku
Big Painted
 Lodge —Wi'ma cats
    co con
Bull Plume —Sta'me ches
    sa'pu a
Butterfly —A'po ni
Comes Back —Pa yo'ta po
    ma'ca
Curly Bear —Ni'na caw yu
    su ches
Eagle Calf —Ni'na pe'ta
    mis ta

Eagle Woman—Pe'ta ki
Feather
 Woman —So'at sa ki
Fisher
 Woman —Pi'na to ya ki
Good Leader
 Woman —Ahk su tah'
    ma ki
Kit-fox —Sin o'pah
Lazy Boy —Pi'ki p ck mi
    pe
Many Tail
 Feathers —A co su'wa
    ches mi
Pretty Head —A na'to ki
Red Cedar —Six in o'ko
Rosebud —Ki'niks

Running
  Wolf   —A pe'so muc
              ca
Singing Long
  Time   —Me sa'min ka
              ki
Star   —Ko'ka to si
Sun Woman —Na'to sa ki
Turtle   —Spo'yie
Two Guns   —Na'to ki na

Wades in
  Water   —So'yi
Water Bird   —Sit'so a ki
White Grass —A po to ye'si
White Quiver—Ches'ches no
              pa
Wolf Robe   —Co ye see'con
Yellow Head —Wi'ta co to
              con

ANIMALS AND BIRDS

Antelope   —sa'ki o wa ka
              si
Beaver   —ksis ksta'ki
Buffalo   —i ni'wa
Coyote   —ksi na'o
Crow   —mai sto'
Deer   —is si ko tu'yi
Eagle, bald   —tsik ki kyi'ni
Eagle, golden —pe'ta
Elk   —pun u'ka
Fox   —ie ku tsi si'no
              pa
Grizzly Bear —kyai'u
Horse   —pun nu ka'mi
              ta

Moose   —sik ki tsi su'
Mountain
  Lion   —o mah ka tai'
              yu
Owl   —si'pis to
Porcupine   —kai i'skahp
Rabbit, cotton
  tail   —si ka'tus ta
Rabbit, jack —o mah ka tsis
              ta
Skunk   —a'pi kai yi
Weasel   —o'ta
Wildcat   —na tai'yu
Wolf   —ma ku'yi

HANDICRAFT

Arrow   —aps'si
Arrow point —ksis sa ko'pun
Bow   —na'ma
Moccasins   —a tsi'kin
Quiver   —pun no pa'
              tsis

Shield   —a'o tan
Spear   —sa pa pis ta'
              tsis
Tipi   —nui'yis

NATURE

Cloud	—so kis tsi ko'	Rain	—so'to
Day	—ksis tsi ko'	River	—ni i'tuh ta
Earth	—chah ko'	Rock	—oh ku'tuk
Fire	—is'tsi	Sky	—spoh'tuh ku
Forest	—a'tsi was ku	Snow	—ko'nis ko
Ice	—kun	Star	—ka ka'to si
Lake	—o'mah si ki mi	Sun	—na to'si
Moon	—ko ko mi'kye	Thunder	—ksis tsi kom'
Mountain	—mis tak'	Water	—oh kiu'
Night	—ko'ko	Wind	—su po'

TREES

Ash	—ka puk'si	Cottonwood	—ni'ta pis tsis
Cedar	—oh ki ni mim' oh tok	Pine	—puh'tok
		Willow	—ma now'

Hopi—Arizona

PERSONAL AND PLACE NAMES

Butterfly Girl	—Po le ma'na	Red Head	—Pa la'ko te
Eagle Claws	—Qua ku'ku	Strong Deer	—Ho'no vi
Eagle Hunter	—Ma'kya	Spring of the	
Flute Maid	—Len ma'na	Sun	—Tawa'pah
Girl of the		Terrace of the	
Sun	—Tawa'ma na	Winds	—Huh'kwat
Little Rabbit	—Kah'ya zhe		we
Rain Clouds		White Flower	—Ko tsa'si
Coming		Yellow Bird	—Sik ya'tsi
Down	—Ha ha'wi		

Navajo—Arizona, New Mexico and Utah

PERSONAL NAMES

Blue Bird	—Do li'	Little Star	—So'ya zhe
Butterfly	—Ka lug'	Medicine	—Ha ta'li
Chief	—Nah'tah ni	Man	
Flower	—Bi lot'ka hi	Morning Star	—So'tso
Little Chief	—Nah'tah ni yez'zi	Sunlight	—Shau'din

ANIMALS AND BIRDS

Antelope	—ju'di	Grizzly bear	—sush
Beaver	—cha	Mountain	
Buffalo	—a ya'ni	Lion	—nash tu i'tso
Coyote	—mai	Owl	—nas'cha
Crow	—ga'ge	Rabbit,	
Deer	—bin	cottontail	—gah
Eagle, golden	—a tsa'	Rabbit, jack	—gah'tso
Elk	—na a'zi si	Skunk	—wo li'zhi
		Wolf	—mai i'tso

NATURE

Cloud	—kas	River	—to
Day	—jin	Rock	—tse
Earth	—ni ho es tsan	Sky	—ya'dilh kih
Fire	—kun	Snow	—yas
Ice	—tquin	Star	—son
Lake	—to	Sun	—che ho na ai'
Moon	—kle ho na ai'	Thunder	—i'ni
Mountain	—tzilh	Water	—to
Night	—kle'je	Wind	—nil'chi
Rain	—nit'sun		

TREES

Cedar	—gad	Pine	—ndish chi'
Cottonwood	—tis	Willow	—ka'i
Oak	—che'chil		

Hupa—California

ANIMALS AND BIRDS

Beaver	—chwa'ai	Mink	—sah'kyo
Black Bear	—sats	Owl	—mis'kyi lo
Coyote	—hon'tehl to	Rabbit	—thoh me'we
Deer	—kihl'hla han	Raccoon	—min na'hoe
Duck	—na to'ai	Salmon	—ha'lo ke
Eagle	—tis'mil	Skunk	—hol'chi
Fish	—to'nai	Squirrel	—mik'kye nes
Grizzly Bear	—mi kys'wi	Wolf	—kihl na'til

HANDICRAFT

Arrow	—na'tses	Moccasins	—yi'chit tal
Bow	—tshihl'tin	Paddle	—kit'to
Canoe	—me'til	Pipe	—kin'ai kyan
House	—hon'ta		

NATURE

Day	—chens	River	—ha'ni
Earth	—nin nis'an	Snow	—nun'til
Fire	—hon	Star	—tsen
Ice	—nun hos'tin	Sun	—hiva chen' hwa
Lake	—mun'ket		
Moon	—hwa	Tree	—kin
Night	—hat'tle	Water	—tan'nan
Rain	—na ai'ya	Wind	—tes'che

TREES

Alder	—keohw	Douglas	
Ash	—cha che'len	Spruce	—nis'kin
Cedar	—i'le tel	Maple	—kit'an
Digger Pine	—na'te tl	Oak	—nihl'tak
Dogwood	—tah'ma a	Redwood	—koh kyo
		Yew	—koh

Yakima—Oregon and Washington

ANIMALS AND BIRDS

Antelope	—chat wi li'	Horse	—ko si'
Beaver	—yu'ha	Mountain	
Buffalo	—mus'us tsin	Lion	—kai'ya wi
Coyote	—spil yai'	Owl	—a'mash
Crow	—a'a	Rabbit,	—aiqs
Deer	—ya'mash	cottontail	
Eagle, golden	—hwai ya'ma	Rabbit, jack	—wi la'lik
Elk	—wi ya pu'nit	Skunk	—ti'skai
Fox	—lu'tsa	Weasel	—wa'tai
Grizzly Bear	—tu'it tash	Wildcat	—pi'chum
		Wolf	—lal la'wish

NATURE

Cloud	—shu'wa tash	River	—chi at'wan
Day	—hlki	Rock	—pshwa
Earth	—ti'cham	Sky	—to'hun
Fire	—i'luqsh	Snow	—pu i
Ice	—ti'tuh	Star	—has'lu
Lake	—wa'tam	Sun	—an
Moon	—al lu hai'uh	Thunder	—i num'hla
Mountain	—ni'pot	Water	—chi'ish
Night	—stat'pa	Wind	—wi sla'tsaik
Rain	—tah'tah		

TREES

Cedar	—nan nuk'	Pine	—ta'pash
Oak	—tsu'nips	Willow	—ti'tahsh

American State Names of Indian Origin

ALABAMA—From Alibamu, the name of a Muskoghean tribe said to mean "Those Who Clear Land for Agricultural Purposes."

ARIZONA—From the Papago word Arizonac, which probably means "Small springs."

ARKANSAS—From Akansea, a name applied by the French to the Quapaw, a tribe whose name means "Downstream People."

CONNECTICUT—Quonoktacut, meaning "River whose water is driven by tides or winds."

DAKOTA (North and South)—Tribal name of the Sioux, meaning "Allies."

IDAHO—From a word said to mean "Gem of the mountains."

ILLINOIS—From Illinek, meaning "Men," the name of a confederacy of Algonkian tribes.

IOWA—The name of a tribe meaning "Sleepy Ones."

KENTUCKY—Said to be derived from the word "kenta," meaning "field or meadow."

MASSACHUSETTS—The name of an Algonkian tribe meaning "At or About the Great Hill."

MICHIGAN—From the Michigamea, a tribe of the Illinois confederacy whose name means "Great water."

MINNESOTA—From a Dakota word meaning "whitish or sky-tinted water."

MISSISSIPPI—From the Algonkian words *misi* ("great") and *sipi* ("water").

MISSOURI—From the name of a tribe meaning "Great Muddy," which refers to the river.

NEBRASKA—From an Oto word meaning "broad water."

NEW MEXICO—From the name of an Aztec god, Mexitli.

OHIO—Derived from an Iroquois word meaning "beautiful river."

OKLAHOMA—A Choctaw word meaning "Red People."

TENNESSEE—From Tanasi, the name of a Cherokee settlement. Its meaning is unknown.

TEXAS—The name of a group of tribes meaning "Friends" or "Allies."

UTAH—From the tribal name of the Ute, the meaning of which is unknown.

WISCONSIN—The name applied to a group of tribes living on the Wisconsin River. Its meaning is unknown.

WYOMING—From the name of a Lenape village in Pennsylvania called "M'cheuwomink," meaning "Upon the Great Plain."

Bibliography

THE following list is not intended as a complete bibliography of the subject. It includes only those books likely to be of interest to boys and girls, teachers, scout and camp leaders.

I. INDIANS OF THE UNITED STATES

CATLIN, GEORGE, *North American Indians.* 2 vols. Leary, Stuart & Company.

FLETCHER, ALICE C., and LA FLESCHE, FRANCIS, *The Omaha Tribe* (27th Annual Report, B.A.E.). Government Printing Office.

GODDARD, PLINY E., *Indians of the Northwest Coast.* American Museum of Natural History, New York.
Indians of the Southwest. American Museum of Natural History, New York.

GRINNELL, GEORGE B., *The Cheyenne Indians.* 2 vols. Yale University Press.

HOUGH, WALTER, *The Hopi Indians.* Torch Press.

KROEBER, A. L., *Handbook of the Indians of California* (Bulletin 78, B.A.E.). Government Printing Office.

LINTON, RALPH, *Indians of the Chicago Region.* Field Museum, Chicago.

LIPPS, O. H., *The Navajos.* Torch Press.

McCLINTOCK, WALTER, *Old Indian Trails.* Houghton Mifflin & Company.

MORGAN, LEWIS H., *The League of the Ho-de-no-sau-nee, or Iroquois.* Dodd, Mead & Company.

PARKER, ARTHUR C., *Indian How Book.* Doran & Co.

PERROT, NICHOLAS, *The Indian Tribes of the Mississippi Valley and the Region of the Great Lakes*. Translated and Edited by Emma H. Blair. Arthur H. Clark Company.

RADIN, PAUL, *The Story of the American Indian*. Boni & Liveright.

SKINNER, ALANSON, *The Indians of Greater New York*. Torch Press.

SWANTON, JOHN R., *The Indian Tribes of the Lower Mississippi Valley and Adjacent Coast of the Gulf of Mexico* (Bulletin 43, B.A.E.). Government Printing Office.

VERRILL, A. HYATT, *The American Indian*. Appleton.

WILSON, MINNIE M., *The Seminoles of Florida*. Moffat, Yard & Company.

WISSLER, CLARK, *Indians of the Plains*. American Museum of Natural History, New York.

II. INDIAN CAMP FIRE STORIES

Legends and adventure stories which may be told almost exactly as they are written.

BORLAND, HAL. G., *Rocky Mountain Tipi Tales*. Doubleday, Page & Company.

DE HUFF, E. W., *Taytay's Tales*. Harcourt, Brace & Company.

EASTMAN, C. A., *Wigwam Evenings*.

GARLAND, HAMLIN, *The Book of the American Indian*. Harpers.

GRINNELL, GEORGE B., *Blackfeet Indian Stories*. Scribners.
Blackfoot Lodge Tales. Scribners.
Pawnee Hero Stories. Scribners.

LINDERMAN, FRANK B., *Indian Old Man Stories*. Scribners.
Indian Why Stories. Scribners.
Kootenai Why Stories. Scribners.

LUMMIS, CHARLES F., *Pueblo Indian Folk Stories*. Scribners.

NUSBAUM, A., *The Seven Cities of Cibola*. Putnams.

PARKER, ARTHUR C., *Skunny Wundy*. Doran.

SCHULTZ, JAMES W., *Blackfeet Tales of Glacier National Park.*
Houghton Mifflin Company.
Friends of My Life as an Indian. Houghton Mifflin Company.
WILSON, GILBERT L., *Indian Hero Tales.* Ginn & Company.

III. STORIES OF INDIAN LIFE

BANDELIER, A. F. A., *The Delight Makers.* Dodd, Mead & Company.
CURTIS, EDWARD S., *Indian Days of the Long Ago.* World Book Company.
In the Land of the Head Hunters. World Book Company.
EASTMAN, C. A., *Indian Boyhood.* Little, Brown & Company.
GRINNELL, GEORGE B., *When Buffalo Ran.* Yale University Press.
JENKS, ERNEST A., *Childhood of Ji-Shib the Ojibwa.* American Thresherman, Madison, Wis.
LAING, MARY, *Hero of the Long House.* World Book Company.
MORAN, GEORGE N., *Kwahu, the Hopi Boy.* American Book Company.
SCHULTZ, JAMES WILLARD, *Apauk, Caller of Buffalo.* Houghton Mifflin Company.
Bird Woman. Houghton Mifflin Company.
My Life as an Indian. Houghton Mifflin Company.
Running Eagle, the Warrior Girl. Houghton, Mifflin Company.
Sinopah, the Indian Boy. Houghton Mifflin Company.
With the Indians in the Rockies. Houghton Mifflin Company.
SNEDDIN, G. S., *Docas, The Indian Boy of Santa Clara.* D. C. Heath & Company.
WILSON, GILBERT L., *Goodbird the Indian.* Revell.

IV. BIOGRAPHIES OF FAMOUS INDIANS

DRAKE, F. S., *Indian History for Young Folks.* Harpers.
EASTMAN, CHARLES A., *Indian Heroes and Great Chieftains.* Little, Brown & Company.

HOWARD, O. O., *Famous Indian Chiefs I have Known*. Century Company.

JOHNSTON, C. H. L., *Famous Indian Chiefs*. The Page Company.

SABIN, E. L., *Boy's Book of Indian Warriors and Heroic Indian Women*. Jacobs & Company.

SWEETSER, KATE, *The Book of Indian Braves*. Harpers.

V. GOVERNMENT RELATIONS

CRANE, LEO, *Indians of the Enchanted Desert*. Little, Brown & Company.

HUMPHREY, S. K., *The Indian Dispossessed*. Little, Brown & Company.

JACKSON, HELEN HUNT, *A Century of Dishonor*. Little, Brown & Company.

LEUPP, FRANCIS E., *The Indian and His Problem*. Scribners.

LINDQUIST, G. E. E., *The Red Man in the United States*. Doran.

MERIAM, LEWIS, *The Problem of Indian Administration*. Johns Hopkins Press.

VI. MUSIC

BURTON, FREDERIC R., *American Primitive Music*. Dodd, Mead & Company.

CURTIS, NATALIE, *The Indian's Book*. Harpers.

DENSMORE, FRANCES, *Chippewa Music*, 2 vols. (Bulletins 48 and 53. B.A.E.). Government Printing Office.

Mandan and Hidatsa Music (Bulletin 80, B.A.E.). Government Printing Office.

Northern Ute Music (Bulletin 75, B.A.E.). Government Printing Office.

Teton Sioux Music (Bulletin 61, B.A.E.). Government Printing Office.

The American Indians and their Music. Woman's Press.

FLETCHER, ALICE C., *Indian Games and Dances with Native Songs.* C. C. Birchard.
Indian Story and Song from North America. Small, Maynard & Company.

VII. INDIAN POETRY

AUSTIN, MARY, *The American Rhythm.* Harcourt, Brace & Company.
BARNES, NELLIE, *American Indian Love Lyrics.* Macmillan.
CRONYN, C. W., *The Path of the Rainbow.* Boni & Liveright.

VIII. INDIAN PLAYS

ALEXANDER, HARTLEY B., *Manito Masks.* Macmillan.
AUSTIN, MARY, *The Arrow Maker.* Duffield & Company.
LORD, K., "The Raven Man," in *Plays for School and Camp.* Little, Brown & Company.
MACKAY, CONSTANCE D., "The Vanishing Race" and "The Passing of Hiawatha," in *Plays of the Pioneers.*

IX. INDIAN CRAFTS

JAMES, GEORGE W., *Indian Basketry.* Malkan & Company.
Indian Blankets and their Makers. A. C. McClurg & Company.
SETON, ERNEST THOMPSON, *Book of Woodcraft.* Doubleday, Page & Company.
TODD, MATTIE P., *Hand Loom Weaving.* Rand, McNally & Company.
WHITE, MARY, *How to Make Baskets.* Doubleday, Page & Company.

WISSLER, CLARK, *Indian Beadwork*. American Museum of Natural History, New York.

X. SIGN LANGUAGE

SETON, ERNEST THOMPSON, *Sign Talk*. Doubleday, Page & Company.

TOMKINS, WILLIAM, *Indian Sign Language*. Published by the author, San Diego, Cal.

XI. REFERENCE

Bureau of American Ethnology—Reports and Bulletins.
These publications, issued during the past fifty years, contain a wealth of information about the Indians. Most of them are out of print, but complete sets may be consulted in nearly all libraries and museums.

Bureau of American Ethnology—*Handbook of American Indians*, 2 vols. (Bulletin 30, B.A.E.). Government Printing Office.
An encyclopedia of Indian life and customs in so far as modern ethnological research has disclosed them.

CURTIS, EDWARD S., *The North American Indian* (20 volumes when completed).
The volumes so far published of this magnificent work may be consulted only at the larger libraries and museums. Each volume contains between one hundred and fifty and two hundred of Mr. Curtis's splendid pictures of Indian life, which offer many suggestions for costume-making and for arranging scenes in plays and pageants.

INDEX

Index

A CATALOG OF SELECTED DOVER
BOOKS IN ALL FIELDS OF INTEREST

CONCERNING THE SPIRITUAL IN ART, Wassily Kandinsky. Pioneering work by father of abstract art. Thoughts on color theory, nature of art. Analysis of earlier masters. 12 illustrations. 80pp. of text. 5⅜ x 8½.   23411-8

ANIMALS: 1,419 Copyright-Free Illustrations of Mammals, Birds, Fish, Insects, etc., Jim Harter (ed.). Clear wood engravings present, in extremely lifelike poses, over 1,000 species of animals. One of the most extensive pictorial sourcebooks of its kind. Captions. Index. 284pp. 9 x 12.   23766-4

CELTIC ART: The Methods of Construction, George Bain. Simple geometric techniques for making Celtic interlacements, spirals, Kells-type initials, animals, humans, etc. Over 500 illustrations. 160pp. 9 x 12. (Available in U.S. only.)   22923-8

AN ATLAS OF ANATOMY FOR ARTISTS, Fritz Schider. Most thorough reference work on art anatomy in the world. Hundreds of illustrations, including selections from works by Vesalius, Leonardo, Goya, Ingres, Michelangelo, others. 593 illustrations. 192pp. 7⅛ x 10¼.   20241-0

CELTIC HAND STROKE-BY-STROKE (Irish Half-Uncial from "The Book of Kells"): An Arthur Baker Calligraphy Manual, Arthur Baker. Complete guide to creating each letter of the alphabet in distinctive Celtic manner. Covers hand position, strokes, pens, inks, paper, more. Illustrated. 48pp. 8¼ x 11.   24336-2

EASY ORIGAMI, John Montroll. Charming collection of 32 projects (hat, cup, pelican, piano, swan, many more) specially designed for the novice origami hobbyist. Clearly illustrated easy-to-follow instructions insure that even beginning papercrafters will achieve successful results. 48pp. 8¼ x 11.   27298-2

THE COMPLETE BOOK OF BIRDHOUSE CONSTRUCTION FOR WOODWORKERS, Scott D. Campbell. Detailed instructions, illustrations, tables. Also data on bird habitat and instinct patterns. Bibliography. 3 tables. 63 illustrations in 15 figures. 48pp. 5¼ x 8½.   24407-5

BLOOMINGDALE'S ILLUSTRATED 1886 CATALOG: Fashions, Dry Goods and Housewares, Bloomingdale Brothers. Famed merchants' extremely rare catalog depicting about 1,700 products: clothing, housewares, firearms, dry goods, jewelry, more. Invaluable for dating, identifying vintage items. Also, copyright-free graphics for artists, designers. Co-published with Henry Ford Museum & Greenfield Village. 160pp. 8¼ x 11.   25780-0

HISTORIC COSTUME IN PICTURES, Braun & Schneider. Over 1,450 costumed figures in clearly detailed engravings–from dawn of civilization to end of 19th century. Captions. Many folk costumes. 256pp. 8⅜ x 11¾.   23150-X

STICKLEY CRAFTSMAN FURNITURE CATALOGS, Gustav Stickley and L. & J. G. Stickley. Beautiful, functional furniture in two authentic catalogs from 1910. 594 illustrations, including 277 photos, show settles, rockers, armchairs, reclining chairs, bookcases, desks, tables. 183pp. 6½ x 9¼.   23838-5

AMERICAN LOCOMOTIVES IN HISTORIC PHOTOGRAPHS: 1858 to 1949, Ron Ziel (ed.). A rare collection of 126 meticulously detailed official photographs, called "builder portraits," of American locomotives that majestically chronicle the rise of steam locomotive power in America. Introduction. Detailed captions. xi+ 129pp. 9 x 12.   27393-8

AMERICA'S LIGHTHOUSES: An Illustrated History, Francis Ross Holland, Jr. Delightfully written, profusely illustrated fact-filled survey of over 200 American lighthouses since 1716. History, anecdotes, technological advances, more. 240pp. 8 x 10¾.
25576-X

TOWARDS A NEW ARCHITECTURE, Le Corbusier. Pioneering manifesto by founder of "International School." Technical and aesthetic theories, views of industry, economics, relation of form to function, "mass-production split" and much more. Profusely illustrated. 320pp. 6⅛ x 9¼. (Available in U.S. only.)   25023-7

HOW THE OTHER HALF LIVES, Jacob Riis. Famous journalistic record, exposing poverty and degradation of New York slums around 1900, by major social reformer. 100 striking and influential photographs. 233pp. 10 x 7⅞.   22012-5

FRUIT KEY AND TWIG KEY TO TREES AND SHRUBS, William M. Harlow. One of the handiest and most widely used identification aids. Fruit key covers 120 deciduous and evergreen species; twig key 160 deciduous species. Easily used. Over 300 photographs. 126pp. 5⅜ x 8½.   20511-8

COMMON BIRD SONGS, Dr. Donald J. Borror. Songs of 60 most common U.S. birds: robins, sparrows, cardinals, bluejays, finches, more—arranged in order of increasing complexity. Up to 9 variations of songs of each species.
Cassette and manual 99911-4

ORCHIDS AS HOUSE PLANTS, Rebecca Tyson Northen. Grow cattleyas and many other kinds of orchids—in a window, in a case, or under artificial light. 63 illustrations. 148pp. 5⅜ x 8½.   23261-1

MONSTER MAZES, Dave Phillips. Masterful mazes at four levels of difficulty. Avoid deadly perils and evil creatures to find magical treasures. Solutions for all 32 exciting illustrated puzzles. 48pp. 8¼ x 11.   26005-4

MOZART'S DON GIOVANNI (DOVER OPERA LIBRETTO SERIES), Wolfgang Amadeus Mozart. Introduced and translated by Ellen H. Bleiler. Standard Italian libretto, with complete English translation. Convenient and thoroughly portable—an ideal companion for reading along with a recording or the performance itself. Introduction. List of characters. Plot summary. 121pp. 5¼ x 8½.   24944-1

TECHNICAL MANUAL AND DICTIONARY OF CLASSICAL BALLET, Gail Grant. Defines, explains, comments on steps, movements, poses and concepts. 15-page pictorial section. Basic book for student, viewer. 127pp. 5⅜ x 8½.   21843-0

AUTOBIOGRAPHY: The Story of My Experiments with Truth, Mohandas K. Gandhi. Boyhood, legal studies, purification, the growth of the Satyagraha (nonviolent protest) movement. Critical, inspiring work of the man responsible for the freedom of India. 480pp. 5⅜ x 8½. (Available in U.S. only.)   24593-4

CELTIC MYTHS AND LEGENDS, T. W. Rolleston. Masterful retelling of Irish and Welsh stories and tales. Cuchulain, King Arthur, Deirdre, the Grail, many more. First paperback edition. 58 full-page illustrations. 512pp. 5⅜ x 8½.   26507-2

THE PRINCIPLES OF PSYCHOLOGY, William James. Famous long course complete, unabridged. Stream of thought, time perception, memory, experimental methods; great work decades ahead of its time. 94 figures. 1,391pp. 5⅜ x 8½. 2-vol. set.
Vol. I: 20381-6   Vol. II: 20382-4

THE WORLD AS WILL AND REPRESENTATION, Arthur Schopenhauer. Definitive English translation of Schopenhauer's life work, correcting more than 1,000 errors, omissions in earlier translations. Translated by E. F. J. Payne. Total of 1,269pp. 5⅜ x 8½. 2-vol. set.   Vol. 1: 21761-2   Vol. 2: 21762-0

MAGIC AND MYSTERY IN TIBET, Madame Alexandra David-Neel. Experiences among lamas, magicians, sages, sorcerers, Bonpa wizards. A true psychic discovery. 32 illustrations. 321pp. 5⅜ x 8½. (Available in U.S. only.)   22682-4

THE EGYPTIAN BOOK OF THE DEAD, E. A. Wallis Budge. Complete reproduction of Ani's papyrus, finest ever found. Full hieroglyphic text, interlinear transliteration, word-for-word translation, smooth translation. 533pp. 6½ x 9¼.   21866-X

MATHEMATICS FOR THE NONMATHEMATICIAN, Morris Kline. Detailed, college-level treatment of mathematics in cultural and historical context, with numerous exercises. Recommended Reading Lists. Tables. Numerous figures. 641pp. 5⅜ x 8½.
24823-2

PROBABILISTIC METHODS IN THE THEORY OF STRUCTURES, Isaac Elishakoff. Well-written introduction covers the elements of the theory of probability from two or more random variables, the reliability of such multivariable structures, the theory of random function, Monte Carlo methods of treating problems incapable of exact solution, and more. Examples. 502pp. 5⅜ x 8½.   40691-1

THE RIME OF THE ANCIENT MARINER, Gustave Doré, S. T. Coleridge. Doré's finest work; 34 plates capture moods, subtleties of poem. Flawless full-size reproductions printed on facing pages with authoritative text of poem. "Beautiful. Simply beautiful."—*Publisher's Weekly.* 77pp. 9¼ x 12.   22305-1

NORTH AMERICAN INDIAN DESIGNS FOR ARTISTS AND CRAFTSPEOPLE, Eva Wilson. Over 360 authentic copyright-free designs adapted from Navajo blankets, Hopi pottery, Sioux buffalo hides, more. Geometrics, symbolic figures, plant and animal motifs, etc. 128pp. 8⅜ x 11. (Not for sale in the United Kingdom.)   25341-4

SCULPTURE: Principles and Practice, Louis Slobodkin. Step-by-step approach to clay, plaster, metals, stone; classical and modern. 253 drawings, photos. 255pp. 8⅛ x 11.
22960-2

THE INFLUENCE OF SEA POWER UPON HISTORY, 1660–1783, A. T. Mahan. Influential classic of naval history and tactics still used as text in war colleges. First paperback edition. 4 maps. 24 battle plans. 640pp. 5⅜ x 8½.   25509-3

CATALOG OF DOVER BOOKS

THE STORY OF THE TITANIC AS TOLD BY ITS SURVIVORS, Jack Winocour (ed.). What it was really like. Panic, despair, shocking inefficiency, and a little hero-ism. More thrilling than any fictional account. 26 illustrations. 320pp. 5⅜ x 8½.
20610-6

FAIRY AND FOLK TALES OF THE IRISH PEASANTRY, William Butler Yeats (ed.). Treasury of 64 tales from the twilight world of Celtic myth and legend: "The Soul Cages," "The Kildare Pooka," "King O'Toole and his Goose," many more. Introduction and Notes by W. B. Yeats. 352pp. 5⅜ x 8½.
26941-8

BUDDHIST MAHAYANA TEXTS, E. B. Cowell and others (eds.). Superb, accurate translations of basic documents in Mahayana Buddhism, highly important in history of religions. The Buddha-karita of Asvaghosha, Larger Sukhavativyuha, more. 448pp. 5⅜ x 8½.
25552-2

ONE TWO THREE . . . INFINITY: Facts and Speculations of Science, George Gamow. Great physicist's fascinating, readable overview of contemporary science: number theory, relativity, fourth dimension, entropy, genes, atomic structure, much more. 128 illustrations. Index. 352pp. 5⅜ x 8½.
25664-2

EXPERIMENTATION AND MEASUREMENT, W. J. Youden. Introductory manual explains laws of measurement in simple terms and offers tips for achieving accuracy and minimizing errors. Mathematics of measurement, use of instruments, experimenting with machines. 1994 edition. Foreword. Preface. Introduction. Epilogue. Selected Readings. Glossary. Index. Tables and figures. 128pp. 5⅜ x 8½.   40451-X

DALÍ ON MODERN ART: The Cuckolds of Antiquated Modern Art, Salvador Dalí. Influential painter skewers modern art and its practitioners. Outrageous evaluations of Picasso, Cézanne, Turner, more. 15 renderings of paintings discussed. 44 calligraphic decorations by Dalí. 96pp. 5⅜ x 8½. (Available in U.S. only.)   29220-7

ANTIQUE PLAYING CARDS: A Pictorial History, Henry René D'Allemagne. Over 900 elaborate, decorative images from rare playing cards (14th–20th centuries): Bacchus, death, dancing dogs, hunting scenes, royal coats of arms, players cheating, much more. 96pp. 9¼ x 12¼.
29265-7

MAKING FURNITURE MASTERPIECES: 30 Projects with Measured Drawings, Franklin H. Gottshall. Step-by-step instructions, illustrations for constructing handsome, useful pieces, among them a Sheraton desk, Chippendale chair, Spanish desk, Queen Anne table and a William and Mary dressing mirror. 224pp. 8⅛ x 11¼.
29338-6

THE FOSSIL BOOK: A Record of Prehistoric Life, Patricia V. Rich et al. Profusely illustrated definitive guide covers everything from single-celled organisms and dinosaurs to birds and mammals and the interplay between climate and man. Over 1,500 illustrations. 760pp. 7½ x 10⅛.
29371-8